Samuel Beckett

Waiting for Godot

A CASEBOOK

EDITED BY

RUBY COHN

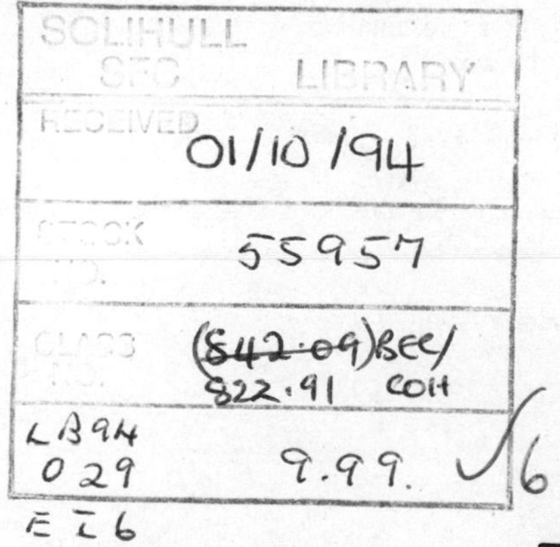

MACMILLAN

First published 1987 by
THE MACMILLAN PRESS LTD
Houndmills, Basingstoke, Hampshire RG21 2XS
and London
Companies and representatives
throughout the world

ISBN 0–333–34489–8

A catalogue record for this book is available
from the British Library.

Printed in Hong Kong

Reprinted 1990, 1992, 1993

CONTENTS

System of Titling: here and in the Selection, exterior quotemarks are used for editorially devised captions. In other cases, the caption employs the original title of the writer's book, chapter or section of a book, article or essay (in some instances abbreviated from that), and it is displayed without exterior quotemarks.

GENERAL EDITOR'S PREFACE

The Casebook series, launched in 1968, has become a well-regarded library of critical studies. The central concern of the series remains the 'single-author' volume, but suggestions from the academic community have led to an extension of the original plan, to include occasional volumes on such general themes as literary 'schools' and genres.

Each volume in the central category deals either with one well-known and influential work by an individual author, or with closely related works by one writer. The main section consists of critical readings, mostly modern, collected from books and journals. A selection of reviews and comments by the author's contemporaries is also included, and sometimes comment from the author himself. The Editor's Introduction charts the reputation of the work or works from the first appearance to the present time.

Volumes in the 'general themes' category are variable in structure but follow the basic purpose of the series in presenting an integrated selection of readings, with an Introduction which explores the theme and discusses the literary and critical issues involved.

A single volume can represent no more than a small selection of critical opinions. Some critics are excluded for reasons of space, and it is hoped that readers will pursue the suggestions for further reading in the Select Bibliography. Other contributions are severed from their original context, to which some readers may wish to turn. Indeed, if they take a hint from the critics represented here, they certainly will.

A. E. Dyson

IN MEMORY
OF

ROGER BLIN (1907–84)

AND

ALAN SCHNEIDER (1917–84)

INTRODUCTION

The Man

When Samuel Beckett, interrupting his fiction, began in 1948 to scrawl *En attendant Godot* in a cheap graph-paper notebook, he could not predict that he was sounding the clarion call of contemporary drama. Far from feeling successful, he later wrote to his American director Alan Schneider that he had breathed deeply of failure's vivifying air all his writing life.

That life began on Good Friday, 13 April 1906 in Dublin. The younger of two sons in a comfortable Protestant family, Samuel Beckett affirms that his parents did everything to make a child happy, but he had little talent for happiness. Yet he mingled easily with family and friends. At the age of six he began to study piano and French; but, hardly a child prodigy, he proceeded to excel in team sports, visit the Abbey Theatre and write unremarkable juvenilia. Not until he attended Trinity College, Dublin, did he display academic brilliance, and it was then also that he composed mannered fiction and sardonic non-fiction. In 1927 Beckett graduated from Trinity with a first in Modern Languages, and the following year he was awarded a two-year exchange fellowship to the prestigious École Normale Supérieure of Paris.

Beckett had earlier bicycled along the Loire Valley but this extended exchange-fellowship in Paris was to be fundamental to his life and work; it not only steeped him in French culture but also plunged him into an international *avant-garde*. He was befriended by James Joyce (though never his secretary, as is often mis-stated), and participated drunkenly in the twenty-fifth Bloomsday celebration. During his tenure at the École Normale he published in *transition*,* and also won a prize for a poem on Descartes. With a French friend, Alfred Péron, he translated into French the 'Anna Livia Plurabelle' section of Joyce's *Work in Progress*, and he wrote a critical monograph on Proust's *À la recherche du temps perdu*.

Expected to conform to an academic career, Beckett was back at

*The *avant-garde* journal edited by Eugene Jolas; Beckett's contribution there in 1929, his first piece of fiction to appear in print, was the short story 'Assumption', and the same issue included a reprint of his essay on Joyce. Thereafter he contributed to several other issues of *transition*.

Trinity in 1930, but he fled to the continent during the long vacation – returning to his alma mater some twenty years later, to receive an honorary degree. In the 1930s, however, he had to confront the problem of supporting himself. His father died in 1933, leaving him a small annuity. He moved to London, hoping to live by writing. In 1934 he began (but did not complete) a course in psychoanalysis at the Tavistock Clinic. That year *More Pricks Than Kicks* was published – a collection of short stories whose title offended the proprieties in Dublin. In 1935 a slim volume of thirteen poems was published in Paris: *Echo's Bones and Other Precipitates*. He also received small sums for book reviews in London and translations in Paris. In 1936, after completing his first novel – *Murphy* (published in 1938), reflecting local colour in a way he subsequently abjured – Beckett visited museums in Germany but was upset by Nazi oppression of Jewish intellectuals. He returned to Paris in the following year, where he renewed his friendship with Joyce. In January 1938, while walking along a Paris street, he was stabbed by a total stranger, narrowly escaping death. While in the hospital, he was visited by the pianist Suzanne Dumesnil, who later became his wife.

Although Beckett was at his mother's home in Dublin when the Nazis invaded Poland in 1939, he returned immediately to Paris, and he has been quoted as saying: 'I preferred France in war to Ireland in peace.' Through Alfred Péron (who was later murdered in a concentration camp), Beckett joined the French Resistance, Irish national though he was (and is): 'I couldn't stand with my arms folded.' When Péron was captured by the Gestapo, Beckett fled to the Unoccupied Zone of France, seeing Joyce in Vichy, for the last time. Beckett spent the remainder of the war as an agricultural labourer by day and a writer at night. Thirty of the eighty members of his Resistance group survived the war.

After a reunion with his family in Dublin, Beckett was able to return to France only by joining the Irish Red Cross, to become a relief worker in war-ravaged Normandy. In an Irish radio broadcast of June 1946, he reported on the horrors he had witnessed (and helped to alleviate). Eventually he made his way back to Paris.

With these harrowing experiences behind him, Beckett exploded creatively; between 1945 and 1950 he wrote four long short-stories, four novels and two plays – all in French and none referring directly to his wartime life. Yet pain seeps through his prose whose surface seemed chaotic at the time, but is now valued as a formal and meaningful pattern.

After the death of his mother in 1950, and that of his brother in 1954, Beckett rarely visited Ireland. It would be only a slight exaggeration to say that, after mid-century, the life of Samuel Beckett becomes his work. Never again would he know the exhilaration of those five fluid years of writing, 1945–50, but through the ensuing decades he carved ever new forms in both drama and fiction. Uniquely, he not only writes in English *and* French, but he also translates each successive work. After other honours, he was awarded the Nobel Prize for Literature in 1969; yet, ever shy and reserved, he did not journey to Stockholm to receive it. Living simply, refusing interviews, avoiding critical controversy, he is generous of both time and funds. Not only has he been a writer and translator, but beginning in the mid-1960s, he has occasionally directed his own plays – in German, French and English. During 1986, the year of his eightieth birthday, celebrations were held in several cities and campuses – none of which Beckett attended.

The Work

Through half a century Samuel Beckett has produced a body of work that some critics reduce to a single theme, although they do not agree on the nature of the theme. Among those proposed are: the search for self; the absurdity of man in the world; the dedication to artistic failure; the erosive force of time; the bankruptcy of the Western cultural tradition; the encroachment of nothingness on being; the treacherous slippage of language; the wavering eye on a hovering object. Serious though these themes may be, Beckett's prose is never solemn, and he has written some of the funniest lines in the English and French languages. Over the years he has pared down plot, probed to the core of his characters, and experimented with syntax, from the periodic sentences in his early stories to floating phrases, incantatory repetitions and simple questions or statements. Finally, a vestigial verbal skeleton feints its articulation.

For convenience one may divide Beckett's work by genre – essays, verse, fiction, drama. Except for the essays, however, all three genres have challenged Beckett throughout his writing life, and often he enfolds into the particular genre a doubt as to its boundaries. Or Beckett's work may be divided chronologically: 1. English writing from juvenilia up to the novel *Watt* (completed in 1944); 2. French fiction and plays composed between 1945 and about 1955 – with progressive concentration and intensity; 3. a return to English in drama and fiction – *Krapp's Last Tape* (1958 completion, published 1959) and *From an Abandoned Work* (completed in 1956) – permitting a radical syntax in either language; 4. after about 1970, denser pieces in both languages, focusing on incisively etched images.

Although Beckett is best known as a dramatist, he considers his fiction a lesser failure. It begins unassumingly with the short story 'Assumption' (written in 1929), but within a year he embarked on a picaresque novel, *Dream of Fair to Middling Women*. From this aborted work he salvaged a protagonist, Belacqua Shuah, for a series of short stories, subsequently published as *More Pricks Than Kicks* (1934). The exotic first name of his Dublin-based hero comes from Canto IV of Dante's *Purgatorio*, where he sits in foetal position 'more indolent than if sloth were his sister'. Having propelled his indolent protagonist through a discontinuous series of stories, Beckett next (in 1936) composed his most traditional novel, *Murphy*. Belacqua's several women crystallise into Murphy's Celia Kelly, an avatar of that cliché, the kind-hearted whore. She prevails upon Murphy to seek employment so that she can relinquish hers. But Murphy, inspired by a Mr Endon, renounces the outside world, including Celia. He is oblivious of the small Irish company who hunt him down, only to discover his charred corpse. They then go their several ways, ignoring Murphy's last wish – that his ashes be flushed down the toilet of Dublin's Abbey Theatre, preferably during a performance.

Murphy is at once Beckett's first English novel and his first French novel, since he translated it before fleeing from Nazi-occupied Paris. In the 'unoccupied' Vaucluse, Beckett wrote *Watt*, whose naïve titular hero uses his senses ('his most noble faculties') and his mind ('whatever that may be') in an effort to understand thing, event and person at Mr Knott's home, where he undertakes service. But senses and reason are incommensurate with Mr Knott, and Watt leaves his abode. At a later date Watt meets Sam, who purports to be the recorder of Watt's adventures, which he narrates in four parts and in Addenda – and which we read.

Watt, a would-be Cartesian, thinks in order to try to be, but his nameless successor in Beckett's fiction, adopting the language of Descartes, deliberately does not think in order to be. He lets the stream of sentences carry him where they will – up to The End that gives Beckett's first French story its name: *La Fin* (1946). After four such stories by feeble but febrile narrators, interrupted by the novel *Mercier et Camier* (completed in 1946), Beckett embarked on what is often considered his major work. Published individually, in French, *Molloy* (1947), *Malone meurt* (1948) and *L'Innommable* (1949) are a trilogy in their progressive concentration and obsessive repetition. *Molloy* is divided into two parts. In the first a grotesque old cripple, hat fastened to his buttonhole by a lace, having somehow arrived in his mother's room, writes a choppy tale of his choppy voyage toward his mother. In the second part Jacques Moran, a middle-aged

Catholic father of an only namesake son, having returned from a mission in quest of Molloy, writes a report for his employer Youdi. In *Malone meurt* (English version *Malone Dies*, 1956), a paralysed hero, confined to his bed, tries to order his dying hours by noting an inventory of his possessions and of the symptoms of his present state, while composing stories. The titular speaker-protagonist of *L'Innommable* (English version *The Unnamable*, 1958) probes behind fictional and linguistic formulae to what may be himself. His utterances, stripped of Moran's determination, Molloy's meanderings and Malone's purpose, attain an incantatory anguish of meaning made music.

After the trilogy Beckett creates lyrics of fiction, which he calls 'texts'. *Comment c'est* (1960: *How It Is*, 1964) traces the itineraries of characters who meet and part, naked in the mud. The grammatical first person dissolves into unpunctuated phrases in irregular verses, permuted and repeated. Thereafter Beckett's lyrics of fiction bear slenderly on referential reality, the quasi-mathematical works (1965–67) in *Residua** leading to *Le Dépeupleur* (1966: *The Lost Ones*, 1972).

Like the three novels completed by mid-century, Beckett's later three (shorter) novels may be viewed as a trilogy. *Company* (1979) dramatises the wavering voice; *Mal vu mal dit* (1980: *Ill Seen Ill Said*, 1981) – pointedly titled – conveys the hovering image; *Worstward Ho* (1983) is Beckett's boldest foray into uncharted prose, at once summoning and shrinking from human trace. In an incantation of monosyllables, negatives, contradictions and qualifications, scene precipitates to image, being to saying, while 'no' reverses to a polyvalent 'on'. And that monosyllable – on – may serve as the watchword of Beckett's ever searching, ever exploring 'wordward ho'.

In the theatre, however, Beckett never forgets that the stage image is more visual than verbal. And that image, for all his formal invention, is always inscribed within the century-old picture-frame stage. But Beckett the dramatist is not limited to theatre; he has also written for radio, television and film. And (with his own love of numbers!), we may tally his one actorless play, one aborted scene, one movie, two mime plays, six radio plays, five television scripts and sixteen plays for speaking actors in the theatre. After an early aborted scene in English (*Human Wishes*, 1937) and, a decade later, a wordy well-made play in French (*Eleuthéria*), Beckett in 1948–49 composed *En attendant*

**Residua* (London, 1967) is the 'group title' for three works (completion dates in brackets): *Imagination morte imaginez* (1965: *Imagination Dead Imagine*, 1966), *Assez* (1965: *Enough*, 1967) and *Bing* (1966: *Ping*, 1967).

Godot (*Waiting for Godot*, 1954). Since this volume is devoted to that play, I will forbear from commentary on it – for the moment.

The master–servant couple of *Godot* are moved to centre-stage in *Fin de partie* (1956: *Endgame*, 1958), but they are also father and son, artist and audience. And the hero's parents are omnipresent in their ashbins, composing a nuclear family. More rigorous than *Godot*, with fewer music-hall routines, *Endgame* rests more gravely on an economy of purposeless play. Passive play is the lesson of Beckett's *Acte sans paroles I* (1956: *Act Without Words I* 1958), written to accompany *Endgame*. In contrast, *All That Fall* (1956), is a radio play that peoples the Irish town of Boghill through sound alone. Radio and mime nurtured Beckett's first stage play originating in English: *Krapp's Last Tape* (1958). Here an invisible voice emerges from tape, while the lone stage character gestures as lavishly as a mime. Bordering on the sentimental if it is not rigorously performed, the monodrama resorts to pattern as a defence against aging.

Beckett's subsequent drama dissolves the familiar world into the context of an eternal void. *Happy Days* (1961) shows Winnie literally sinking into her grave, and yet she prattles on under a blazing sun. She calls on four main resources to help her through what she insistently designates as her happy day: the stage props, her husband Willie, the composition of a story, and involuntary recollections through which thread snatches of English verse. By Act II, Winnie is buried up to her neck and her resources shrink. Indomitable, she is rewarded by the most startling climax in all Beckett's drama – the entrance of her husband Willie on all fours, in morning clothes. He utters a single syllable – 'Win' – at once an abbreviation of her name and a thrust against their lives of loss.

Play (1962) views a lovers' triangle from the perspective of eternity, but it also introduces what I have called Beckett's 'theatereality', in which stage fact and fiction almost converge. In *Play* the inquisitorial light is an actual theatre light, which ignites speech as it shifts from urn to urn, but fictionally it is a mysterious force that elicits confession. Beckett's plays of the 1970s dazzle the senses with resonances of this device. Thus, a light beam and the buzzing within the discourse of Mouth of *Not I* (1972) are also a theatre spotlight and the words of the rapid discourse. Similarly, in *That Time* (1974) we see the head of a white-haired old man, and we hear about a white-haired old man in two of the three voice-strands that finally dissolve 'that time' into no time. The very title *Footfalls* (1975) describes what we hear and hear about in the theatre. *Rockaby* (1980) engraves the titular action on the audience's eyes, while a voice-over tells about a woman who retraces the way of her mother from a world outside into a cradling rocker that is also a coffin. *A Piece of Monologue* (1977) is a monologue about a man, a lamp of the same height, and the corner of a bed, which is more or less what we see on stage. *Ohio Impromptu* (1981) confronts us with two identical white-haired, black-coated men, Listener and Reader, who read aloud about a listener and a reader. Yet theatereality is always slightly out of focus with theatre reality.

Catastrophe (1982: English version, 1983) is overtly polyvalent. Dedicated to the imprisoned Czech playwright Vaclav Havel, the play is – on one surprising political level – a scene about a dictatorial director treating his actor as a property, in order to achieve commercial success with a catastrophe; it is a stage image of totalitarian control, over which the actor's rebellious spirit nevertheless triumphs: 'P raises his head, fixes the audience.' At another level, the play mocks Beckett's own role as a director, manipulating artifice, but finally at the mercy of the performing actor. To that role as director, we now turn.

Although Beckett has advised on, and occasionally directed, productions of his plays in English and French, it is mainly in German that he has assumed full directorial responsibility: *Endgame* in 1967, *Krapp's Last Tape* in 1969, *Happy Days* in 1971, *Waiting for Godot* in 1975, *Footfalls* and *That Time* in 1976 – all in West Berlin – as well as the late television plays in Stuttgart. Beckett's German is fluent, but Elmar Tophoven has been his translator since the time when, as a student, he first undertook *Waiting for Godot* on his own initiative. Beckett, not having actually penned each word of the German texts, views them from a desirable distance.

Beckett has approached his several German stage productions in the same methodical way: 1. meticulous examination of Tophoven's translation, so as to correct work toward the original French or English; 2. intense visualisation of the play in space – what Beckett calls 'trying to see'; 3. commitment of the re-viewed German text (with stage directions) to memory; 4. composition of a Director's Notebook to which he does not refer during actual rehearsal; 5. transmission of staging ideas to the designer (usually Matias). Only when these steps are completed does Beckett arrive in West Berlin, where the plays have already been cast. At his first meeting with the actors, Beckett never speaks about the play but plunges right into it. Although the production is complete in his mind's eye, he asks for and sometimes accepts actors' suggestions during the course of rehearsals.

'Waiting for Godot'

Of his several productions in West Berlin, *Waiting for Godot* in 1975 was the most difficult for Beckett. Not only does it contain a more intricate plot and more active characters than his subsequent plays, but Beckett himself lacked stage experience when he wrote it (1948–49). 'Messy', and 'not well thought out', he has said impatiently of his play that is now considered a model of form and meditation (but he never viewed it as a commercial venture). In production, he tried to compensate for what he considers textual weaknesses.

Beckett's main changes were deletions. He pared away much of Pozzo's Act I business with pipe and whip, as well as his conversation about Lucky's burdens, dancing and rebellion. The puzzling 'knook' vanishes, as well as the music-hall joke about the weak and sound lungs. In Act II, when the four men sprawl on the ground, Didi and Gogo lose a few lines, and when they prop Pozzo up, they no longer discuss evening and friendship. In contrast, Beckett made one remarkable addition to the dialogue. When Didi in Act II asks the Boy whether Mr Godot's beard is fair or black, the German question becomes: 'Blonde or . . . *he hesitates* black . . . *he hesitates* or red?' Thus, Mr Godot is pointedly related to Gogo's smutty story about the Englishman in the brothel, juxtaposing – as so often in *Godot* – the physical and the metaphysical, the vulgar and the visionary.

For Beckett as for Artaud, stage space is empty, and much of his *Godot* reflects his characters' valiant efforts to move through it. That valour is evident in stylised standing, sitting, walking, and especially falling. Beckett's directing notebooks amplify his texts with many diagrams of the movements of his characters. This is not only traditional blocking but also a concern with who faces where at every moment of time, with each actor's movement-by-movement victory over stillness, with the counterpoint of word against gesture, with visual echoes, symmetries and oppositions. In *Godot*, Beckett's characters manoeuvre through stage space to pass the time. For it is, of course, with time that Beckett's classic is obsessed – the time of waiting.

The seed of *Waiting for Godot* is St Luke's account of the crucifixion, as summarised by St Augustine (although no one has found the passage to which Beckett refers): 'Do not despair: one of the thieves was saved. Do not presume: one of the thieves was damned.' The two thieves are Didi and Gogo; the two thieves are Pozzo and Lucky; the two thieves are Mr Godot's goatherd and his off-stage shepherd brother; the two thieves might be you and me. Beckett shaped the play to reflect that fearful symmetry – in text and performance. There are two acts, one repeating the other. There are two couples, one contrasting with the other. Within the acts, within the couples, symmetries and oppositions recur. A résumé of either act yields a parallel pattern. Two friends meet by a tree at twilight to wait for Godot. A burdened menial and his master arrive, dally a while, and then leave. When the friends are alone again, a messenger arrives to inform them that Godot will come not today but tomorrow. The moon rises as the boy departs. Although the friends agree to go, they have not gone when the curtain falls.

Beckett submitted this unlikely play to several theatre managers and publishers in the Paris of the early 1950s. To this day he attributes his subsequent good fortune to the almost simultaneous enthusiasm of Jérôme Lindon (owner of the Resistance-founded publishing company, Les Editions de Minuit), and Roger Blin, nominal manager of the Gaîté-Montparnasse Theatre (but with no power to impose his taste on the actual owners). In the event, Blin took so long in finding a theatre he could afford that *Godot* reached print before it took the stage. Once Beckett's characters stepped on 'The Board', however (opening at the Théâtre de Babylone on 5 January 1953), they proceeded to command the stage in many languages of our shrinking globe. Part One of the present volume presents reactions to several performances.

Surprisingly, some dozen reviews took notice of that first *Godot* by an unknown playwright, and in a weekly publication *Godot* drew fulsome praise from the most successful playwrights of Paris, Jean Anouilh and Armand Salacrou. The former proclaimed *Godot* 'a vaudeville sketch of Pascal's *Pensées* as played by the Fratellini clowns'. Monthly periodicals ushered in more meditated criticism, and by the 1960s many critics sank their teeth into Beckett, and they – we – have been gnawing away ever since. Part Two of our selection garners a variety of approaches to what has become a classic text.

Not only scholars but, more importantly, artists have been inspired by *Godot* – painting, song, dance, and especially drama. From Wole Soyinka's 1965 *The Road* to Jim Cartwright's 1986 *Road*, the *Godot* setting is emblematic of human life. In Tom Stoppard's *Jumpers* his sinister academic jubilates: 'Wham bam! Thank you Sam!' in homage to Sam Beckett, from whom Stoppard borrowed phrase and form for *Rosencrantz and Guildenstern are Dead*. Harold Pinter has thanked Beckett for freeing the stage for his own enigmatic couples, like Goldberg and McCann in *The Birthday Party*, or Hirst and Spooner in *No Man's Land*. David Storey's *Home* is peopled, like *Godot*, by two couples and a loner. Tennessee Williams's *Out-Cry* is set in an entropic theatre in an unnamed country which recalls the stage of *Godot*, bared for performance. Sam Shepard cites *Godot* as the first play he remembers reading, and its playfulness is echoed in his *Cowboys #2*. David Mamet's *Duck Variations* echo the rhythms of Didi and Gogo. And beyond art, *Godot* has resonated into daily events, a few of which are adumbrated in Part Three of this Casebook.

The concluding paragraphs of this Introduction seek to trace the thread of *Godot* through Beckett's subsequent work. Precise, economical word and gesture in an unlocalised but specific setting become Beckett's theatrical hallmark. Twinned contrasts also structure his *Fin de partie* (1956: *Endgame*, 1958), *Acte sans paroles II* (1959: *Act Without Words II*, 1959), *Fragment de théâtre I* (1959: *Rough for Theatre I*, 1976), *Fragment de théâtre II* (1960: *Rough for Theatre II*, 1976), *Happy Days* (1960), *Not I* (1972) and *Ohio Impromptu* (1981). The ghost of a couple hovers over *Krapp's Last Tape* (1958), *Footfalls* (1975), *A Piece of Monologue* (1977) and *Rockaby* (1980), as well as the television pieces before *Quad* (1982). Vladimir prevents Estragon from narrating his dreams, but later Beckett characters compose compulsively – Hamm, Krapp, Winnie, to name a few. Like Didi and Gogo, several of the later mobile characters walk distinctively: Krapp, M of *Footfalls*, the figures of *Quoi où* (1983: *What Where*, 1983), and the television figures from *Ghost Trio* (1976), *. . . but the clouds . . .* (1976) and *Quad*. Although Pozzo is the only *Godot* name found in a later Beckett work – in 'Text 5' of *Texts for Nothing** – *Godot* refrains become titles of later works: 'happy days', 'enough'. The several references to the audience in *Waiting for Godot* are the seed of Beckett's later theatereality, where the physical and the fictional converge. Lucky's stones freeze into a deathbed in *Eh Joe* (1965) and his 'unfinished' may be applied to Hamm's chronicle, Willie's intention and Mouth's monologue. Some critics affix it to all Beckett's works, which avoid closure.

Beckett's recent masterpiece in fiction, *Worstward Ho* (1983), mines *Godot*. The four adults of that tragicomedy utter the word 'on', obverse of 'No'. *Worstward Ho* opens and closes on 'On' – although 'there's no lack of void' in either setting. Residual pipe, boots and hat (though not a bowler) figure in the later work. The shifters 'true' and 'enough' spatter both *Godot* and *Worstward Ho*.

Beckett translates the 'charnier' of the original French *Godot* as 'charnel-house', after the bone and graveyard imagery has conveyed the climate and even the susurration of a moribund cultural tradition.

* 'Text 5 for Nothing' is one of the thirteen fiction-pieces in *Textes pour rien*, all written in 1950 (*Texts for Nothing*, 1967). *En attendant Godot* was completed in January 1949.

Lucky, whose monologue encapsulates that tradition, repeats the word 'skull' eight times, four in merciless sequence. In *Worstward Ho*, the head that holds and is held in the fiction is stripped down to a skull, after bones and mind have been cited as loci of pain. Toward the end of Lucky's speech 'skulls' and 'stones' thud pell-mell, but by the end of *Worstward Ho* the stones are tempered to stooping humanised gravestones, and the skull with its single pinhole for three pins barely sustains the waning words: 'What left of skull not go. Into it still the hole. Into what left of soft.'

In Act II of *Godot* Estragon observes: 'Everything oozes', and a few minutes later he explodes: 'All my lousy life I've crawled about in the mud!', correcting the original French 'sables' (sands). By *Worstward Ho*, the ooze – repeated some dozen times – is that of plaintive words. Estragon intuits his world as a primeval slime from which he has never evolved: 'Look at this muckheap! I've never stirred from it!' By *Worstward Ho* all stirring fuses into the sense and senses of the soft within the skull. In *Godot* the opening announcement breaks silence: 'Nothing to be DONE': that is, to be given a time, place and form through a dramatic action. In *Worstward Ho* 'Nothing ever unseen. Of the nothing to be seen', because seeing is a constant, iterative, revisionary process of wording, mis-wording, for-wording 'On' by the seer who is Samuel Beckett.

PART ONE

The Stage

Eric Bentley (1964)

AN ANTI-PLAY

. . : Samuel Beckett's *Waiting for Godot* has established itself as the most original contribution to dramatic literature since 1950. The distinction of the writing is undeniable. All kinds of good things may be said about the dialogue, 'but is it dramatic?' Let us set aside the fact that very little happens in the play, for this is true of so many good plays. And many good plays have wrongly been found undramatic ('not a play') by their first critics. The first critic to make the point, and repeatedly, that Beckett's dialogue is not dramatic is Beckett himself – in that dialogue. For this 'criticism' is inherent in the recurrent joke of letting the conversation simply dry up and having one character tell the other to say something. In this, Beckett has put into a play what 'cannot be put into a play'. For in a play, the dialogue cannot conceivably dry up. A play is, so to speak, a much longer piece of dialogue, reduced to the number of lines one sees in the final text by the craftmanship of compression. Pauses can only occur when they are equivalent to dialogue, when their silence is more eloquent and packed with meaning than words would be. The dramatist fights against time. He cannot 'get it all in'. His craft is the filling out of every nook and cranny that each second as it passes may offer him, just as the painter's craft is the filling in of each square inch of canvas. That any part of the dramatist's precious couple of hours should stand empty, and that there should be any difficulty about filling it, is absurd. But *Waiting for Godot* is 'drama of the absurd'.

Not to settle the matter with a pun, let me add that on the face of it, Beckett's work is too Naturalistic for drama. It is in life, not in drama, that there may be a problem about filling in the time. It is in life that we 'kill time'; in drama, time kills us. A dramatist will show the sands running out on Dr Faustus and hell approaching. He will not show time stretching endlessly, inorganically out, and Godot not coming. And, as far as dialogue is concerned, a dramatist cannot use garrulousness (talk, talk, talk) except incidentally and framed by nongarrulousness. (If a Mr Jingle breezes in, he must soon breeze out again.) *Waiting for Godot* seems anti-dramatic in that garrulity is the all-but-declared principle of its dialogue. These men talk to kill time, talking for talking's sake. It is the opposite of *azione parlata*, which implies 'a minimum of words, because something more important is going on'. Here we seem to have a maximum of words because nothing at all is going on – except waiting.

But this is a big exception, and it saves Beckett's play. It makes no difference that the waiting may be for nothing. Here is a play with a very slight Action, with only the slightest movement from beginning to middle to end, and yet there *is* an Action, and it enables us to see the totality, not as *un*dramatic, but as a parody of the dramatic. After all, Beckett is not himself finding it hard to fill two hours with words. His play is actually jampacked and like any other good play could easily be thought of as a compression of some five-hundred-page version. He is *presenting* people who have trouble filling up *their* time. In the theatre, the moments where Vladimir and Estragon dry up are not gaps *for the audience*: Beckett has made comic points of them. And so *Waiting for Godot* is not, after all, 'the end of the line', it is only one of many modern works *about* the end of the line. Now an art is never threatened with extinction by good works of art *about* extinction. It is threatened only by bad works of art, though they cry nothing but: Eternal life!

Waiting for Godot is not, I suspect, a tombstone but a landmark. If the form of the dialogue is derivative (from the music hall and so, one might say, from the *commedia dell'arte* tradition), there is freshness and originality in the application of that dialogue to these purposes. Behind the mordant flippancy of the clowns we are made to hear – if in the distance – another voice: Beckett's own perhaps, or that of the Lamentations of Jeremiah, desolate and dolorous, a voice of cosmic doom not untouched by human dignity.

SOURCE: extract from section ('Anti-Plays') in *The Life of the Drama* (New York, 1964; London, 1965), pp. 99–101.

Marcel Frère (1953)

ROGER BLIN'S PRODUCTION OF 'EN ATTENDANT GODOT'

SAMUEL BECKETT'S FIRST PLAY WILL BE PERFORMED AT THE THÉÂTRE DE BABYLONE where Estragon and Vladimir will wait for Godot at the foot of a tree.

For three years Roger Blin looked in vain for a theatre in which to produce Samuel Beckett's *Waiting for Godot*. It must be admitted that this play by the novelist of *Molloy* and *Malone Dies* offers nothing to reassure theatre directors in the throes of current difficulties – according to Roger Blin.

'This work is a gamble; imagine a play that contains no action but characters who have nothing to say to one another.'

One might be tempted to call it an 'anti-play', especially since its theme is boredom. But there's the miracle: if the characters are bored, the audience should not be bored for an instant. *Waiting for Godot*, which is not a laboratory play, often moves at the pace of farce. Its realistic dialogue consists of everyday words in short lines. Without an ounce of literature – I mean self-conscious literature – Samuel Beckett gives us a profoundly poetic work, the desperate work of an author animated by a great epic breath, who paradoxically proclaims his love of life.

Four men (and a boy) will play *Waiting for Godot* at the Théâtre de Babylone, awarded a subsidy toward production of a first play. Pierre Latour and Lucien Raimbourg (who has been playing cabaret) will enact two tramps. Roger Blin and Jean Martin will enact a squire and his servant. At least, on the surface, for their clown names – the tramps are called Estragon and Vladimir, the others Pozzo and Lucky – and their circus lines make us hesitate between dream and reality.

By patient and gradual work, Roger Blin strives to create the climate of this play that lacks the idea of time, expressing the pauses of a reticent and spare dialogue. Nothing artificial or external enters his direction. No lighting effects or set, except for a tree at whose foot the tramps wait for Godot.

'Who is Godot?'

'That's the secret of the play.'

I learn, however, that a boy arrives as a messenger from the Godot upon whom Estragon and Vladimir base their hope. But it seems as though we are never to know what to believe about this mysterious character.

Source: article in *Combat* (7 January 1953); translated by Ruby Cohn.

Mary Benson (1978)

Blin on Beckett

Roger Blin is convinced that reality is only attained through poetry, a conviction that informs his work in theatre. One of the great European directors of our time, he is habitually labelled *avant-garde* by writers on theatre and by critics. '*Avant-garde*?' he mocks, 'I don't know what that is. It's a word that escapes me completely. I have a text or subject in my hands; I try to follow it, to give it the greatest possible effect by rapport with the author, and in reaction to the playing of the actors. I have no ideas – no theories – on theatre at all.'

It was in this spirit that he chose to direct a work by an unknown playwright twenty-five years ago in Paris: a play that was to create a revolution in theatre and change the course of modern English drama. The play, of course, was *Waiting for Godot*. But for Roger Blin, it might never have been performed. . . .

. . . One hand tensely gripping a small clay pipe, he overcame his persistent stammer to recount how it had all come about, back in 1949: 'Beckett didn't know me. I had a little theatre – the Gaîté Montparnasse – somebody told him I was a director who might put on the play he's just written. I'd directed Strindberg's *Ghost Sonata* and Beckett came to see it. He came a second time.' Beckett who [it is rumoured] chose Blin because his production was faithful to the text and because the theatre was nearly empty every night, then sent a copy of *En attendant Godot* to Blin.

'I read it at once without understanding it very well, but I felt a kind of mysterious voice which shook my natural laziness, which said it must be put on and I must direct it, I absolutely must. I proposed it to associates who didn't want to do it. I took it to a number of theatre-managers in Paris – they laughed in my face.' In 1950 Blin first met Beckett – 'We liked each other at once'. Meanwhile he had found friends willing to work with him on the play: 'Beckett himself hadn't seen his characters really in writing them, he had heard their voices but hadn't visualised them, so it fell to me to choose the actors and, among them, those who liked the play and to find those also who would work without being paid and without hope of performing it.'

In an afterthought he adds: 'I was quite mad about Keaton, Chaplin, above all – Harry Langdon – those early American comics; when I first had Godot in my hands, that's what I thought of.' He cast an out-of-work music-hall artist as Vladimir – 'Raimbourg, a small man, he was a quite extraordinary Vladimir'. . . .

All these years later Blin can speak philosophically about the three years' search for a theatre: 'We had plenty of time to work on the play, to examine all the questions, and many false trails were avoided. Also, talking with Beckett, though he didn't want to give me much information on it.' One of Beckett's clues was that 'godot' came from *godillot* – hobnailed boot – chosen because of the importance of boots in the play. . . . Blin continues: 'I had seen the religious context – the tree representing the Cross, the two tramps the two thieves and the stories of being saved or not, etc. Some were to say "At last, a Christian play!" but I soon came to the conviction that for Beckett it was a mockery. The four characters represent one, who is Man. One is more lucid than the other, one exploits the other, etc. I didn't want to press the symbolic side – I know that at the end of the day the audience must get the play at the second level but to arrive there, it's necessary to achieve the first level. I didn't bother the actors by saying, "Look, careful, this is very important, it means something other than it seems." I wanted them to discover it for themselves; through the rehearsals they should give something surpassing the everyday realism of tramps – who finally are not tramps but you and me.'

Little by little they succeeded in 'raising' the play. The actors soon got its melody, the pauses, the rhythm. 'Then, for the movements, I first thought of something quite elementary, of beginning with their ailments: Estragon has bad feet and is always falling asleep so is more static, while Vladimir has bladder trouble and is therefore much more mobile, going from time to time to relieve himself – or try to – he succeeds or he doesn't. And Pozzo is carried along by his stomach – I imagined also he has flat feet, while Lucky is completely gaga, an ex-intellectual who gives a lecture; this lecture is not without meaning, based on three principal phases: the absence of God, then the dwindling of humanity and, following that, matter – stones and such things. If in this speech of Lucky's which takes seven pages – if you cut out all repetition, you come to something which really stands up.'

Finally they understood the play – Blin and three of the actors that is – there still was no satisfactory Pozzo. 'And really there was a kind of work done which wouldn't have happened if it had been immediately taken by a theatre.' . . . Two weeks to opening and no Pozzo. An experienced actor himself, as he knew the lines, he plunged into the part. (Amazingly, when it comes to acting he completely overcomes his stammer through a technique of breathing.) Not that he was right for Pozzo – Beckett had imagined the character as a kind of mass of flesh – 'But I put on a bald pate and a false belly and a "fat" voice; it was a total creation, the nearest I could get to the ideal Pozzo.'

[Thanks to a small subsidy, Blin eventually found a theatre for the play.] *En attendant Godot* was launched at the Théâtre de Babylone on January 5, 1953 – 'Without knowing what it was going to turn out as. I was convinced it was a great thing, and the actors also. Beckett had absolutely no idea – he hadn't been in on the production but had attended some rehearsals.' The outcome, as Blin puts it, was a 'surprise'.

A sensation actually: wild applause broke out from some in the audience, others sat in baffled silence, fisticuffs were exchanged by pros and cons; most critics demolished play and production but a handful wrote prophetically – among them the playwright Armand Salacrou; 'We were waiting for this play of our time, with its new tone, its simple and modest language, and its closed, circular plot.' Anouilh described it as 'the music-hall sketch of Pascal's *Pensées* as played by the Fratellini clowns'. Significant that playwrights were the first to value *Godot* – it is they who ever since have most radically felt its influence – to mention only Pinter and Fugard. It is all now a part of theatrical history, and Beckett was set on the path that led to the Nobel Prize for Literature in 1969. . . .

SOURCE: extracts from article, 'Blin on Beckett', *Theater* (Fall, 1978), pp. 90–2.

Elmar Tophoven (1953)

A French Dramatist from Ireland

The German translator of the play *Waiting for Godot* gives information about the life and work of Samuel Beckett, who is expected in Berlin for the German première of that play, that has sparked so much discussion in France.

All who know Samuel Beckett find it difficult to amplify the bare dates of his biography with anecdotes or remarks about his character. Not only because the slim Irishman is taciturn, but above all because his special discretion and sober avoidance of self-indulgence command restraint and attention. Roger Blin, the Paris director of *Waiting for*

Godot, who rehearsed for months in the author's presence, recently wrote: 'If you know someone who knows someone who knows Samuel Beckett, maybe you could, I mean, perhaps you could ask him whether, by chance, naturally only if it occurs to him, he might take it into his head to write a new play.'

That doesn't mean that Beckett is unapproachable, but Beckett is one of those authors who keep quiet if they have nothing to say. One needs a little of the patience of Vladimir and Estragon if one wants to learn more about Beckett's world than can be read in his work. At the Paris première Beckett was not to be found. He withdrew from success and the interviews that entailed. When he returned to Paris after a few weeks, he said little about the most enthusiastic, but often contradictory, interpretations of *Waiting for Godot*. . . .

'His voice sounds in our ears like our own, finally recovered voice', wrote Maurice Nadeau in *Les Temps Modernes*, and this comment contains more than mere admiration of the language mastery on the part of an author whose native tongue is English. This skilful and nuanced ability also characterises the Russian exile Arthur Adamov and the Roumanian-born Eugene Ionesco, two playwrights who, along with Beckett, are often called 'Le Théâtre Insolite' – surely because they appropriated the French language more deliberately than their native tongues.

One looks in vain for *bons mots* or wise quotable sayings in Beckett's play that premiered on 4 January 1953 in Paris, and then during more than 150 performances introduced the author to a broad Parisian public. And yet the playwright Armand Salacrou wrote: 'This new dialogue becomes immediately familiar to us and henceforth accompanies us.' This unusual play contains a variety of experiences that at first glance are not easy to pierce but then have a lasting effect, and these are staged so economically and yet unobtrusively that the effect is at once breath-taking and liberating.

Vladimir, Estragon, Pozzo and Lucky, the characters that Beckett puts on the stage, are more than parts of his own personality. The variety of their names indicates that they represent all humanity. A pitiful tree, on which a few leaves sprout during the intermission, offers the imagination only a slender clue in the playing space that is scarcely separated from the wings. The play's playing time is as endless as human waiting for salvation; it stretches back into the past before the beginning of the play and out into the future after the end of it.

One can anticipate nothing about the plot of the play because there is no plot in the usual sense. And yet something happens during the performance of both acts, where the second seems to be the repetition of the first. It happens between the stage and the spectators if, after its initial discomfort, the public increasingly recognises its own fate in the almost inescapable hopelessness of Didi and Gogo. The large question about the sense of Being moves all those who come into contact with Beckett's world. 'It is a play that I read and saw again and again. It continues to excite me', wrote Jacques Lemarchand in the Paris weekly *Figaro Littéraire*. There are indeed few texts for the stage which already in reading drive toward theatrical configuration, and which, after the final curtain, make one want to read it so as to penetrate more deeply into Beckett's world, which is our own.

SOURCE: article, 'Ein französischer Dramatiker aus Irland', *Die Neue Zeitung*, no. 208 (6 Sept. 1953), p. 12; translated by Ruby Cohn.

Peter Hall (1961)

WAITING FOR WHAT: FIRST LONDON PRODUCTION, 1955

. . . How did I come to direct *Waiting for Godot*? Well, I'd been director of the Arts Theatre for a few months, and during that time I'd been looking out for new experimental plays. I'd just done the first Ionesco play in England, *The Lesson*, when the script of *Godot* arrived – a bit dog-eared, I must confess, because it had been the rounds of the West End managers who'd expressed interest, and many leading actors had expressed interest too, but no one had quite dared to do it. Anyway, we decided that we would, and we set about casting it, and a very wonderful cast we had. We were under such stress and duress. . . . The play was so difficult – we didn't understand it – that we absolutely had to pull together. Perhaps it's a help to a director when a play is obscure. The actors can't have their own pet theories or argue too much. Mine didn't anyway. They trusted me, and off we went. The director of course shouldn't waver or doubt or not know his mind. Or at least if he does, he shouldn't show the actors. I must admit I didn't really know all of *Godot*, and I couldn't say in precise or literal terms that I understood it, but then I don't think one can say about this kind of writing or this kind of play that there is a literal or final meaning. I remember that I read it first between two dress rehearsals of a previous play at the Arts. I was immediately struck by the enormous humanity and universality of the subject, and also by the extraordinary rhythms of the writing, and it was these rhythms and almost musical flexibility of the lyricism which communicated itself to me and which I tried to pass on to the actors. I'm an instinctive director. Maybe I don't sometimes know why I do something, and a play like this I respond to very much, and my actors responded with me.

Looking back on the production, some of the things make me feel very hot and embarrassed. I used a lot of music, and I believe that I shouldn't have. Also, the stage had too much scenery on it; it should have been much more bare and barren. But anyway the play worked and was a great and significant success because it went into the West End and in fact was part of a movement of the 50s. I think the two plays which really broke through in our theatre in the 50s were, first, *Godot*, which brought back the use of the word and a frank theatricality which we're still living on and using; then *Look Back in Anger*, which brought back themes of social relevance – plays about that time. Both plays, it's interesting to remember, got more or less very bad notices when they opened. More than that, *Godot* is the only play I've ever encountered – up to that date anyway – which made a dramatic use of boredom. I remember when Samuel Beckett came to see the play, he said: 'It's fine, but you don't bore the audience enough. Make them wait longer. Make the pauses longer. You should bore them.' Now this is dangerous talk, dangerous country in the theatre. But undoubtedly, he has broadened theatrical language – the sense of time, the sense of waiting, the sense of hopelessness, the sense of boredom had never actually been used on the stage before, to create tension, and he did create tension. It was the happiest experience of my early years as a director, and I've often thought that I would like to revive it. If I do ever, I hope I shall be able to do it with Messrs Daneman, Bateson, Woodthorpe and Bull. . . .

SOURCE: extract from interview on the BBC Third Programme (14 April 1961) – BBC LP 26900A.

Philip Hope-Wallace (1955)

Two Evenings with Two Tramps

Waiting for Godot at the Arts Theatre Club is a play to send the rationalist out of his mind and induce tooth-gnashing among people who would take Lewis Carroll's Red Queen and Lear's nonsense exchanges with the food as the easiest stuff in the world. The play, if about anything, is ostensibly about two tramps who spend the two acts, two evenings long, under a tree on a bit of waste ground 'waiting for Godot'.

Godot, it would seem, is quite possibly God, just as Charlot is Charles. Both tramps are dressed like the Chaplinesque zanies of the circus and much of their futile cross-talk seems to bear some sort of resemblance to those music-hall exchanges we know so well. . . . One of the tramps is called Estragon, which is the French for tarragon herb; the other is called Vladimir. On the first evening their vigil is broken by the arrival of a choleric employer called Pozzo (Italian for 'a well'), and a downtrodden servant Lucky, who looks like the Mad Hatter's uncle.

On the second evening this pair reappears, the former now blind and led by the latter, now a deaf mute. As night falls on both sessions a boy arrives to announce that Godot cannot keep the interview for which the tramps so longingly wait. And at the end of it, for all its inexplicit and deliberately fatuous flatness, a curious sense of the passage of time and the wretchedness of man's uncertainty about his destiny has been communicated out of the very unpromising material.

The allegorist is Sam Beckett, who was once James Joyce's secretary[1] and who writes in French for preference. His English version bears traces of that language still. The language, however, is flat and feeble in the extreme in any case. Fine words might supply the missing wings, but at least we are spared a Claudelian rhetoric to coat the metaphysical moonshine.

The play bored some people acutely. Others found it a witty and poetic conundrum. There was general agreement that Peter Hall's production did fairly by a work which has won much applause in many parts of the world already, and that Paul Daneman in particular, as the more thoughtful of the two tramps, gave a fine and rather touching performance. Peter Woodthorpe, Timothy Bateson,

Peter Bull and a boy, Michael Walker, the mysterious Godot's messenger, all played up loyally. There was only one audible retirement from the audience, though the ranks had thinned after the interval. It is good to find that plays at once dubbed 'incomprehensible and pretentious' can still get a staging. Where better than the Arts Theatre?

SOURCE: review article, 'Two Evenings with Two Tramps', *Manchester Guardian* (5 Aug. 1955).

NOTE

1. [Ed.] As mentioned in the Introduction, this 'secretary' appointment is incorrect.

Alan Simpson (1962)

FIRST DUBLIN PRODUCTION, 1956

. . . In his letter to us, telling us we could do the play, Beckett said at the end, 'You had better, as a matter of courtesy, inform my London agents of your plans'.

Thinking this a mere formality, we wrote gaily to London, telling them that we proposed to present the play the following year. We were horrified to receive an apologetic but firm note from London, informing us that they could not consider granting us permission to present the play in Dublin, as they were hoping for a London production. This depressed us, but we carried on with our immediate plans, which took us well into the following summer. Cheered by the success of our spring season, we decided we could manage a short trip to Paris in June. I don't know at what stage it was when, worrying over the problem of how to bring *Godot* to the Pike [Theatre], I started to wonder whether in fact the London agents had any right to prevent us going ahead with a Dublin production. Anyway, I decided to try and have a look at the contract while I was there.

To my delight, on reading it, I found that the English language section specifically covered, on the one part, the U.S.A. and Canada, and on the other, the British Commonwealth of Nations. In 1948, the Prime Minister of the Irish Coalition Government then in power, in an attempt to 'take the gun out of politics' and to placate the extreme

Republican wing of his Cabinet, had declared the Republic of Ireland and had seceded from the British Commonwealth. This historic occasion had passed unnoticed by the London agents, and I realised there was nothing to stop us presenting the play, provided Sam would stand [firm] over his original permission. . . .

There was a good deal of shilly-shallying about the production in London. The London rights were held jointly by Peter Glenville and Donald Albery. Glenville, I believe, visualised the play in terms of stars of the calibre of Sir Ralph Richardson, but for one reason or another, things didn't work out for him. In the meantime, Sam asked us to hold our horses for a bit because, while it was clear that he was perfectly within his rights to let us go ahead, there was obviously so much money involved in the London production that it would have been disastrous if we had irritated them to the point of losing their already not very firm resolve to put on the play. However, ultimately Mr Glenville retired from the scene of action and Donald Albery decided to go ahead with a production in the Arts Theatre Club, without the publicity assistance of big stars. By this time, it was autumn 1955. . . .

In the event, of course, we benefited from having delayed our opening until after London. The play created an instant furore at the Arts. Almost without exception, the popular press dismissed it as obscure nonsense and pretentious rubbish. However, it was enthusiastically championed by Harold Hobson and Kenneth Tynan. As in Paris, it made the news columns of the daily papers, when indignant and respectable members of the community were moved to walk out of the theatre, or shout epithets at members of the cast. This sort of thing was by no means confined, of course, to London. In the Brussels production, a scandalised old lady stood up and shouted to her astonished companions in the stalls: 'Why don't they work?' Some wit in the upper part of the theatre, shouted back: 'Because they haven't time.'

In Dublin, the critical appraisal of the play was, as far as I can judge, more universally favourable than in any other city. This, I think, was partly due to the fact that . . . the dialogue is more entertaining in Dublinese, so it is easier for the audience to enjoy the play, even though they may not appreciate its subtleties; and partly, dare I say it, because many of the Dublin critics were regular readers of the *Sunday Times* and the *Observer*. Of course, we didn't get off scot free. The *Evening Herald* said, 'Some of the grosser crudities, which were omitted or glossed over in London, were included here. They add nothing to the atmosphere, and are merely an attempt to out-Joyce the Joyce of *Ulysses*.'

We had, in fact, stuck to the original bargain with Sam, and played the play more or less exactly as he had translated it. In the London production, there had been a number of small cuts made by the Lord Chamberlain. After considerable pressure had been put on him, Sam reluctantly agreed to allow the play to be presented, omitting these passages and words; for he realised that, after such a long wait, there was not much point in cutting off his nose to spite his face. . . .

Donal Donnelly was Lucky. He gave a magnificent performance, but the famous long speech was marred, I am afraid, by inadequate preparation. This was not Donal's fault. I had been most anxious to have him in the play, but he had contracted to play in Belfast during the greater part of our rehearsal period, and the only production I was able to give him before he left was five minutes in what surely must be the most unusual venue ever used for a theatrical rehearsal.

I cannot now recall the exact reason for this state of affairs, but we were unable to get together until a few minutes before his train left for the north, and the arrangement was that he should learn the speech during his period in Belfast. In order to give us the longest possible time at the job, we went into the toilet on the train, and went over the speech until the carriage was actually in motion, when I leapt out. I have always found that slow preparation in rehearsals is the only way for an actor to get full value out of the subtleties of a difficult part. Actors who have played a lot in repertory, tend to learn a part quickly – in some cases even before rehearsals have started. This has the effect of crystallising any inadequacies in their own personal reading of the lines, and it is impossible for any producer to readjust the interpretation at a later stage. With a speech like Lucky's, which is words of gibberish, the sheer enormity of the task of memorising made it imperative that the golden rule be broken. However, his mime was superb, and the intensity of feeling he brought to the slave's pathetic situation made it a landmark in his career and an event in the history of the Pike. . . .

As the run progressed, various problems of an unusual nature presented themselves. First of all, there was the supply of bowler hats. Both tramps wear bowler hats, and at one point, a bowler hat is jumped on and generally maltreated as part of the action of the play. So we had to comb the Dublin secondhand clothes shops to satisfy the steady demand. Another problem was chicken. In Act I, Pozzo eats a portion of chicken in front of the hungry eyes of Vladimir and Estragon, and subsequently presents Estragon with the bones. In the small confines of our auditorium, there was no possibility of faking, so the families of those connected with the management of the theatre had a constant supply of chicken soup – a by-product of the property department – for as long as the run continued. However, occasionally some slip up would occur, and the stage manager would have to rush to the nearest hotel and beg an astonished manager for a leg of chicken 'to take away'.

There is something about the title of the play which captures the public imagination and in Dublin, even to a greater extent than in other cities, *Godot* became a catch-phrase. If anyone, from Jimmy O'Dea in the Gaiety Pantomime to a corner-boy propping up a betting office in one of the poorer quarters of the city, was asked for what they were waiting, the inevitable reply would come back, 'I'm waiting for Godda'. At the same time, there had been a lot of controversy about Henry Moore's reclining figure, and the *Irish Times* cartoonist 'N.O'K,' captioned a cartoon of a Civic Guard eyeing a tramp recumbent against a tree, reporting to his superior, 'I'm afraid it's going to be no run of the mill vagrancy case, he claims he's the Reclining Figure waiting for Godot.'

The phrase crept into journalistic usage over all sorts of irrelevant subjects. A letter in a daily paper, headed 'Idle Youth', read:

> Sir. Your columnist, Aknefton, was in extraordinary mood in your issue of November 19th. His column was headed 'Idle Youth waiting for Godot'. As his story unfolded, he was referring to corner boys, as he described them, loafing outside public houses and betting offices.
>
> That description would be more appropriate for another kind to be found lounging in the coffee-houses and lounge bars around Grafton Street, St Stephen's Green and Baggot Street. They are the people waiting for 'Godot'. They have no problem as to where the next meal or night's shelter is to come from. It is they who have the time and money to bother about and discuss for hours the inane, purposeless philosophy of *Godot*. Not so the young persons that Aknefton saw loafing at public houses and betting offices. They are the 'Unemployable' and they 'deserve censure' said Aknefton. One would imagine we had employers crying out for idle, youthful hands. . . .

The more serious writers, too, couldn't let the subject drop. Profiles of Beckett were published in the glossy monthlies. The Irish poet, Patrick Kavanagh, contributed a newspaper article entitled 'Some Reflections on *Waiting for Godot*', and Vivian Mercier reviewed the Faber publication. All this was unsolicited. The Public Relations Department of the Pike hadn't to resort to any of the stunts normally in the repertoire of a theatre publicist. . . .

SOURCE: extracts from *Beckett and Behan and a Theatre in Dublin* (London, 1962), pp. 75–6, 77–8, 79–80, 81–3.

Alan Schneider (1986)

Miami Production, 1956

. . . The first week's proceedings went reasonably well. We read the play several times, trying to catch its rhythms and tones. Bert [Lahr] soon discovered that what I called 'Ping-Pong games' between Estragon and Vladimir were very much like vaudeville routines, and began to have a little fun. With both Wilder and Beckett behind me, I managed to come up with enough illuminating comments daily to keep everybody satisfied – at least on the surface. Every two minutes, Bert would smile and say, 'It's all opening up, kid. It's opening up!' I would feel good for a couple of minutes, until Bert would come up with the idea of replacing the end of the 'Let's go. / Why not? / We're waiting for Godot' sequence with his old vaudeville 'Ohnnnngggg' instead of Beckett's 'Ah'. Or ask me to cut the Lucky speech because no one understood it. And, anyhow, the audience was coming to see him and not the guy playing Lucky, wasn't it?

There was a lot to 'open up'. And four actors who had entirely different ideas of the best way to do the opening up. Bert kept saying he was the 'top banana', and that the 'second banana', Tommy [Ewell], was really the straight man who should be feeding Bert his laughs. Tommy (and I) kept trying to explain to Bert that this show had two bananas. (I was afraid to tell him that perhaps the character of Vladimir was slightly more central to the play's thematic core than the character of Estragon. 'Thematic core' was not an expression calculated to win Bert's heart) Jack Smart kept struggling with Pozzo's complicated stage business, finding himself almost unable to co-ordinate whip, pipe, atomiser, watch, etcetera, with his lines. Charles [Weidman] stood still and moved beautifully but kept delaying the moment of his speech. I was getting encouraged and discouraged simultaneously.

Somewhere during those early rehearsals, which he occasionally attended, sitting silent and saturnine away from us, Myerberg sprang his big surprise. We had originally been booked in Washington and Philadelphia prior to opening at the Music Box Theatre (partly owned by Irving Berlin, one of Bert's good friends). Our advance sale at both locations had not been going well. Myerberg had cancelled both and was instead taking us for two weeks to open a new playhouse, the Coconut Grove in, of all places, Coral Gables, Florida, near Miami. His only explanation was that it was a fine new theater with very comfortable accommodations next door for all of the actors and the director. We also discovered that he had been offered a generous two-week guarantee.

It was only years later that I got the whole story from Tommy Ewell. The owner of the Coconut Grove, a Miami businessman named George Engel, had been hoping to open his newly furbished and enlarged playhouse with some kind of Broadway splash. Engel had approached Tommy, whom he knew and who was then at the top of his commercial career, having recently played *The Seven Year Itch* both on Broadway and, with Marilyn Monroe, on the screen. Would Tommy come down to Miami to open his new theater with that same play – and Marilyn? As inducement, Tommy told me, Engel was offering an oil well apiece to both him and Marilyn. Tommy approached Marilyn, who agreed to come for two weeks; but at the last minute either she or her Studio got scared of her appearing on a stage, and she pulled out. Tommy then suggested to Myerberg that Engel might be persuaded to take Ewell and Lahr as a substitute for Ewell and Monroe. Engel, desperate for 'name' stars, grabbed on to the idea.

I don't know if Engel ever offered Myerberg an oil well in addition to his two-week guarantee. Tommy says he never got his. Perhaps there were no oil wells to begin with. Whatever the details, we did go to Miami, with most of us – from Thornton Wilder on down – fighting and kicking to get Myerberg to change his mind. He didn't.

After two weeks of rehearsal in our hotel ballroom, the play very roughly on its feet, we took a train down to Miami – or was it Samarkand? The theory was that we would at least rehearse the lines on the way down, but Bert's wife, Mildred, and especially his about-to-be-teenage son, John, kept him occupied. Any hour of the day or night, Bert and Mildred's voices could be heard through the walls of their compartment. And at one point, I recall preventing Bert from tossing his son off the train – a humanitarian action I have had some occasion to regret in recent years since John became a theater critic. I have no memories whatsoever of the rest of our cast on that train except that Charles was hidden away somewhere trying to learn Lucky's speech – which he still had not come close to delivering – and Jack was somewhere else trying to learn Pozzo's business – which he had never gotten right.

Arriving at the Coconut Grove Playhouse complex – architecturally best described by my wife as 'Miami Beach ungepotched' – we found our apartments to be indeed comfortable and convenient, right next to the theater. There was also a fancy restaurant, a fancy foyer with a fountain which eventually contained real live goldfish, a fairly conventional eight-hundred-seat auditorium fronting on to a Broadway-sized stage – and no dressing rooms. Tommy and Bert et al. had to dress in a couple of trailers set up in an alley off the stage door. The Miami audience was being informed, in large type, that Bert Lahr, 'Star of *Harvey* and *Burlesque*', and Tom Ewell, 'Star of *The Seven Year Itch*', were about to appear in their midst in 'the Laugh *Sensation* of Two Continents, *Waiting for Godot*'. The name of the author appeared only in very small print. My name, luckily, hardly appeared at all.

Rehearsals went like a snowstorm in an orange grove. We never seemed to be able to get through a single day's rehearsal as planned. The closer we got to opening, the more Bert insisted on his 'top banana' prerogatives. My telling him that Tommy was also supposed to get laughs made me the enemy. Tommy, who had persuaded Bert to do the show in the first place, was well acquainted with his colleague's insecurities and idiosyncrasies; he kept reassuring me (and himself) that he could deal with them.

Every day we came closer to our January 3rd opening, and every day Bert got more and more away from the play, from himself, from all of us. Like all good comedians in vaudeville or revue, Bert was an inveterate worrier off-stage, the saddest of all men. With us he gradually got himself into such a state that he could not remember a line or a move. Nor could he rehearse for as much as an hour at a time without some kind of physical complaint requiring medical attention. The action of the play required Bert as Estragon constantly to return to his mound to go to sleep or just to sit down. Bert never came back to the same location twice, even though the stage manager had marked the location of the mound with a taped x on the floor. (Years later, critic John Lahr accused me of tying down his father's freedom of movement to a mark on the floor.) When Bert finally had to accept the fact that I would not consent to cutting Lucky's long speech in its entirety, he insisted on going off-stage during the speech so that he would not have to listen to it. And he kept ad-libbing lines and sounds which had worked for him in the past.

Our Pozzo kept getting weaker rather than more secure in his role, never did anything the same way twice, and refused to pay any attention to my comments. At the same time, Jack had a strong voice and presence; if I could keep him from falling down, he might get away with his performance. Poor Charles understood Lucky's speech perfectly but could not learn it, could not speak it even after he learned it, and was absolutely riveting in his silent moments. Each day, he would manage to go a sentence or two further into the speech and then – literally shaking – run off the stage to hide in the wings. For years one of America's most accomplished dancers, a pioneer in the transition from ballet to modern dance, Charles knew exactly what he had to do in the part of Lucky, but his fundamental shyness and his own inner demons made it impossible for him to speak on stage.

Tom Ewell went on searching for the reality of the play and the truth of his own character. Like Bert, he was a natural comic, but he cared about the play and understood it as something larger than himself. As Vladimir, he suggested a modern Malvolio; I told him more than once that he should be playing Shakespearean clowns. We worked well together, talked about the play and about Bert, solved some of our problems together, and at least were sometimes able to share some of our frustrations. Bert tended to feel that I always took Tommy's side against him. I felt I wasn't on anyone's side – except the play's.

During those first days, Tommy still felt that he could evolve a way to work with Bert. By the end of a week, he realised that it was hopeless. Bert had to dominate, and Bert had to get the laughs. We might have been able occasionally to fool the audience into thinking they were working together, but Bert could not fool Tommy. Bert would just not look at Tommy or listen to him. He was never concerned with the scene or the situation; he just wanted Tommy to feed him the line so that he could get a laugh out of his response. If Tommy's line seemed to be getting the laugh, he would find a way of topping it. Tommy tried to explain to Bert that this play was different, that it was vaudeville all right but a different kind of vaudeville, in which the laughs were to be shared. I'm sure that Bert tried to understand – even though he couldn't. Nor could I really get to him, even when he managed to get to rehearsal. Maybe Jed Harris – or Garson Kanin – could have pulled things together. I couldn't. All I could do was provide the doctors and nurses and dentists who kept getting in the way of our rehearsals. Every morning, in rumpled gray pyjamas, Bert came over to our kitchen, to drink Jean's coffee and tell me, 'It's opening up, kid!' His wonderful rubber face was sadder than ever, and my own face trying hard not to let him know that I felt it was all impossible.

Three or four days before our opening, we had what was called a run-through, although stumble-through would have been a more accurate description. Myerberg's eyes were more cavernous than ever, but I don't remember that he had much to say. My most severe critic, my wife Jean, thought that the production had possibilities – if only Bert would realise that his serious moments were as important as his laughs. Tennessee Williams, who happened to be staying down at his Key West residence, thought the second act was wonderful. The first 'needed work'.

Soothed by some friendly comments, Bert began to feel his oats. He even enjoyed the play a little. Tommy, on the other hand, realising that Bert was taking everything away from him, making Estragon instead of Vladimir the center of everything, grew more worried daily about the play's future and his own part in it. He must have decided then that he would not go on with Bert and the production beyond Miami if Bert did. I kept trying to hold on to both of them, but in my heart I knew that going on with Bert would be impossible for me. Those last days before our opening, with the constant shiftings and manoeuvrings going on between Bert and Tommy, as well as among Myerberg, Bert, Tommy, Lester Shurr (who happened to be both men's agent and who was not happy that either one of them was in the play) and myself were positively Byzantine in their proportions. I despaired of ever making it through our opening night.

I was almost right.

Nine o'clock of 3 January 1956 arrived on time in Miami. The audience didn't. Everyone who owned a Cadillac or who could wear a mink coat descended on the Coconut Grove Playhouse at dusk and paraded through its goldfish-infested foyer to eat and drink at length in its ultra-posh dining room, all done up in special decorations for the occasion – although the dressing rooms were still not ready. In fact, the play and production seemed secondary to the rest of the evening's performance. Everyone knew everyone, and everyone kept talking to everyone else through all the wining and dining – and, eventually, the seating, which didn't take place until almost ten o'clock, more than an hour after it was scheduled. When they all got seated, they still would not stop talking, even though the house lights went off and stayed off for about five minutes.

Up went the plush gold curtain, and instead of *The Seven Year Itch* or *Harvey*, that audience got *Waiting for Godot*, not the 'laugh sensation of two continents' but a very strange sensation indeed. At first they laughed – at Bert trying to take off his shoe, at Tommy realising his fly was unbuttoned; but as soon as they realised that the actors were on to more serious matters, they stopped. By the time they got to the Bible and the thieves, they were laughless. As they realised what they were in for, a few of them started to whisper, a few to groan, more and more of them more and more audibly. Somebody walked up the aisle, muttering, to get another drink. Someone else joined him. Whole groups started to sneak out. Then droves, driving right up the aisle to the goldfish. On-stage, Tommy and Bert, aware and not exactly aware that something was happening, tried to continue. Familiar with the activities of audiences in burlesque houses, Bert tried to stem the tide by broadening his stage business. He got a few laughs and stepped on a few of Tommy's. I remember having to hold on to Tommy's wife to keep her from charging forcibly onto the stage to hit Bert. I couldn't stop her from doing some forceful muttering of her own.

By the intermission, at least a third of the house had left. Another third didn't come back afterward; they were too busy drowning their resentment in the theater bar, where the dialogue was more familiar. I slunk into our trailer camp in the alley. Tommy was tight-lipped and grim, Bert no different than he had ever been. Jack Smart, as usual, was a tower of whipped cream. Our Lucky, played that night by understudy Arthur Malet because by that time everyone, including Charles himself, had realised that it was impossible for him to deliver, had done reasonably well – being rewarded with stunned silence during his long speech and a small round of faint applause afterward.

How they ever got through Act II, I have no idea. Presumably only the diehards or those whom the steak dinner and whiskey had rendered immobile stayed on, awake or not. We wound up with three mild curtain calls, and both Tennessee and William Saroyan standing up in different sections of the audience shouting 'Bravo!' Afterward, we wended our way home next door for a cup of tea and lots of sympathy from Jean.

The next morning, there was a straggle of a line at the ticket booth, which lifted our spirits immensely until we realised that they were waiting to get their money back. More people cancelled their tickets, and many just didn't pick them up. The reviews for the audience and the building were excellent – and extremely unfavorable for anything that took place on the stage. The goldfish got raves. Walter Winchell, who covered the evening, accused us of being both indecent and immoral, and suggested we should all be tarred and feathered and ridden out of town on a rail. . . .[1]

. . . [*Godot*] could not be done by four actors, no matter how good they were, in four different ways. At least I learned that lesson for the five productions [of the play] I was to direct in later years.

. . . I wrote to Sam in Paris, taking full responsibility for the failure in Miami, and hoping he would understand something of what had happened. I didn't go too much into detail. His almost immediate answer was so startling that I have never fully recovered from it. Nor has any other playwright ever had his generosity under the circumstances, although one or two have come close. Sam told me that the failure was all his fault; he had, after all, written the play. Besides, he didn't mind failure. He had breathed deep of its vivifying air throughout his life. He was concerned about the failure in Miami only because it caused me pain. . . .

SOURCE: extracts from *Entrances: An American Director's Journal* (New York, 1986), pp. 227–33, 236. A shorter account of the Miami production was written by Schneider for the *Chelsea Review* in 1962.

NOTE

1. [Ed.] In justice to some theatre-goers in south-east Florida, Alan Schneider subsequently remarks that later performances in the two-week run were better received. '. . . though our audiences remained relatively small . . ., they grew in interest and staying power. Our nightly reception became almost enthusiastic – especially from the ushers, most of them students from the University of Miami . . . . A few days into the run . . . an absolutely ecstatic mimeographed review from one of the hotel news sheets . . . called our show "astonishing. . . . It is a play so enormous in scope, so compelling, as to require complete attention and, in a sense, devotion." . . . It cheered us up.'

Jack Anderson (1956)

Mink-clad Audience Disappointed: Miami, 1956

I felt almost sorry for the first-night audience which attended the elegant opening of the Coconut Grove Playhouse Tuesday night. Dressed in their best bib and tucker, wined and dined to a state of high-spirited anticipation in the superbly redecorated theater and restaurant, the ladies and gentlemen were sandbagged by an allegory entitled *Waiting for Godot*. You could almost hear the painful state of the audience, howling with disappointment as the principals on stage, Bert Lahr and Tom Ewell, failed to say or do anything funny within the audience's frame of reference.

What unfolded was an actually rather profound play by Samuel Beckett, dealing with life and death. The audience was more in a mood for *Guys and Dolls*. I was perhaps the sole spectator who was prepared. I had seen *Waiting for Godot* done before – early last fall at a private theater in London.

Beckett's play is a real feat of theatrical legerdemain in which the symbolism is apt to be quicker than the eye unless the playgoer has all of his wits about him. The average playgoer has had a hard time just 'getting' the more specific symbolism of Topic A which pervades most of modern drama without having to cope with Mr Beckett's more abstract purposes. But if he is of an intellectual turn of mind (just medium-domed will do) and absent himself from souped-up opening nights, he will enjoy this at least novel departure from all the recognisable structures of playwriting.

Waiting for Godot – if I am absolutely with it – concerns two bums in a limbo between life and death. They represent humanity at its shabbiest, finished with life and waiting for death – or God (hence Beckett's title) to summon them. On an almost stark stage on which stands only a barren tree trunk, bathed in blue light, the bums . . . pass their time in a sort of aimless buffoonery.

In the first and second (the last) acts, a brute of a man . . . enters, whipping ahead of him a forlorn wisp of a man . . . whom he has tethered to a rope. They symbolise the slave / master relationship of life. At the crack of a whip Lucky moves expressionless in obedience to Pozzo's orders. And almost at a crack of the whip, Lucky breaks into speech-making in which he intones all the inanities, the windy pomposities of human utterances in a rising crescendo of pitch until Pozzo shuts him off. . . .

For those members of the audience who failed to stick it out to the end, I might tell them that Godot never does summon them. At final curtain, Estragon and Vladimir are still waiting.

Lahr and Ewell did the very best they could in the roles of a play which I'm not entirely certain wasn't as baffling to them as it was to the audience. They lacked the polish of the actors I saw do the parts in London.

The Miami production, I understand, is a try-out for New York. I wouldn't try to second-guess the imponderables of a New York audience reaction, but it would be my guess that *Waiting for Godot* would be safer attempted in one of the experimental theaters off Broadway.

SOURCE: review article, 'Mink-clad Audience Disappointed in *Waiting for Godot*', *Miami Herald* (4 Jan. 1956).

Antonia Rodríguez-Gago (1987)

Beckett in Spain: Madrid (1955) and Barcelona (1956)

Beckett's theatre arrived in Spain in the late fifties when the fascist censorship exerted a stifling effect on the performing arts. Almost everything was banned, especially if it came from abroad. Comedies, melodramas and the 'poetic theatre of the already known', defended by the 'official' playwright, José María Pemán, contributed to the poor theatrical atmosphere of the fifties. Dramatists like Unamuno or Valle-Inclán were rejected; their plays being suspected of 'intellectualism'. A kind of cultural xenophobia was encouraged by the establishment: Everything coming from abroad was bad, especially if it came from France or Britain – nations which had helped the 'wrong' party in the Civil War.

In this kind of cultural desert only a few groups – 'Teatros de Cámara y Ensayo' – were able to inject some oxygen into the stifling theatrical atmosphere. Experimental groups such as: 'Arte Nuevo', 'El Duende', 'El Candil' or 'Dido Pequeño Teatro' in Madrid – and other similar groups in other parts of the country – managed to introduce in Spain the plays of Camus, Sartre, O'Neill, Miller, Claudel, Schéhadé, Ionesco, Beckett, etc. to very limited audiences. These groups were given 'a performance licence' only for one day, and for very small theatres, to protect the morals of the 'new Spanish Society'. The list of the suspected playwrights who could undermine the moral principles on which Spanish society was being built, was incredibly long.

It is not surprising then that in this rather special cultural atmosphere, *Waiting for Godot* was not even granted a 'one-day' performance licence, but the play was secretly produced on 28 May 1955, by the group 'Pequeño Teatro de Madrid' in the Assembly Hall of the Faculty of Arts of the Universidad Complutense of Madrid, thanks to the cunning of the play's director, Trino Martínez Trives. After being refused a licence by the censors, who considered the play 'obscure and obscene, not worth the trouble', Trives – a key figure in the introduction of 'avant-garde' theatre in Spain – went to see the Rector of the University of Madrid, Pedro Laín Entralgo and asked for his permission to perform *Esperando a Godot*, in the Faculty of Arts. Permission was granted, and in this unusual way the Spanish clandestine *Godot* was born.

The première of the play was as much a political as a theatrical event. It was an act in support of the freedom of artistic expression. Trives confesses that he thought that the right-wing demonstrators who were in the theatre were going to stop the performance at any moment. The great support of the majority of the audience (including students, theatrical people, intellectuals, artists etc.) prevented the right-wingers from jeering. The play was received enthusiastically and many people congratulated Trives, among them the playwright Fernando Arrabal who told him: 'If this is the kind of drama being performed in Paris, I shall go there.' Trino Trives staged the play around the idea 'no es vacío lo que falta', (there is no lack of void). The setting was very simple: a bare stage with a leafless tree. To make this tree more visible, given the technical limitations of the theatre, they hung a rectangular white cloth behind it. This was, Trives says, their only innovation; apart from this they followed the stage directions of the text very closely. The lighting was 'pale grey' until the end of each act when 'it faded gradually, engulfing the characters in shadows'.

This production, with the same cast was presented in Barcelona on 8 February 1956, in a 'real' theatre, the Teatro Windsor, and later in Madrid on 28 March in the theatre of the Círculo de Bellas Artes, produced now by 'Dido Pequeño Teatro'. Audiences and critics alike were divided in their wild enthusiasm or utter rejection. Beckett was, for critics, 'a fraud admired by the Spanish cultural snobs', and also 'a theatrical genius, true inheritor of Calderón, Unamuno and Valle-Inclán'.

SOURCE: originally delivered as a study-group paper in Paris, and sanctioned by Dr Gago for inclusion in this Casebook.

Friedrich Luft (1975)

BECKETT PRODUCES BECKETT: WEST BERLIN, 1975

It was a merry evening. Critics looked on with astonishment and laymen with enjoyment at Samuel Beckett's fifth production at Berlin's Schillertheater – his play *Waiting for Godot*.

When the Schillertheater last staged the play almost ten years ago to the day, Beckett was so concerned that he travelled to Berlin for the final weeks of rehearsals and decisively influenced the production of his friend Deryk Mendel. This time he was responsible for production from the very outset.

It was an evening of surprises and one of extreme intellectual pleasure. Philologists, literary critics and scholars have long waited for Beckett definitively to provide them with the interpretation of his play. But once again they have been fooled, enlightened or edified, depending on how they approach the work.

Beckett's production of *Godot* does not raise the supposed veil of mystery surrounding the play. He has not broken his silence. He merely puts on the stage what he has already recorded in his script. His four wonderfully human protagonists give a truly sensational performance, but none of the puzzles are solved – wisely enough.

Beckett has once again refused to pass any comment on the play – apart from the comment that he does not wish to make any comment. People who try to find some hidden meaning in this play about tragicomic persons waiting for nothing only have themselves to blame. . . .

Bollman and Wigger have belonged to the ensemble for almost a generation and though they are good foils they are also twins in melancholy and humour, like Castor and Pollux, each equipped with a false nose to underline their foolishness. Both are well-qualified and enchanting clowns.

Beckett allows them to play their parts as if they were set to music. He constructs comic or hideous fugues of dialogue. 'Constructs' is the right word. Even the shortest scene has something like architectural precision. Beckett's composition is painstaking. He always strikes the right rhythm for a scene and has it executed precisely as he wishes.

Nothing escapes Beckett's eye. Not even the slightest movement is left to chance. The rate of movement is calculated precisely, executed to a point of perfection and accommodated to the most favourable pace.

Beckett is a perfectionist. The pleasure contained in the play ticks like clockwork and cannot be arrested. Neither can the thoughtfulness, melancholy and sadness that automatically emerge from the clowning of Beckett's production.

The production could have been paced by a metronome . . . the comedy was constant, despite its desperate nature.

Klaus Herm, who played the hapless Lucky as he did ten years ago, received an ovation after his long and terrible monologue when, attached to the long lead of exploitation, he 'thinks' demonstratively and for purposes of entertainment. It was like being in a circus.

The same was true in the case of Carl Raddatz in the role of Pozzo, the depraved representative of the master race, the ruin of power and false grandeur. The actor evidently found some difficulty at first in jumping through the hoop that Beckett held up. For a few moments he acted the traditional comic – and that strikes a false or disturbing note in *Waiting for Godot*.

But he soon overcame that and fitted into the strict and merrily complicated pattern set by Beckett. In the end Raddatz is majestic. . . . He is a profoundly comic monument of decay, a figure of power robbed of his power. He managed to make Pozzo one of the most evil characters of all four tightrope walkers in this existential comedy.

The production never fails to fascinate, be it in an apparently extremely simple or then highly complicated way. The audience is presented with a technically sober and always comprehensible piece of magic.

SOURCE: extracts from review article, 'Beckett produces Beckett in West Berlin', *The German Tribune* (10 April 1975).

James Knowlson (1987)

BECKETT'S PRODUCTION NOTEBOOKS

For each of his own productions of his plays, Beckett has prepared one or two meticulous notebooks which go into intricate detail concerning the movements, gestures and other characteristics of the actors' roles.[1] These notebooks offer important sources of information about the author's attitudes towards his own play and are often more revealing than Beckett himself may have realised, since he was composing them very much with the practical aim of helping himself in the practical staging of the play.

Beckett has commented that the key word in his theatre is 'perhaps' and the *Godot* production notebooks direct our attention, first, to the radical uncertainty that characterises the entire play. In a well-known statement Beckett said: 'I think that anyone nowadays, who pays the slightest attention to his own experience finds it the experience of a non-knower, a non-can-er'. Estragon and Vladimir are certainly non-knowers and non-can-ers. They try or want to hang themselves; but they cannot. They try to leave the spot; but they cannot, detained as they are by their hope that eventually Godot will arrive. Even at the end of the play, they do not leave the stage, although the boy has told them that Godot will not be coming that night: '*They do not move*'. They are failed or foiled rationalists in that their efforts at reasoning lead only to uncertainty, disappointment or failure, and their rational conclusions are no conclusions at all. They keep an all-important vigil, waiting for a meeting that is apparently all that matters to them. But it is an appointment made at some point, in some form or other, at some time in the past. It is an appointment that they think (though they cannot be sure) they also kept yesterday in a place which, again, they think (though they cannot be sure of this either) is the same as the spot at which they now wait.

This uncertainty characterises every element of their vigil. They return in the second act to find that (they think) the shoes that Estragon left behind him have gone or at least that others (they think) have taken their place. But when Estragon seeks for epithets to describe his own boots, he cannot remember their colour and it is with the greatest difficulty that he confers on the present shoes an adjective that will serve to identify them in the future. A similar uncertainty surrounds their encounters with Pozzo and Lucky and with the Boy, who does not recognise them on either of his two visits. Indeed, on each occasion, he claims that it is the first time he has been there. But scepticism is pushed to its very limit when Vladimir (employing an argument already voiced by the philosopher, René Descartes, in the *Meditations*) questions the entire distinction between sleeping and waking, implying that there may be no more reality in the experiences of the day than there is in the dreams or nightmares of the night.

Questions are found scattered throughout the entire text of the play. For *Waiting for Godot* is not (in spite of efforts by some early critics to make it appear so) a philosophical tract which has been given a top-dressing of theatrical fertiliser. The essential qualities of uncertainty, ignorance and impotence that define the lives of the characters emerge in the form of hundreds of questions that receive no answers – some of them indeed almost seem to expect none, since, although interrogatives, they are followed by no question mark. In an unpublished linguistic analysis of the play that I have seen, it has been calculated that 24 per cent of the utterances are questions, while only 12 per cent are replies. And many which seem to take the form of answers are not answers at all, since they leave the troubling problems that provoked the questions entirely unresolved. The same qualities of uncertainty and irresolution emerge in the form of stories that are never concluded, actions that are left deliberately unexplained, and in the form also of concrete, visual images that reveal man as essentially befuddled, disorientated, lost and bewildered.

This aspect of the play is underlined very precisely by Beckett in his red production notebook in a section headed 'Doubts, confusions'.[2] Here he lists for three whole pages all the examples where doubt and confusion cause bewilderment in his characters. There are some dozen separate examples, such as 'E. [Estragon] casts doubts on appointment, asserts they were there evening before, though place not familiar, and perhaps Godot too, admits he may be wrong'; 'E. casts doubts on yesterday and does not recognise place'; 'E. denies they were there evening before, V. [Vladimir] asserting contrary and doubts on yesterday'; and 'E. denies his boots'. Such 'doubts and confusions' are not confined, however, to this single section; they find their way into many of Beckett's other notes relating to the characters' behaviour, starting with the question as to who are the beings who beat Estragon during Vladimir's absence and extending to doubts concerning the nature of the tree or even whether it is a tree at all. Such radical uncertainty about both the natural world and the world of human knowledge could, of course, be defined in terms of the theories of philosophical scepticism. But the production notebooks show very clearly that such scepticism is concrete, physical and all-pervading. They provide, indeed, in most instances, a powerful antidote to the tendency in some criticism to begin with the abstract and the philosophical rather than with the human and the physical in Beckett's plays.

Another section of the *Godot* notebook casts light on the relationships between the four main figures in the play. It is headed 'HELP'.[3] Here Beckett lists the many occasions on which one of his characters asks for help from another of his fellow ceatures. There are, he counts, '21 in all', of which, he notes, 14 are ignored, 4 are answered, 1 attempt [to give help] is made, 1 is not known, 1 is 'answered on condition'; and then he tires of distinguishing between them, commenting 'et j'en passe'. This section focusses attention, of course, on the relatively high proportion of calls for help that go unanswered in the play. But it also shows the unpredictable and ambivalent nature of human sympathy and compassion. For, in their behaviour one to another, Beckett's 'people' can be both tender and compassionate. Yet, at other times, they can be bitter, cruel, unfeeling, even sadistic. More disconcerting still – and this is surely the value of Beckett's notes – they are by turns inhumane and tender, and for no understandable reason either the one or the other. Yet, in spite of frequent rebuttals and disappointed pleas for help or comfort, his 'people' seem forced to seek for a degree of solace in the Other, since the solitude of the individual is even less bearable than are the frequent frustrations and irritations of togetherness. Again we are usefully reminded of how much Beckett's plays reflect observed experience of practical, everyday reality, rather than abstract theorising.

Many details of production set out in the notebooks echo the crucifixion imagery that is found deeply embedded within the play. There are cruciform patterns formed by moves along the up-stage horizontal line and back down the vertical centre line on a raked stage. The bodies of Pozzo and Lucky after their fall from the vertical lie in the shape of yet another cross. There are several tableaux of Pozzo and Lucky supported between the two friends – recalling, in Ruby Cohn's words, 'the many paintings of a crucified Christ between two thieves'.[4] Estragon and Vladimir often stand one to either side of the tree and Estragon, in particular, stretches out his arms – in John Donne's words, 'mine own cross to be' – even passing through the cross, as he takes up the Yoga position of the Tree. In the San Quentin Workshop production of 1984, which was supervised by Beckett,[5] where the same cruciform images prevailed, the production set them in the context of a long drawn-out martyrdom where the painful waiting was relieved by fewer and less animated 'little canters' than in Beckett's Schiller production of nine years earlier. Balletic vaudeville numbers have become a few tired 'wriggles', as the nails go in.

Finally, another important feature of both the Schiller and the San Quentin productions was that the central theme of desire for fulfilment and unity, yet actual experience of incompletion and separateness, meet in the organised patterning of movements into semi-circles, arcs and chords, and triangles. So Estragon and Vladimir moved in opposed patterns of curved paths and straight lines – in Fehsenfeld and McMillan's words, 'like a geometric arc and chord [they] connect cardinal points and define the boundaries of a closed circular world'.[6]

The image of circularity has understandably tended to dominate critical discussion of both the shape of *Waiting for Godot* and the view of human existence that is portrayed in the play. The Beckett production notebooks suggest another image which is, I believe, just as important. In discussing Estragon and Vladimir's movements, Beckett writes in the green notebook that the 'general effect of moves especially V's [Vladimir's] though apparently motivated that of those in a cage.*[7] And, at one moment, he contemplated having 'the

*To clarify the meaning of Beckett's 'shorthand' note to himself: the intended sense here is that the general effect of the moves is as if the characters are in a cage, although they appear to be otherwise motivated [J.K.].

faint shadow of bars on the stage floor', in the end deciding against this degree of explicitation. In the red notebook, he writes: 'Thus established at outset 2 caged dynamics E[Estragon], V[Vladimir] restless + perpetual separation and reunion of V/E [Vladimir/Estragon]'. For Beckett's man is, as Lucky's dance suggests, imprisoned in a net, able only to move along the strands of the mesh in the particular compartment which the two friends find themselves occupying. On a few occasions, they do sketch out circles, but these circles are traced within the spatial delineation of a larger net or mesh. When, in Beckett's production, Vladimir and Estragon go off-stage during Lucky's 'think', they merely beat their wings like birds trapped in the strands of the net and bounce back, as if on elastic, into the stage space to which they are inextricably tied. The theme of imprisonment is one which pervades the whole of Beckett's theatre. By means of the *Godot* production notebooks, we may then see Lucky's dance as expressing in a dramatically arresting way a much wider view of man as what might be termed a 'prisoner of life'.

SOURCE: specially revised and expanded for this Casebook by Professor Knowlson from an article published in the *Revue d'Esthétique*. The same subject is examined by him in a *Modern Drama* article (1987).

NOTES

1. These notebooks are all in the Beckett Archive of Reading University Library, England.

2. Reading University Library MS. 1396/4/4, pp. 79, 81, 83 (Beckett's pagination). 3. Ibid., p. 89.

4. Ruby Cohn, *Just Play: Beckett's Theater* (Princeton, N.J., 1980), p. 260.

5. *Waiting for Godot*, San Quentin Drama Workshop production directed by Walter Asmus, under the supervision of Samuel Beckett; rehearsed at Riverside Studios, London (20–29 Feb. 1984) for the opening performance at the Adelaide Festival, Australia, on 13 March 1984.

6. *Beckett at Work in the Theatre* (London, 1987; New York, 1987). [See also the following excerpt – Ed.]

7. Reading University Library MS. 1396/4/3, facing p. 1.

Dougald McMillan (1987)

THE MUSIC IN 'WAITING FOR GODOT'

. . . The music of *Godot* is treated in the *Regiebuch* (Production Notebook) as Beckett dealt with the series of four 'tunes' in Act II. (Act I is contrastingly without music.) Beckett's original plan was to have four repetitions of 'the dog tune', once 'with words', three times 'without' them. Vladimir's mechanical delivery of the march rhythms of the round beginning the act would have established the 'tune' for the whole series. The lullaby, the 'nightmare march' immediately following it (as Vladimir and Estragon try to walk off the effect of the bad dream), and the 'reconciliation waltz' (when Vladimir and Estragon reunite in a circle after a brief separation), were all to have been sung in the same martial rhythm. The machine-like rhythm and tune for round, lullaby, march and waltz would thus have made a four-part motif suggesting the unrelieved tedium and repetitions underlying even ostensibly different activities. This was the effect of the music in the 1964 Royal Court production. With Beckett's approval, Nicol Williamson as Vladimir sang the round to the rhythm of 'Carnival in Venice' [but delivered] the 'Bye, Bye, Bye, Bye, Bye' of the lullaby in just two alternate high and low tones – 'like the siren of an ambulance'. . . .

Beckett crossed out his first plan and introduced instead four different tunes. The dog tune remained unchanged. For the lullaby he chose *Schlafe mein Prinzchen, schlaf'ein.* The walk following is to the wordless accompaniment of Chopin's 'Funeral March' and the 'reconciliation waltz' is to the hummed strains of 'The Merry Widow Waltz.' These four tunes make a typically balanced set of similarities and contrasts. The series opens with the verbal circle made by the words of the round, which has no definite end and only fizzles down to a stage whisper after false starts and new beginnings. The series closes with the physical circle of the wordless waltz. Between these two come the paired lullaby associated with infancy – without words but so familiar that the tune suggests them – and the wordless funeral march associated with the end of life which follows it. The first two songs with lyrics sung, or implied, balance the second two which have no lyrics. The sombre round about the dog's grave and the funeral dirge alternate with the soothing lullaby and the merry waltz. Long silent tableaux, which Beckett called *Wartestelle*, follow the lullaby and the waltz to set up a further correspondence between them while also breaking the series into two sections defined by the long silence in the middle and at the end. Rather than the effect of one underlying mechanical rhythm of the first plan, the alternation of sombre marches and happier melodies gives the sounds of a life overshadowed by unhappiness and endless monotony lightened by brief moments of solace and joy. The concluding waltz, though different in spirit from the opening march, still has a heavily stressed, unsubtle rhythm which conveys in a more comical way some of the same sense of automatic repetition.

The distinction made in the *Regiebuch* between songs with words and tunes without them is not incidental. Vladimir sings in the play but the four pieces of music in the second act make it clear that the progression from Act I, in which there is no music, to Act II still does not produce a musical resolution. Everything does not 'end in song' according to the French proverb alluded to in *Endgame*. The series of 'tunes' begins with the dog song with lyrics about an ending but in a form that is endless, and it continues with a remnant of a lullaby. In the original German text Vladimir sings only the empty syllables 'Ei a po pi a' of the first line of the lullaby; but in the green notebook which preceded his final *Regiebuch*, Beckett wrote out the words of the first half-stanza of the lullaby. Unsung lyrics are still implied. The series closes with two progressively shorter bits of music, Chopin's funeral march and the 'Merry Widow Waltz', which are not 'sung' at all. Far from a musical resolution, the one quick turn of the waltz evokes a sense of musical form left incomplete.

Not only the pattern of the music but the thematic relevance of the implied lyrics of the lullaby seem to have occupied Beckett's attention. Although he copied out the text of 'Eia Popia' in the green notebook, the lullaby was changed in the red *Regiebuch* to *Schlafe mein Prinzchen*. It was necessary to find a lullaby familiar to the German audience and one with appropriate connotations. These connotations are largely absent in the original French where the 'do, do, do' of the text are merely musical syllables with no specific connection to any text. In English 'bye, bye, bye' echoes part of 'Rock-a-bye baby' which is further established by the melody. The words of that song –

> Rock a bye baby on the tree top
> . . .
> When the bough breaks the cradle will fall:
> Down will come baby, cradle and all.

– relate directly to Estragon's dream of falling from a high place and thus to the theme of the fallen state as well as to the tree. Those connections were not inherent in lullabies most familiar to a German audience.

In a German context, [the famous *Weigenlied* (cradle song) by] Brahms, *Guten Abend. Gute Nacht* (Lullaby and Good Night) would have been the most obvious selection. Its reference to a benevolent Christian God watching over the sleeper and its emphasis on waking in the morning would have made an appropriate, but perhaps too blatant, ironic commentary on the situation in the play. 'Eia Popia' of the original German translation was familiar enough to be recalled and served a more specific function – connecting the lullaby thematically with the round. The dog of the round is given an endless existence in the eyes of those 'to come' by a burial and tombstone usually reserved for humans. The lyrics of the lullaby copied out by Beckett in the green notebook show a similar misattribution of human needs and customs to animals:

> Eia Popia
> What rustles in the straw?
> The goslings go barefoot
> for they have no shoes.

In light of Estragon's boots, it would be more appropriate to lament that men are not shoeless like geese rather than to lament that geese have no shoes.

The change from 'Eia Popia' to *Schlafe mein Prinzchen, schlaf'ein* forfeits the contrast between men and animals. It introduces a greater note of concern for the sleeper.

> Sleep, my Princeling, go to sleep,
> the lambs and small birds are at rest.
> Garden and meadow are silent,
> not even a Bee is still humming.
> Luna with silver light
> peeps in through the window.
> Sleep in the silver light.
> Sleep, my Princeling, go to sleep
> go to sleep, go to sleep.
>
> All in the Palace's lain down,
> all is cradled in slumber.
> No mouse stirs about any more,
> cellar and kitchen are empty.
> Only in the chambermaid's room
> there sounds a yearning 'Ach!'
> What kind of 'Ach' can it be?
> Sleep, my Princeling, etc.

Who is more lucky than you?
Nothing but pleasure and rest,
full up with toys and sugar
and wagons still on the go.
All is prepared and ready
so that my Princeling won't cry.
And think what the future will bring.
  Sleep, etc. [our literal trans.]

There is something precarious about his sleep and uncertain about the future. The palace is quiet, he is at rest, but all must be prepared to keep him from crying. And in the second verse there is after all the background sound of a yearning, '*Ach!*' (as in Estragon's repeated refrain '*Ach ja*' (Ah yes) that follows Vladimir's announcements that they are 'waiting for Godot'). The singer asks, 'What kind of an "Ach" can that be?' The third verse concludes with the imperative question 'Think what the future will bring?' – an assurance of a safe and happy awakening, but also with a note of ambiguity appropriate to the situation in the play. *Schlafe mein Prinzchen* thus provides much more direct commentary on sleep as a temporary respite from a world of activity, desire and uncertainties. It also indicates an even more tender concern of Vladimir for Estragon than 'Eia Popia'.

Although it may work as subliminally as the visual patterns of the stage movements and so has received little attention, the organised pattern of the music is also a part of the 'shape that matters' to Beckett in *Godot*, and was an effective part of his direction.

SOURCE: extract from Martha Fehsenfeld and Dougald McMillan, *Beckett in the Theatre* (London, 1987).

Dan Sullivan (1977)

WAKING UP 'GODOT': LOS ANGELES, 1977

– Charming evening we're having.
– Unforgettable.
– And it's not over.
– Apparently not.
– It's only beginning.
– It's awful.
– Worse than the pantomime.
– The circus.
– The music hall.
– The circus.

That's a passage from *Waiting for Godot*, one of the great texts of the modern theater, but not always an easy play to sit through – particularly when it is being performed as one of the great texts of the modern theater. We have all endured *Godots* where flat voices, monotonous *mise en scène* and an inability to set the timing on passages like the above, were presented as aesthetic virtues. Beckett (we were advised) was supposed to be boring.

Gwen Arner's production of *Waiting for Godot* at the Los Angeles Actor's Theatre gives the lie to that. Ms Arner and her five players have done the simple and revolutionary thing of approaching *Godot* as a play that will not only work but amuse, if you pay strict attention to its rhythms and to the inner lives of its characters, leaving its larger implications to the audience.

Twenty years ago, when the play was new, everybody was trying to figure out what it meant. Not even its characters understood it. 'Nothing happens, nobody comes, nobody goes, it's awful.' It all had to be a symbol of something else.

At LAAT the question of 'meaning' never comes up. Like any good story, it means itself. Once upon a time, there were two tramps named Didi and Gogo who had an appointment to meet a man called Godot. While they were waiting they had many small adventures, such as trying to pull off Gogo's shoes (very much an adventure when your feet have swollen up like balloons) and meeting a genuine slave-driver pulling a poor devil around on a rope. Finally, the moon came out and it was time to meet Godot . . . .

The tramps at LAAT (Donald Moffat and Dana Elcar) may stand for all mankind, but first they're tramps. Godot may stand for God, but first he's the man they have the appointment with. Where is it all happening? Why, here. And just as we suddenly find it a clear play, simple in the way that many of the great myths are simple, so we find it a lively one. 'Nothing happens'? Nonsense. With actors like these, something is happening every minute. 'Return the ball for once, Gogo, can't you?' But in fact the ball is in constant motion.

In a sense, *Godot* is the longest music-hall routine ever written: a play for a great comedy team rather than mere actors. It was considered daring back in the 50s to lure Bert Lahr to star in the first American production, but the producers should have gone further than that – they should have hired Bobby Clark, too. The Lunts would have known what to do with Beckett's play, and so would Laurel and Hardy. Failing them, Elcar and Moffat are practically perfect.

Elcar as Vladimir (Didi to his intimates) is a soft, bandy-legged chap who believes in not making waves and in hoping for the best. Moffat as Estragon (Gogo, at home) is a skinny, long-faced chap who is always ready for the worst, and always gets it.

They are chalk and cheese, Mr Inside and Mr Outside, Jack Sprat and his lady: every great team who ever stuck together out of sheer polar attraction. And they have polished their routine to the point where it's like one half of a mind talking with the other half. They've kept it fresh, too. *Godot* isn't commonly thought of as a passive play, but at LAAT it seems an affirmation of the importance of putting on a class act even if you're not sure anybody's out there. It has always been Beckett's rationale for writing rather than being silent. If all we're doing here is waiting, we might at least wait with style. . . .

Friends? Not always. But partners. It's a healther relationship than the master/slave thing between Ralph Waite's Pozzo and Bruce French's Lucky. Here again our actors play the line and the situation without going for big meanings. Waite especially takes care not to be too heavy. He suggests a circus ringmaster (Liza Stewart's togs help) rather than a Simon Legree.

But it's clear that Pozzo and Lucky are in a more painful place than Didi and Gogo, that the rope claims them both. French is obviously in a bad way (his manic aria on philosophy suggests a learned man becoming some kind of horrible talking dog), but Waite's irrational outbursts show that he is, too. Beckett's hell – if this is hell – has levels. Pozzo and Lucky seem to have been churned up from the bottom.

Yet maybe it isn't hell. Waite consults his watch when he wants to remember how many years ago something happened, and we think of *Alice in Wonderland*, another strange story about strange people in an unidentifiable landscape. Where we know we are at all times, is in a theater. Robert Zentis's setting and lights tell us that.

It is a marvellous set, just wrong enough at first to catch our eye and make us wonder what Zentis is thinking of. Beckett sets the play on a country road. Zentis gives us a loft with ten walls, two doors (one with a transom), a ladder and a floor whose diamond-shaped tiles have almost been worn away. Though it has the skimpy tree that Beckett calls for (Didi and Gogo spend some minutes wondering whether to hang themselves from it), it isn't a country road. It isn't any place you could tie a name to. It is simply an empty box to do *Waiting for Godot* in – bare but not blank, the light walls setting off our black-derbied little men as distinctly as the screen did Charlie Chaplin. The transom has the cryptic quality of a Beckett line. Is it for Godot to look through, or is it part of the theater's architecture – a 'found' element made into art? Somehow one doesn't want to know. It's there. It works.

So does the paper moon – blue, naturally – that's hauled up at the end of each act, making Didi and Gogo suddenly feel solemn, on the brink of a great encounter. Somebody's coming! Is it Godot? No, it's Godot's boy (Ricco Williams). He says that his master has been delayed but will certainly arrive tomorrow.

Didi and Gogo are no good at abstract thinking – as in *Alice*, nobody in this production can keep his mind on anything for more than two minutes – but it does seem strange that Godot never keeps his appointments. On the other hand, if there is no Godot, *who sent the messenger?*

Nevertheless, says Moffatt, 'let's go'. 'Yes', says Elcar, '. . . let's go.' So they wait.

SOURCE: review article, 'Waking Up Godot at LAAT', *Los Angeles Times* (30 Jan. 1977).

Kenneth Rea (1978)

'EN ATTENDANT GODOT': AVIGNON, 1978

When the noted Czechoslovakian director, Otomar Krejca was invited to mount a production for this year's Avignon Festival, he chose Samuel Beckett's *Waiting for Godot*, and then decided to do it in the Cour d'Honneur – a 3,000 seat outdoor theatre in the courtyard of the medieval Palace of the Popes. Throwing out all the intimacy of the play, Krejca has concentrated on its universal aspects. The set, a huge white disc endowed with only a rock and the obligatory tree, is matched by an acting style more akin to Wagner than Beckett. On such a scale, the characters become remote (from the back of the auditorium it must have been like watching a flea circus) and archetypal. What is surprising is that the play appears to fit this interpretation quite comfortably.

The opening image is of utter desolation – two creatures dressed in black, roaming a bare planet, with no sound but the scraping of their boots. This becomes a recurrent motif, punctuating every verbal exchange. When Pozzo appears, Vladimir and Estragon scurry about, looking for a hiding place, but the tree is too thin and the rock too flat; they can take refuge only in each other's arms.

While this production achieves some stunning effects, much of the credit is due to its exceptionally strong cast. All the actors are well known in French theatre. Michel Bouquet is a Pozzo of tremendous authority. Most memorable is his exit in Act I. 'En avant! En avant!' (Forward! Forward!) echoes around the courtyard as he leaps from the disc, reins in hand, and gallops off to other worlds like a lost Valkyrie. Georges Wilson and Rufus make a dignified pair of tramps, precise in their timing and clear in delivery. And José Maria Flotats as Lucky provides one of the finest moments in the play with his great speech on the nature of God. For once it is not treated as so much nonsense, but a coherent argument, starting slowly and building to a heroic climax.

Krejca's production may not be very close to what Beckett has in mind, but it combines tight discipline with a boldness that shows *Waiting for Godot* in a genuinely new light.

SOURCE: review article, 'En attendant Godot', *Guardian* (8 Aug. 1978).

Mel Gussow (1980)

SOUTH AFRICAN VERSION AT NEW HAVEN, 1980

As a true international masterpiece, *Waiting for Godot* can adapt itself to different languages, environments and acting styles. The definitive production, for example, is in German, directed by the author. . . . Audiences at the Long Wharf Theater [New Haven, Connecticut] are having an opportunity to see a South African version, first produced at the Baxter Theatre in Cape Town and starring John Kani and Winston Ntshona, those two remarkable actors who collaborated with Athol Fugard on *Sizwe Banzi Is Dead* and *The Island*.

Beckett's text has been minimally altered. When Didi (Mr Kani) opens the second act with a song, it sounds like an African tune. There are certain embellishments in performance. At one point, the two leading actors toss a handkerchief back and forth, turning a small moment into a silent-comedy caper. With a multiracial South African cast, the play assumes different tonalities, but the core of the tragicomedy remains perdurable. Two tramps, born 'astride of a grave', wait out their lives, sharing familiar routines and rituals while looking to the unseen Godot for promised release.

Didi and Gogo are Beckett's Laurel and Hardy, the first a figure of some intellect and propriety, the second a rustic clown wedded to the ground. Mr Kani stresses Didi's academic fastidiousness. Peering through spectacles, pretending that his garments are not tattered, he faces life as one might prepare for a final examination. He is armed for exigencies, even to stuffing his pockets with radishes and turnips. With his voice raised to a slightly higher pitch, he trills his r's. To make a point, he lifts his index finger as if to acknowledge a student in a back row. To an outsider, he might seem imperious. To his friend, Gogo, he is an attendant nursemaid, shepherding him through their endless journey in limbo.

Mr Ntshona's Gogo is a man of earthly appetites and annoyances. He eats, begs, sleeps and snores – and his shoes are woefully tight. Didi's bowler hat is neat; Gogo's is like a squashed cabbage. This Gogo is easily mollified. When he remembers, 'Yesterday evening we spent blathering about nothing in particular', he wreaths his face with a smile.

The two actors, who have frequently performed in tandem on screen as well as on stage, have an almost conjugal connection as artists. Alternately, one acts and the other reacts. Gogo snores; Didi tries to wake him with a glare. Didi reiterates that they are waiting for Godot; Gogo sighs in exasperation (rather than, as suggested by the author, in despair). This Gogo seems irrepressibly good-natured.

In direct contrast to the partnership is the relationship of Pozzo and Lucky, master and slave, keeper and carrier. Even as they switch roles, they retain their essential personality traits. Bill Flynn's Pozzo is a provincial foreman, a bully boy, and Lucky is the target of his boot of command. Peter Piccolo plays Lucky as a figure of limberness. With his arms and legs akimbo, it as as if he were posing for a portrait of a scarecrow.

Godot is a play of infinite resources, and each version that I have seen accents specific motifis. Among other things, Donald Howarth's production appears to underscore Beckett's biblical references as well as the play's concern with questions of personal history.

Didi consults a Bible, extracting it from deep in his pockets where it resides along with all those vegetables; it is a book as thick as a loaf of bread. The two tramps are searching for signposts of their humanity, certification that they have visited this place before, that they exist in a certain time and place. The tree sprouting leaves, Lucky's lost hat and Gogo's boots all become assurances of a continuing life. Mr Kani and Mr Ntshoma are warm-blooded incarnations of archetypal characters.

Staging the play on a hilly landscape rather than on the usual open plain, Mr Howarth, as designer and director, offers a tangible *Godot* that also has a sense of playfulness. One could imagine this invigorating production appealing to a wide and appreciative public.

SOURCE: review article, 'South Africans in *Godot* at Long Wharf', *New York Times* (5 Dec. 1980).

Anne C. Murch (1984)

ICONS FOR A THEATRE DELIGHTING IN QUOTING ITSELF

. . . In its 1979–80 season, the National Theatre of Strasbourg (TNS) featured a play inspired by Samuel Beckett's *Waiting for Godot*. The text of this play was made up of extracts from the dialogue of the original French version. Such an event obviously constitutes a striking demonstration of the status achieved by Beckett's play in Western culture. But it also throws light on some of the changes which have occurred in Western drama since the end of the Second World War. . . .

The first performance of *En attendant Godot* in Paris, at the Théâtre de Babylone in 1953, was received with indignation and scorn. The scorn and the indignation were reminiscent of the treatment meted out to that other revolutionary play, *Ubu-Roi*, at the Théâtre de l'Oeuvre in 1896. Yet, a quarter of a century later, *Godot* continues to be performed throughout the world. Starting from the stage and the shelves of bookshops it has reached amphitheatres and classrooms, first as a prescribed text in universities, then as a text for secondary school students. Reaching an ever wider public in terms of cultures, age-groups and social classes, it seems to have thrived on, rather than suffered from, the delicate process of translation and interpretation. It has successfully survived the linguistic and cultural differences and distortions which such a process unavoidably entails. This very resilience confirms its universality.

What seems to have occurred in this singular rise to fame is that the *dramatis personae* – first given life by Beckett's writing, then, as it were, given a second birth through their incarnation on stage – have rapidly left the narrow precincts of art to become, perhaps subliminally, part of the collective imagination of our time. They have become crystallised into living images which Western or Westernised man in the troubled second half of the twentieth century recognises: he is moved by them and he identifies with them. Pozzo and Lucky as the master and the slave, functionally interdependent, are to be found in all walks of life. Estragon and Vladimir, as the ineffectual, likable, incredulous losers bonded in friendship, waiting for the miracle which tomorrow must bring, are also present everywhere.

The *personae* may have become somewhat simplified in the process. Their metaphysical dimension has lessened as the period has turned its back on metaphysics. Their comic strip features have been exaggerated as the world has turned to ever more simplistic, manicheistic representations of itself. And the detached quality of their irony has sometimes been overshadowed by their simpler, rough-and-tumble humour, so that the physical 'gags' are better remembered and better understood than some of the subtleties of dialogue. But the characters still stand firm as representatives of an existential malaise, epitomes of man's floundering in the prison of time and space, troubled by the riddle of mortality, the focus of a bewilderment and pain daily experienced and rejected. Thanks to their powerful *iconic*[1] quality, they can be used as *models* to give concrete expression to instances in the here and now of a plight whose universal dimension they initially articulated. They have become, it seems, a cross between archetypes and stereotypes, inviting identification over a wide spectrum of existential situations.

An early example of this, and one which has been much quoted, was the immediate success of the play with the inmates of San Quentin penitentiary in the U.S.A. The *dramatis personae*, prisoners of the human condition, were received as *icons* of the prisoners in the penal institution. The *personae's* general plight became equated in literal terms with the life imprisonment which was their audience's *particular* fate. Hence the immediate identification.

Another instance of this process, operating in reverse this time, was seen in an Australian production of the play in Melbourne

(Alexander Theatre, Monash University, 3–20 March 1976; director, Peter Oyston). In this particular case it was the *staging* which iconised the particular and the specific. Beckett's abstracted *personae* were made to fit the realities of the Australian outback. Vladimir and Estragon were presented as 'no-hopers' wandering aimlessly in the bush, deafened by the roar of omnipresent cicadas, clinging to each other in a hostile environment which emphasised the rejection of man. Pozzo became the *icon* of the colonial oppressor; Lucky, an Australian aborigine, the colonial slave. The audience, entirely white and urban, had no difficulty in transcending the regionalist *parti-pris* and identifying with the plight of the *personae*. It was experienced as their own malaise in a rootless culture in which they groped unsuccessfully for some life-giving, structuring principle in a big city, urban but not urbane.

Beckett's play, through a wide range of differences in stage realisation and audience reception, has come to offer a structured substitute for the apparently unstructured complexity of raw experience in any one reality. The substitute at once simplifies and clarifies this reality. It takes its place in the collective imagination and operates as a *stereotype*. I am henceforth using the term *stereotype* as positive and implying in my context the presence of an archetypal element.

The antipodean 'tampering' with the play in the Monash production was minor by comparison with the much more radical 'tampering' undertaken in *Ils allaient obscurs sous la nuit solitaire*, the title of the Strasbourg production.[2] In the latter, the performing space was a disused hangar, rented by the company in order to free itself from the traditional architecture of its own theatre. The spectators were forced to walk across the actors' performing area to their seats when the hangar door was finally opened. The whole length of the hangar, and about half its width, were used as performing area. The remaining space accommodated a few tiers of wooden benches for the spectators. The wide performing area thus set up was lost in fog (this artificial fog spread through the hangar while the spectators waited to be let in; water had been poured on the concrete floor across which they had to walk). The fog remained during the performance, though it began to disperse towards the end. The lighting was dim throughout, with no use of light effects of any kind. All the light originated from the props themselves. Surrounding a vast empty area in the centre, the set consisted of a neon-lit bar on the left with large windows through which could be seen a barman, endlessly washing and drying glasses and serving some newly-weds who were the only people entering the bar. There were two cars parked diagonally by the curb in front of the bar, the main façade of which was perpendicular to the audience; the bar occupied a street corner; a number of parking meters were aligned on the pavement. Facing the bar on the opposite side of the stage were two shops, apparently closed, but with their display-windows lit; in one of them a television set was turned on, as was the set displayed in the bar opposite. Another shop, neon-lit and glass fronted, stood along the back of the stage; but from what could be glimpsed through the fog, it turned out to be a dentist's consulting room with patient's chair, drill and the usual equipment. Between the bar and the shop opposite, and closer to these, a row of stacked supermarket trolleys divided the performing area, structuring the space with the props of a consumers' society already hinted at in the rest of the set. Against the back wall and to the right, a door was just noticeable, with two lighted windows high above it.

This space, marked by diffusion, and therefore quite unlike traditional concentration of dramatic space, was animated, not by four actors and the brief appearance of a fifth one (as in Beckett's play), but by ten actors. Four of them bore the names of *Gogo*, *Didi*, *Lucky* and *Pozzo*. The others were: *the owner of the Citroën*, *the barman*, *the bridegroom*, *the bride*, *the man with the Ricard*, *the man with the clubfoot*. The dialogue, consisting of extensive quotes from the original, was distributed in segments among the ten actors, not necessarily following the order of the original. The circular structure of Beckett's play was retained, though it was much less readily apparent due to the fragmentation of the dialogue. Perhaps in order to compensate for this, the circularity was underlined in powerful visual terms in the finale, where all ten actors filing across the stage suddenly stopped, frozen in suspended animation, in a grim version of a game of 'statues' in which no move forward could allow the player to reach his goal. The action, as in Beckett's play, was marked by repetition and deterioration. However, the clear binary repetition engineered through the two-act structure of the original was abandoned here. The show was performed without interruption. The repetition appeared fragmented over the micro-structures.

In Beckett's *Godot*, the deterioration is shown mainly through the changes suffered by Pozzo and Lucky in Act II. Pozzo has gone blind, Lucky can no longer sing or dance, much less, presumably, think. The change is presented by Beckett as wrought by life itself, by a fate common to all mankind. The perspective changes in the TNS play, which introduces the following added *peripeteia*: Pozzo and Lucky disappear through the door at the back of the stage into the area indicated by the lighted windows; the play continues without them (as in the original); then a huge explosion is set off in that area, sending bricks and rubble flying in all directions; out of the wreckage cries for help are heard, answered by Vladimir and Estragon's memorable statements about being called at last; when Pozzo and Lucky are finally dragged out of the ruins, they are in the same condition as the pair in Act II of Beckett's play. The explosion is associated with an act of terrorism by the audience. In other words, the deterioration is ascribed here to a human agency at a particular moment of history, rather than to man's condition viewed in universal terms and apparently transcending history. . . .

This use of pre-existent material may be seen (as in certain comparable Brecht plays) as a kind of vast *quotation* from a product of the incriminated culture. The product itself is incriminating, but in universal terms. Here it is inserted more pointedly in history. Quoting is usually a privileged terrain for irony. Not so here, where it is used both referentially and deferentially. Yet it would obviously be wrong to see it simply as a homage to a writer, for the 'grafting' is also a transgression of the cultural taboo which sets up works of arts as sacred and untouchable. The quoting, here, acknowledges the fact that Beckett's work, by its exceptional resonance, has broken free from such constraints. It confirms its passage into that category of the collective imagination in which it appears truer than life. But in addition to being a comment on the work's impact, the process of quoting is clearly a comment on life itself. Offering the 'show of a show' as a *faithful picture* of that life, it suggests that life itself has become a show which can only be apprehended through the mediation of the spectacular, i.e. the mediation of the alienating culture. A society celebrating its own finality in narcissistic fascination, vampirising in so doing the individual and his natural environment, is mirrored in a theatre about itself – a theatre delighting in quoting itself. . . .

The now frequent phenomenon of *quoting* in theatre may be linked with the increased dominion of a culture alienating the individual from himself and the world. Extensive quoting, in a creative work, however interpretive and critical, ackowledges this alienation in submitting to the power of the cultural mediation which only mediates back to itself. Such a process points to a refinement, but also an impoverishment, of invention. Furthermore, its appeal is necessarily limited – the quotation used as subject-matter only fully speaks for an audience conversant with the original; there is a real danger of theatre becoming a cult for the initiated few. One might view in the same light the present favour enjoyed by the classics of the repertoire and see them as subjected to similar limitations. They do not escape the principle of quoting because of the cultural mediation required for their full understanding.

The struggle of theatre over the last few years confirms its state of crisis. We may indeed be reduced to 'quoting from *Godot*', and we may be tempted to accept that in our bankrupt cultures the truly seminal power of theatre is also spent. Except that, as a rose is a rose is a rose, theatre is theatre is theatre, conjuring up in the multi-layered complexity of its signs the memory of man's mythical appurtenance to the world; briefly healing, through the physical immediacy of its message, the mediate character of contemporary man's experience of this world: re-incarnating him through the flesh and blood of the ritual of performance, even when the starting point is quoting from *Godot*.

SOURCE: extracts from article, 'Quoting from *Godot*', *Journal of Beckett Studies*, 9 (1984), pp. 113–17, 118–19, 128–9.

NOTES

1. 'The iconic is that which exhibits the same quality, or the same configuration of qualities, as the object denoted – for instance, a black spot for the colour black; onomatopoeia; diagrams reproducing relations between properties': O. Ducrot and T. Todorov, *Dictionnaire encyclopédique des sciences du language* (Paris, 1972), p. 115. (My translation).

2. With, as its subtitle, 'D'après *En attendant Godot* de Samuel Beckett'. The director was André Engel, the 'Dramaturg' Bernard Pautrat. I shall henceforth refer to it as the TNS play.

Linda Ben-Zvi (1987)

ALL MANKIND IS US: 'GODOT' IN ISRAEL, 1985

Without any preliminaries, the play begins. Two Arabs wearing knit and cotton caps, open-necked work shirts and baggy pants arrive singly at a construction site, one of the many that dot the landscape of Israel in the 1980s. They have probably been brought from their homes in the occupied lands to what is commonly referred to in Israel as 'the slave market' – an area skirting major cities where Arab workers wait to be hired by Israelis for day labour, most often to work on housing projects and settlements in the territories from which the workers come.

Behind the pair there is a steel skeleton of the concrete column they will pour that day, and a few cinder blocks on which they occasionally sit or stand. While they wait, the pair talk in Arabic: trading stories, telling jokes, making small talk. Finally, the Israeli foreman – in white shirt, blazer, khaki pants and sunglasses – strides in. He is preceded by his carrier, a poor Arab slave who is attached to his master by a retractable ruler fastened to his neck and who is carrying his paraphernalia of construction: surveyor's equipment and blueprints, as well as an attaché case and luggage.

With the arrival of the builder, the language of communication shifts from Arabic to Hebrew – his language. He talks to the workers in the slow, laboured form one uses with those unfamiliar with a language and they answer him in broken Arabic-accented Hebrew phrases. The carrier, however, in the one set-speech he recites, speaks in literary Arabic, a variation of the spoken vernacular form. Apart from this speech and brief verbal exchanges, little happens. The group stands for a period of time, and then the latter pair depart while the original workers remain and wait.

There is nothing extraordinary about the general outline of the play. It resembles a number of works written by Jewish and Arab Israeli playwrights during the past decade: plays which condemn the government's handling of Arabs, illustrate the evils of occupation and its effects on the occupier as well as the occupied; mourn the failure of the Zionist dream about the dignity of work and the commitment to self-help; abhor the class distinctions that have emerged in the society, and the material acquisitiveness of the new generation. The dialogue echoes words and ideas found in modern literature, the media and on the street. When one worker says, 'We've lost our rights', the other replies, 'We got rid of them'. Although the foreman asks the pair what they are doing ('Here? On my land?'), he grudgingly admits, 'The road is free to all'. The pair recoil from his treatment of his carrier – 'To treat a man . . . like that . . . I think that . . . no . . . a human being . . . no . . . it's a scandal!' – yet they feel impotent and incapable of intervening, and they are not even certain who is ultimately to blame for the condition. When one asks, 'Well? What do we do?', the other answers, 'Don't let's do anything. It's safer'. Both repeat the hope, 'Tomorrow everything will be better', and echo the phrase – the most common expression in modern Hebrew – 'Nothing to be done' (*ain ma l'asot*).

The play offers a comment – a painful, familiar comment – on the muddled mess of the Middle East in the 1980s, but it does so through highly unusual means. It never once mentions the combatants, Jews and Arabs; the expressions 'Zion', 'Palestine', or 'Israel' do not appear. It also offers no solutions to the stark realities it presents, ending as it begins, with the workers frozen in place, still waiting. It is not even a contemporary creation or written by an inhabitant of the region. It was composed in 1948 – the year the state of Israel was established – by an Irishman writing in French, a man who had never been to the area but knew instinctively that here 'they crucified quick'.

The transportation of *Waiting for Godot* to Israel was the idea of the talented young Israeli director Ilan Ronen, who had previously won Israel's Producer of the Year award for C. P. Taylor's *Good.* His cast, members of the Haifa Municipal Theatre, reflect the racial mix of the sponsoring city. Makhram Khouri and Youssuf Abu-Warda, who play Vladimir and Estragon, are two leading Arab Israeli actors; Doron Tavori and Ilan Toren (Lucky and Pozzo) are both Israeli Jews – Toron having played Lucky in the 1968 Habimah production of *Godot.* The original conception, described above, was 80 per cent Arabic, although the audience was predominantly Hebrew-speaking and had to read the distributed mimeographed translations of the play if they wished to understand the words. This alone was a daring act for the theatre company, replicating for the audience the experience of confronting an unmastered language in their own country: something Arabs face in the nominally bilingual but traditionally Hebrew-speaking society of Israel. In a second version of the production, which ran after the close of the first – and was perhaps a response to the confusion that the mimeographed form engendered – Vladimir and Estragon speak Hebrew, one in an Ashkenazi or European accent, the other in a Sephardic or Levantine form, and both revert to Arabic when in the presence of the Hebrew-speaking Pozzo. Lucky continues to declaim in literary Arabic, with his monologue reproduced in Hebrew for the audience to read. In this form of the production, the emphasis shifts slightly from racial and political to economic and class confrontations among the characters. However, the central image – Pozzo the Jewish master and Lucky the Arab slave – remains.

It is this second version of the play that I saw in a labour union hall in a small town of Nes Tziona, near the centre of Israel, in the summer of 1985, eight months after the original production had opened to wide acclaim. Following a tradition in Israeli theatre, the Haifa group had travelled there, as they travel to all sections of the country, to bring people living outside urban areas the experience of professional theatre. This audience, comprised of the mixed ethnic working population of the area, received *Godot* unreservedly: they laughed, whispered running comments, sat in rapt albeit pained attention as Lucky spoke in a language few knew, and applauded strongly – not always a gratuitous response of Israeli audiences – as the lights faded on the last tableau. Most important, no one in the sold-out house left, something Beckett audiences in far more sophisicated venues still do; and no one I overheard asked the often parrotted question of Shower/Cooker[1]: 'What's it meant to mean?' They knew.

SOURCE: specially written for this Casebook by Dr Ben-Zvi.

NOTE

1. [Ed.] Winnie, in *Happy Days*, twice speaks of the last passer-by name Shower or Cooker – punning on the German words *schauen*, *kuchen*.

Peyton Glass III (1977)

BECKETT: AXIAL MAN

. . . *Waiting for Godot*, according to Vivian Mercier, is a play 'in which nothing happens, twice'.[1] The number is important since it implies both progression and continuity. The play gives us two time segments of indeterminate length, perhaps days, which occur with certain evidences of sequentiality, and it invites us to find connections between them. The search for links between two moments in time, ostensibly the thread of the drama's 'plot', is in effect only a facet of a much larger search for connective threads which will link the four isolated and encapsulated characters to some kind of universalising and on-going process.

Beckett's description of the scene in *Waiting for Godot*, 'A country road. A tree', establishes, even before the entrance of the characters, the primary axes on which the play is to be charted. Since they lead both into and away from the stage area, the horizontal and vertical axes might be characterised as concrete expressions of explorational possibilities, avenues of potential discovery. Perhaps the clearest of the symbols is the road. As a line stretching away from the static point at which Vladimir and Estragon . . . find themselves, the road offers a clear alternative to their condition.

If the road visually articulates the horizontal axis, then Pozzo and

Lucky are embodiments of its directional characteristics. . . . They are capable only of forward motion. Pozzo's costume and manner suggest a ring-master and, indeed, there is something of the circus processional in their entrance: Lucky's cry precedes Lucky who, in turn, precedes Pozzo. The Pozzo-Lucky relationship, as indicated by Pozzo's commands, is also directionally oriented. Lucky is ordered to bring, to stoop, to get up, to get back, and, most significantly, to go on.

The symbiotic bond between Pozzo and Lucky is represented by the rope which joins them together. Beckett emphasises this symbolic link by making the rope long enough for Lucky to be at center-stage before Pozzo appears. Thus the rope, stretching from one character to another, is . . . a visual articulation of the horizontal axis of the play.[2] It must be remembered, however, that although Pozzo and Lucky are in constant forward motion, their freedom is only that of movement. They are forever linked to one another. This condition echoes that of Vladimir and Estragon who are similarly inextricably fixed.

The forward-oriented motion of Pozzo and Lucky contrasts with the tentative movements of Vladimir and Estragon, movements which appear to be directed only toward discovering the limits of stage space. Estragon, for example, shortly after the beginning of the play '. . . *rises painfully, goes limping to extreme left, halts, gazes off into distance with his hand screening his eyes, turns, goes to extreme right, gazes into distance*'. Later, Estragon '. . . *turns, advances to front, halts facing auditorium*'. Still later, he follows Vladimir '. . . *as far as the limits of the stage*'.

The various expressions of the vertical axis of the play take less time to explain. Its primary symbol is the tree. Mircea Eliade has noted the importance of a sacred pole representing a 'cosmic axis' in tribal religions.[3] Hugh Kenner points out that the tree suggests not only crucifixion, but also the Tree of Life.[4] There is a suggestion as well that, because of its pronounced axial properties, it may also be related to the 'World tree' of Norse mythology. The tree likewise gives tentative evidence of chronological stability and, hence, links between one point in time and another. In Act II, the tree which was previously bare has produced leaves, a change which implies a refutation to the understood hypothesis of the play that 'nothing happens'.

As with the horizontal, representation of the vertical axis is an identifiable *motif* of the play. It is seen primarily in the thematic inferences that Beckett draws from a standing figure as opposed to one at rest or collapsed. Erect, the body is itself a vertical plane, marked at either end by the head and feet. This particular distribution allows for the delineation of characters in terms of hats and boots, two of the major symbols of the play. Vladimir, the 'thinker' of the two, is associated with the hat. . .; the more prosaic Estragon is identified with the boots. In Act I, Vladimir takes off his hat, looks inside and shakes it as if to dislodge something while Estragon repeats these motions with his boots. Lucky does not 'think' until the bowler has been put on his head.

Activity along a vertical plane is also seen in the large number of falls which pervade the play. (In a lovely stroke, the final fall of the play is not of man, but of trousers.) Niklaus Gessner has noted that there are forty-five stage directions in which characters leave the upright position.[5] As Martin Esslin has pointed out, these falls are of a highly symbolic nature, carrying with them overtones of the Original Fall and the destruction of the dignity of man.[6]

. . . Death in *Godot* is generally depicted in terms of vertical movement. Thus we find suicide contemplated by means of hanging or jumping. A similar vertical directionality is seen in Vladimir's description of the life/death matrix: 'Astride of a grave and a difficult birth. Down in the hole, lingeringly, the grave-digger puts on the forceps'. Death is seen as an avenue of escape, a line leading away from the condition of nothingness; however, like the other avenues of escape in the play, it is eliminated as a possibility. Suicide fails; death, like Godot, will not come; and the characters remain exactly where they are.

The emphasis on the axes suggests the basic strategy of *Waiting for Godot*: the frustration, visually presented, of movement along any line which might lead away from the immediate condition. We have thus far seen the establishment of two of these lines in the various articulations of the horizontal and vertical axes of the play. To these must be added two other concepts, time and language, each of which offers the possibility of a system of linkages which is potentially liberating, and each of which in the play is rendered invalid.

Time in *Godot* is primarily a function of memory; its invalidation takes the form of amnesia. If a temporal connection between the two 'days' which constitute the two acts of the play can be proven, then time is demonstrably in motion and the waiting of Vladimir and Estragon, by virtue of its sense of 'progress', is justified. But this is precisely what does not happen. Estragon cannot remember whether they were there the day before or not; Vladimir is uncertain, Pozzo is too wrapped up in his present agony to care, and Lucky is once again mute. Since Beckett's cast list calls for one boy rather than two, the boy who appears at the end of Act II is clearly the same boy who appeared at the end of Act I; yet he is incapable of recalling any previous encounter with Vladimir and Estragon.

Describing what he calls Beckett's 'characteristic comedy of impasse', Kenner discusses the architectural relationship between the arrangement of words in a sentence and the idea that the sentence expresses.[7] Such relationships, which may be seen clearly in poetry, are less apparent in drama. Nevertheless, such a concept does exist and is particularly important in a play such as *Waiting for Godot* which attempts to define (shape) its spatial context. Just as stage movement suggests the visualisation of dramatic lines of force, so dialogue may be conceived of as a verbal 'movement' expressing in auditory form the dynamics of a particular relationship. Viewed in this sense, the term 'line' takes on a special significance; it suggests a tangible expression of the concept of communication, a concept not unlike the Renaissance notion of eye beams or the comic-strip convention of visualising conversation in balloons.

Two of the clearest examples of such expressions suggesting movement in *Waiting for Godot* are Lucky's 'thinking' in Act I and the 'round' which Vladimir sings at the beginning of Act II. In the former instance, the tortured convolutions of Lucky's 'argument', a parody of the linear progression of formal logic, may be read as a verbal analogue to the similarly twisted set of movements which comprise the dance Pozzo calls 'the Net'. Vladimir's song is important because it deals with the themes of death and repetition, and because its form, like that of the play as a whole, denies any possibility of progress or resolution. . . . A similar instance is seen in the lullaby in Act II: a lullaby which, like practically everything else in the play, exhibits a resistance to linear development. . . .

In exchanges of dialogue, Beckett reaches his 'comedy of impasse' by organising the speeches of his characters in patterns that tend to destroy the momentum of normal discourse. Generally, dialogue may be conceived of as flowing back and forth from one character to another but moving 'forward' to the extent that one speech responds to material in another. This mode is reflected in the question-and-answer dialogue that constitutes most of the play. . . .

. . . Like a tennis match, lines of dialogue cross back and forth between the participants across an intervening space. Silence, or failure to respond, destroys the game's continuity (*Vladimir*: 'Come on, Didi, return the ball, can't you, once in a way?'). As the play progresses and Vladimir and Estragon become more compulsively involved in the games, the emphasis shifts from content to form ('That's the idea, let's ask each other questions') reducing substantially the information-imparting aspect of the game and hence its forward motion. The result is illusory rather than substantive progress.

An intensification of the word game is the verbal 'duel' which takes place in Act II. . . . The duel is clearly a conversational impasse which, like other activities in the play, gives only the impression of continuity. There is an increase in tempo and volume, but no progress is made; one line cancels out the other.

Opposed to the word duel is another conversational game with directional overtones. This game we might call 'Synonyms'. . . . Esslin notes that such conversations derive from the 'cross talk' of vaudeville. A more accurate directional description might be parallel conversation, since the lines of cross talk do not, in fact, cross but rather proceed in the same plane without making contact with one another. Parallel conversation is the result of a dialogue between characters who refuse to be untracked from an individual train of thought. There can be no real progress in 'Synonyms' since, as the name implies, the object of the game is to locate alternatives rather than to establish relationships. This, again, is very much in keeping with the major ideas of the play. The form of the dialogue, then, might be rendered as:

QUESTION:	What do dead voices sound like?	
ANSWER:	*Vladimir:*	*Estragon:*
	Wings	Leaves
	Sand	Leaves
	Whisper	Rustle
	Murmur	Rustle
	Feathers	Leaves
	Ashes	Leaves.

As might be expected, the real games of *Godot*, those involving movement as part of play, have clearly defined spatial properties and serve, as do the majority of movements in the play, to confound forward motion. In Act II, Vladimir finds Lucky's hat on the ground and, finding this corroboration of their presence there the day before, is pleased. A game ensues in which the hats are passed back and forth between the two characters. As with most of the activity in the play, function is subsumed in form; whatever practical value might adhere to the exchange is obscured by its compulsive repetition. Like the word duel, the hat exchange is a shuttle, a repeating transversal of space. Symbolically, the shuttle demonstrates one of the key considerations of the play, pointless activity and the ultimate negation of movement. Sustained movement along the horizontal plane is impossible. Pozzo and Lucky, identified with resolutely forward movement in Act I, return in Act II to the same place along the same line.

Movements along the horizontal axis, then, cancel themselves out: those along the vertical are overwhelmingly downward, generally ending in an inert lump on the floor of the stage. Here the game, played for the amusement of both stage characters and spectators, is 'All Fall Down'. The assumptions of this fall are both tragic and comic: Pozzo down epitomises all fallen men (he answers to both Abel and Cain, and Estragon remarks that he is 'all humanity'); he is also the source of slapstick humor . . . .

The systematic elimination of outward-extending axes suggests an accompanying centripetal movement toward the intersection of these two lines. Hugh Kenner has noted that the tree and road are coordinates o, o, 'the intersection of the Cartesian axes'.[8] Rather than a fixed point, however, the core of the Beckett play is emptiness, a nucleic area of dead space at its absolute center. It is this encapsulated space which is the basis of the theatre images most often associated with Beckett: the sacks of *Act Without Words II*; the literally entombed figures of *Endgame* and *Happy Days*. In *Godot* it is seen in the recurring sequence of containers and circles – hats, boots, the low grave-like mound on which Estragon sits; in Lucky's dance, 'The Net'; and in the circular structure of the play itself. Echoing the thematic paradox of the play, the circle is simultaneously endless and constricting, infinity and a cage.

The images of encapsulated space lead us once more to the place where we began: to an empty stage where man will struggle, not so much with the characters who occupy the same space, as with space itself. For Beckett, the question of existence is inextricably linked with the question of location; this is reflected in his plays in an almost obsessive concern with measuring and orientation. Ultimately, however, the attempts of the individual to define himself by fixing his position within the void must be regarded as failures. Orientational axes exist, but only to indicate what might be, not what is. For all his attempts to move along these lines, he will end, as the two tramps in *Waiting for Godot*, unmoving and alone.

SOURCE: extract from article, 'Beckett: Axial Man', *Educational Theatre Journal* (Oct. 1977), pp. 366–76 (play quotes excised).

NOTES

[Reorganised and renumbered from the original – Ed.]

1. Vivian Mercier, 'The Mathematical Limit', *The Nation* (14 Feb. 1959), pp. 144–5. In this article on Beckett's *The Unnamable*, Professor Mercier

discusses the 'co-ordinates' of the novel and concludes that its mathematical limits are, 'content zero, length infinity'. He then recommends as an exercise attempting to represent graphically the action of *Waiting for Godot*. The present essay represents such an attempt.

2. Martin Esslin has pointed out the extent to which *Godot* employs music-hall routines. One such routine features a man who enters hauling mightily at one end of a rope. He pulls the rope all the way across the stage and disappears into the wings. The still-taut rope continues to move across the stage as if still being pulled, whereupon the same man emerges tugging its other end. See his *Theatre of the Absurd* (1961; 1968 edn), pp. 26–7.

3. Mircea Eliade, *The Sacred and the Profane* (New York, 1959), p. 33.

4. Hugh Kenner, *Samuel Beckett: A Critical Study* (Berkeley, 1968), p. 133; cf. Eliade's remarks on the cosmic axis.

5. Niklaus Gessner, *Die Unzulanglichkeit der Sprache* (Zurich, 1957), p. 32; quoted in Esslin, p. 27.

6. Esslin, p. 27. 7. Kenner, p. 10. 8. Ibid., p. 10.

John Fletcher (1972)

The Play's Balance

. . . The vital thing for any production of this play to achieve, in fact, is a proper tautness. It may not be constructed along traditional lines, with exposition, development, peripeteia and dénouement, but it *has* a firm structure, albeit of a different kind, a structure based on repetition, the return of leitmotifs, and on the exact balancing of variable elements, and it is this structure which must be brought out in production. The sort of repetition the audience must be conditioned to respond to can be seen in the following example. Pozzo, having eaten his meal and lit his pipe, says with evident satisfaction, 'Ah! That's better' . . . . Two pages later Estragon makes precisely the same comment, having just gnawed the remaining flesh of Pozzo's discarded chicken bones. But the circumstances, though similar, are not identical: Pozzo has fed to satiety, Estragon has made a meagre repast of his leavings. The repetition of the words in different mouths is therefore an ironical device for pointing a contrast, like that between Pozzo's selfish bellow 'Coat!' to Lucky in Act I, and Vladimir's selfless spreading of *his* coat round Estragon's shoulders in Act II.

The entire movement of the play, therefore, depends on balance. 'It is the shape that matters', Beckett once remarked apropos of the

Augustinian saying which underlies so much of the play's symbolism: 'Do not despair – one of the thieves was saved; do not presume – one of the thieves was damned.' It is certainly the shape that matters here: the director must bring out the 'stylised movement' which Beckett himself stressed in discussion with Charles Marowitz: a movement which relies heavily on asymmetry, or repetition-with-a-difference. In both acts, for instance, Pozzo's arrival is curiously foreshadowed by one of the men imagining he hears sounds of people approaching; and whereas in the first act the two prop Lucky up, in the second they serve as 'caryatids' to Pozzo. But the most poignant example is the ending of the two sections, where the wording is identical, the punctuation varied only slightly to slow down delivery the second time, but the roles reversed: in Act I Estragon asks the question, but Act II gives it to Vladimir:

VLADIMIR: Well? Shall we go?
ESTRAGON: Yes, let's go.

The first time round, these two sentences can be delivered at more or less normal speed, but on the second occasion they should be drawn out, with three- to six-second pauses between their consistent phrases. When this is done, the intense emotion generated in the auditorium as the last curtain falls is redolent of great sadness.

But the asymmetrical reproduction of nearly everything in two acts of unequal length is not the only structural feature in the play. Another is the manner in which the counterpointing of the act-structure is mirrored in the contrasted characterisation. Estragon's name is composed of the same number of letters as Vladimir's; the same applies to Pozzo and Lucky. Hence, they find themselves associated, and have been joined in a complex sado-masochistic relationship for many years. But their natures obviously conflict: Vladimir is the neurotic intellectual type, Estragon the placid intuitive sort; Pozzo is the bullying extravert, Lucky the timorous introvert. Vladimir instinctively sympathises with Lucky, and for Pozzo Estragon experiences a degree of fellow-feeling. Vladimir and Pozzo, like Lucky and Estragon who kick each other, are at the extremes of the poised poles. Estragon is afraid of being 'tied', Lucky is tied in effect; Vladimir kow-tows to authority, Pozzo asserts it forcibly. The characters, in fact, like the occurrences both major and minor, are held in uneasy equilibrium within this play.

Yet another of its structural features is the way the writing modulates continually from one tone to its opposite. Pozzo's declamation on the night, for instance, shifts almost violently from the false sublime to the prosaically ridiculous, and after rising to 'vibrant' heights lapses to 'gloomy' depths, and ultimately to inevitable silence. After a long pause, Estragon and Vladimir strike up and swap vaudeville remarks . . . . The transition is masterly, almost musical in subtlety, like the sound of the strings when the brass dies away. Similar modulation occurs between the high jinks of the business around Lucky in Act I and the high grief of Vladimir's cross-examination of the Boy in Act II, culminating in the great cry from the mass, 'Christ have mercy on us!'. . . . Farce and pathos are closely mingled throughout, but perhaps most obviously at the start of Act II in the clowns' loving embrace which ends, appropriately, in a grotesque pratfall.

The whole of Act II, in fact, shows a slightly different tone from Act I. The cross-talk is of a more 'intellectual' and less overtly music-hall kind; the confident Pozzo of the first act is changed into the sightless decrepit of Act II; and the words of the Boy, delivered 'in a rush' in Act I, have to be dragged out of him by Vladimir the second time round. The entire second panel of this diptych is less naturalistic, and assumes familiarity with the two down-and-outs and their ways which permits a briefer restatement of the theme. Pozzo enters later, and is sooner gone. Lucky's monologue of Act I, despite its repetitious and garbled jargon, made a point: that man, notwithstanding the existence of a caring God of sorts and progress of various kinds, is in full decline; even this statement from a degraded man of reason cannot recur in Act II, because, we learn with terror, he has gone dumb.

Lucky's speech, however, like so much else in the play, is calculatedly deceptive if we expect it to yield a significant key to the work as a whole. Those who are perplexed by the play's 'meaning' may draw at least some comfort from the author's assurance that it means what it says, neither more nor less. . . .

SOURCE: extract from chapter ('Bailing Out the Silence') in John Fletcher and John Spurling, *Beckett: A Study of His Plays* (London, 1972; New York, 1972), pp. 65–8.

PART TWO

The Study

Colin Duckworth *Godot*: Genesis and Composition (1966)

... The first page of the manuscript of *En attendant Godot* bears the date '9 October 1948'; the last '29 January 1949'. Between these dates Beckett put aside *Malone meurt* and wrote the play which was due to cause as much controversy among scholars and critics as Goethe's *Faust* and Kafka's *Castle*. 'I began to write *Godot*', Mr Beckett told me, 'as a relaxation, to get away from the awful prose I was writing at that time.' Although *Godot* was in many ways – structurally, stylistically, thematically – a new development in Beckett's writing, it expressed his basic concerns as faithfully and sincerely as his novels.

In *L'Avant-Scène* of June 1964, P.-L. Mignon wrote: 'Pour Samuel Beckett chaque travail nouveau procède du précédent, chaque travail secrète le suivant.' It was with this in mind that I asked Beckett if he would throw any light on the way *Godot* might have grown out of his previous works which might illuminate the study of the genesis of the play. In the first place, he confirmed that, as Mignon records, the source of the dialogue between the boy and Vladimir is to be found in the unpublished play *Eleuthéria*. He then added: 'If you want to find the origins of *En attendant Godot*, look at *Murphy*.' The most significant connexion between the two works – but far from being the only one – can be discerned in the description of Murphy as 'split in two, a body and a mind. They had intercourse, apparently, otherwise he could not have known that they had anything in common. But he felt his mind to be bodytight and did not understand through what channel the intercourse was effected nor how the two experiences came to overlap. He was satisfied that neither followed from the other.' The description continues with a detail which one cannot help associating with the unfortunate Estragon crippled by Lucky: 'He neither thought a kick because he felt one, nor felt a kick because he thought one.'

Murphy, then, feels his body and mind to be divided into separate entities. This idea has its roots in a very respectable philosophical tradition. . . . Beckett has readily acknowledged the profound effect upon him of the occasionalist Arnold Geulincx. In *Godot* Beckett consummates the division, thus making the monologue of the novels – the exploration of the depths of one central solipsistic character – into dialogue. It is too simple to call one of the two tramps 'the Mind' and the other 'the Body', as Ruby Cohn does ('mental versus physical man').[1] They are nevertheless a *pseudocouple*. It is not without significance that Beckett applies this term, in *L'Innommable*, to the protagonists of the unpublished novel *Mercier et Camier* – the only one of Beckett's French novels not to be written from the point of view of 'I'.

A careful reading . . . of *Mercier et Camier* discloses many clues to the 'making' of *En attendant Godot*, but it should be stressed at the outset that to compare them is not to infer that the play is in any way a deliberate transposition or adaptation of the novel. Such a conclusion would misconstrue the purpose of the comparison, which is twofold: to show the uses to which elements common to both works were put; and to throw light on the artistic superiority of *Godot* by showing what it grew out of and what it might have been but for the magical transformation wrought by a true artist. . . .

When I told Mr Beckett that I was struck by the similarities between the two works and that, to put it crudely, they seemed to have come out of the same stable, his only comment was to the effect that he could remember nothing about *Mercier et Camier* ('a dreadful book'), and had cast it completely out of his mind. Seeing that it was written in 1945, four years before *Godot* (with *Molloy*, *Eleuthéria* and *Malone meurt* in between), it is quite credible that a writer with a handful of dying worlds crying out to be drawn into existence should drive an unwanted embryo from his conscious mind. But any work of art, once it has been created, never leaves its author intact, whatever he might think of it. As Dr Fletcher points out, for example, Part II of *Molloy* derives from *Mercier et Camier* and in places follows it quite closely. The resemblances between *Mercier et Camier* and *Godot* are of quite a different order, however. That they are unconscious similarities one need have no doubt, but they are none the less highly informative and, together with the manuscript of *En attendant Godot*, throw some new light upon the question of the making of *Godot*.[2]

There are many coincidences of style and theme in *Mercier et Camier* and *Godot*. Particular attention will be paid to the most interesting points illuminated by the unpublished documents – namely, the setting of the play; the origins and meaning of the tree; Godot; the rendezvous and the theme of waiting; the creation of the characters and the relationships between them; the perfection of the dialogue and the suppression of certain precise details to be found in the manuscript.

The essential difference between *Mercier et Camier* and *Godot* is that the two old men in the novel are completely *disponibles*, able to wander aimlessly on their vague quest, whereas the two tramps in the play are tied to one spot. This results in radical dissimilarities in structure. Mercier and Camier dissipate their energies in the search for divers objects – their bag, their umbrella, their bicycle – as well as for the ultimate unspecified thing or person motivating their wanderings. In *Godot* all this is streamlined, as all the hopes of Vladimir and Estragon are concentrated upon one objective: the meeting with Godot, with whom a rendez-vous has been arranged. Vladimir and Estragon do, in fact, go away from the meeting place at night, and they lose sight of each other during the action of the play, greeting each other like long-lost friends a few moments later. Similarly the journey of Mercier and Camier is punctuated by regular returns *chez* Hélène (a singularly accommodating acquaintance). The centre of interest in the novel is in the time spent away from 'base'; in the play, the centre is in the returning and the waiting. The importance of waiting and meeting is a notable feature of the novel too, together with the questing theme which Beckett took up again in *Molloy*. . . .

Mercier and Camier wait in a public shelter for the rain to stop. Their conversation has the same qualities as that of their two counterparts in *Godot*; it is that of two people forced into passive waiting by something beyond their control. The 'agent complaisant de la malignité universelle' which forces them to wait is in this case nothing more mysterious than the rain; the strong term applied to it might seem more appropriate to Godot.

Mercier and his companion argue about what kept whom waiting. Camier replies, 'On n'attend ni ne fait attendre qu'à partir d'un moment convenu d'avance'.

This statement is the very core of *Godot*. The very fact that Vladimir and Estragon are waiting presupposes that a time was fixed. In the manuscript of the play this arrangement is not just verbal, as in the published text [p. 9], but *written down by Godot himself*:

– Tu es sûr que c'était ce soir?
– Quoi?
– Notre rendez-vous.
– Diable! (*Il cherche dans ses poches.*) Il l'a écrit.
[*He pulls out a number of pieces of paper and hands one over.*] Qu'est-ce que tu lis?
– 'Samedi soir et suivants.' Quelle façon de s'exprimer!
– Tu vois!
– (*rendant le papier*). Mais sommes-nous samedi?

For Godot to have written the words himself, he must have a physical reality; this obvious consequence led to the omission of the piece of paper. But we see from this first version something not entirely without significance, that Beckett originally envisaged the two characters to be waiting for a real person. . . .

The manuscript reveals that none of the characters is individualised to the extent of having names when they first appear on the written page – proof enough that it is the original draft. The opening stage direction reads, 'Un vieillard assis' . . . 'Entre un deuxième vieillard, *ressemblant au premier*' (my italics). Differentiation between them only gradually crystallises. Vladimir is the first to receive his name. The other *vieillard* is called 'Lévy' right up to the end of Act I. The word 'Estragon' is written on the back of the last page of Act I, and he becomes Estragon from that point on.

The first entrance of Pozzo and Lucky reads thus in the manuscript: 'Extrent deux messieurs, un très grand et un petit'. They are then referred to as 'le grand' and 'le petit'. Pozzo is not given a name until he introduces himself – which he does in the manuscript with the words 'Je m'appelle Pozzo'. Of particular interest is the fact that the reason why Lucky is so named is clarified by the context in which he first receives his name. Pozzo is explaining the protocol with regard to the bones: 'Mais en principe les os reviennent au porteur' – the manuscript reads '. . . à Lucky'; that is to say, he is lucky *because he gets the bones*. Just to keep the spirit of contradiction alive, however, it must be stressed that this is not the only 'official' explanation. Mr Beckett's verbal reply to my question, 'Is Lucky so named because he has found his Godot?' was: 'I suppose he is Lucky to have no more expectations.' . . .

The dialogue of *Godot* is a great improvement on that of *Mercier et Camier*. The manuscript of *Godot* shows that Beckett has an infallible ear for what to cut. In Act II, for example, there were originally about ten additional pages of dialogue inserted between p. 125 and p. 129 of the final text. They contain an argument (of which the 'Oh pardon' routine is the essence) elaborately built round the sentence 'Est-ce que c'est la peine'. This sentence takes them ten pages to complete, just as it takes them many pages to ask Pozzo why Lucky does not put down his bags. Beckett rightly saw the danger of tedium and repeated effect here – although it would have stood in a novel, as it is a true *tour de force*.

Another example occurs on p. 69 of the final text of *Godot*. Between the juxtaposed words 'Enchaînez' and 'Assez' the following originally appeared:

POZZO—Ou bien il ne fait rien.
LÉVY—Le salaud.

VLADIMIR—Et quand vous ne lui demandez rien?
POZZO—Ça ne change rien.
LÉVY—Il sait ce qu'il veut.
VLADIMIR—Quand il veut.
LÉVY—Comme il veut.
VLADIMIR—Que vous lui demandiez ou non.
POZZO—Plus ou moins.
LÉVY—Et quand vous lui demandez de s'arrêter?
POZZO—Ça ne change rien.
LÉVY—Il ne s'arrête pas.
POZZO—Quelquefois.
VLADIMIR—Mais pas toujours.
POZZO—Non.
LÉVY—Et il a toujours été comme ça?
POZZO—Non.
VLADIMIR—Depuis quand?
POZZO—Je ne sais pas.
LÉVY—Assez.

This long quotation is given because it is instructive. It shows how miraculously the final text of *Godot* manages to avoid the tedium of this suppressed page even though the intellectual substance of much of the play is no greater than this. The danger of taking the quality of the dialogue for granted, of failing to appreciate the manipulation of language and the flow of words, is diminished by the realisation that a lesser writer would have finished with a book full of passages like the suppressed one quoted, no doubt congratulating himself on creating the Theatre of Inaction in a massive prefatory note. . . .

Mercier et Camier illuminates the situation of the characters in *Godot* by showing that Beckett does not push them to the extreme suffering of self-aware solitude. Those who think *Godot* depressingly morbid, exploiting *ad nauseam* the basic misery of a godless universe, would realise on reading the novel that the hours or days of anguish on the *haute lande*, when the narrative becomes turgid and incoherent, mark the mysterious transformation of the *pseudocouple* Mercier/Camier into the *pseudocouple* Vladimir/Estragon. They become imbued with a totally different quality. Whereas Mercier and Camier rarely rise above the level of two rather dirty old men, Didi and Gogo positively *glow* by comparison; their condition is so infused with timeless, tragic quality that it acquires a density and depth quite lacking in the novel. . . .

SOURCE: extracts from the Introduction to the Harrap edition of *En attendant Godot* (London, 1966).

NOTES

[Reorganised and renumbered from the original – Ed.]

1. Ruby Cohn, *The Comic Gamut* (New Brunswick, 1962) p. 213.

2. The manuscript of *En attendant Godot*, which Mr Beckett kindly allowed me to read, thus making this study possible, consists of an exercise book measuring 8½ in. × 7 in. Beckett wrote on each right-hand page to the end of the book, then continued on each left-hand page beginning at the beginning of the book again. He told me that there were several typescript versions between the manuscript and the first edition. The 2nd edition (also 1952) contains minor textual changes, and constitutes the definitive edition upon which the present text is based.

Hersh Zeifman The Alterable Whey of Words: The Play's Texts (1977)

Although the British were the first to stage Samuel Beckett's *En attendant Godot* in its English translation (London, 3 August 1955), they were not the first to publish the English text of the play. That honor belongs instead to the American firm Grove Press, which published *Waiting for Godot* in the United States in 1954; the first British edition (Faber) did not appear until two years later, in 1956. The translation in both cases is Beckett's own, but, interestingly enough, it is not the same translation. Some of the differences are attributable to the fact that the British text was the one used in the London production and therefore partly bowdlerised, certain cuts having been demanded by the Lord Chamberlain before the play could receive a licence for public performance. Thus, where the American text reads 'arse', 'farted' and 'the clap', for example, the British edition substitutes the presumably more genteel 'backside', 'belched' and 'warts'. Such censorship accounts for perhaps a dozen minor emendations, but does nothing to explain the literally hundreds of other variations between the two texts. Simply to list all of these variations, most of which are very slight indeed, would be a rather pointless, not to mention tedious, task. A discussion of some of the more significant of them, however, might prove to be helpful, if for no other reason than to draw attention to the subtly and surprisingly different texture of those two early editions.

Compare, for example, the first occasion on which Godot's name is mentioned in the text:

ESTRAGON: Let's go.
VLADIMIR: We can't.
ESTRAGON: Why not?
VLADIMIR: We're waiting for Godot.
ESTRAGON: Ah!

The above quotation is from the 1956 British edition;[1] in the 1954 American edition, Beckett adds a most revealing stage direction – Estragon is to deliver his 'Ah!' '*despairingly*'.[2] Why should Estragon despair at this point, unless he already knows from past experience that Godot never keeps his appointment? From the very initial mention of Godot's name, then, it is suggested that the tramps are caught up in what appears to be an infinitely extended, infinitely repeated series of actions. The American edition of the play is thus seen to begin *in medias res*: obviously this is not the first evening the tramps have spent waiting for the arrival of their elusive savior.

A similarly significant variation in stage direction may be noted towards the end of Act I when Pozzo confesses that he finds it difficult to leave the scene. In the British edition, Pozzo comments, 'I don't seem to be able . . . (*he hesitates*) . . . to depart' [47].* The American edition shifts the stage direction ever so slightly: 'I don't seem to be able . . . (*long hesitation*) . . . to depart' [31]. This insistence on a specifically *long* hesitation adds an important emphasis to the American text. Pozzo's struggle *with* the words parallels the struggle *in* the words; the sentence is as difficult to complete as the action it speaks of. And the marked silence further emphasises Pozzo's inability to leave by suggesting that the fragment spoken before the hesitation is a complete phrase in itself, thereby focusing clearly on Pozzo's essential impotence.

When we turn to a consideration of the actual dialogue of the play, we discover a number of interesting, occasionally puzzling, variations. Some passages get entirely lost in the shuffle. For example, in the British edition of *Godot*, Pozzo's homey bit of wisdom in response to the disappearance of his pulveriser, 'No matter! What can't be cured must be endured!' [40], is omitted from the American version (nor does it appear in the original French). Vladimir's comment about the fallen Pozzo, 'He must get used to being erect again' [84], likewise appears in the British text but not in the American, although in this instance it *does* appear in the French: 'Il faut qu'il se réhabitue à la station debout.'[3] Other passages find their

*[Ed.] The references within square brackets relate to page numbers in the versions cited. For explanation of the subsequent 'B' indicator in references to the American edition, see n. 2 in the concluding NOTES section, below.

way into both editions, but curiously altered along the way. Thus the British Vladimir comments that it is pointless for the tramps to lose heart now: 'We should have thought of it when the world was young . . .' [10], while the American Vladimir chooses different words to express the same thought: 'We should have thought of it a million years ago . . .' [7B]. (The French reads 'il y a une éternité . . .' [13].) In the British edition, Estragon notes that Lucky is puffing 'like a walrus' [29], and later declares of the suffering Pozzo, 'He's all mankind' [84]; the American edition substitutes 'like a grampus' [20B] and 'He's all humanity [54]. (Cf. the original: 'comme un phoque [47] – i.e., a seal – and 'C'est toute l'humanité [142].) Monetary units are shillings and pence in the British text, francs in the American. The British Vladimir sums up the evening's entertainment with 'It's worse than being at the theatre' [34]; his American counterpart drops a couple of words and narrows the image: 'Worse than the pantomime' [23B]. (The French is 'spectacle' [56].)

Perhaps the most important dialogue variation in these first editions of *Waiting for Godot* is Estragon's response to Pozzo's 'What is your name?'; in the British text, Gogo identifies himself as 'Catullus' [37] – cf. the French 'Catulle' [60] – while in the American text he answers 'Adam' [25]. The shift is surely significant, particularly in light of the play's repeated emphasis on sin and redemption. In this connection, it is also instructive to compare the different ways in which Beckett translates the tramps' discussion concerning the Apostles and the thieves on the Cross. In the British edition, Vladimir explains to Estragon that one of the Apostles speaks of a thief being saved: 'But the other Apostle says that one was saved' [13]. The line is an almost word-for-word translation of the French: 'Mais l'autre [évangéliste] dit qu'il y en a eu un de sauvé' [19]. In the American edition, however, the line has been subtly altered: 'But one of the four says that one of the two was saved' [9B]. The apparently positive nature of the statement is thus eroded by its own syntax; the deliberate parallelism ('one of the four / one of the two') emphasises the fortuitousness of grace by drawing attention to the heightening of the odds, implying that the presumably even chance for salvation is in reality much less.

Note, too, the scene in which the tramps discuss, obliquely, the concept of original sin. In his early book on Proust, Beckett wrote: 'The tragic figure represents the expiation of original sin, of the original and eternal sin of him and all of his "socii malorum", the sin of having been born.'[4] For Beckett's characters, birth is irrevocably linked with guilt, punishment and repentance; thus Estragon wonders, in both the British and American editions of *Godot*, whether perhaps he and Didi should repent their being born [Faber, 11, Grove, 8B]. A few pages later, however, the texts diverge significantly. In response to Gogo's query 'We've lost our rights?', the British Didi replies, 'We waived them' [19], whereas his American counterpart answers '(*distinctly*) We got rid of them' [13B]. (Cf. the French: '[*avec netteté*] – Nous les avons bazardés' [29].) Both the addition of the stage direction and the switch from a rather passive involvement ('waived') to a more active one ('got rid of') emphasise the tramps' guilt. Each of them has somehow *conspired* to be born, and in that conspiracy lie the seeds of his doom. MacMann, one of the characters in Beckett's novel *Malone Dies*, similarly laments his fate: 'And no doubt he would have wondered if it was really necessary to be guilty in order to be punished but for the memory, more and more galling, of his having consented to live in his mother, then to leave her.'[5]

Although some of the above variations (and many others could have been chosen) may hold great interest for the dedicated Beckett scholar, none of them is, in itself, particularly earth-shattering. Still, there is a kind of cumulative effect when one is dealing with literally hundreds of variations, however minor – their presence *does* ultimately make a difference, if only in terms of a play's texture and rhythm. The play is essentially the same, and yet somehow not the same. And there remains as well a lingering question as to which version is preferable. When the British Gogo identifies himself as 'Catullus' in contrast to the American Gogo's 'Adam', we want to know which name represents the 'improvement' in Beckett's mind. One must be a considered revision of the other – but which? In 1965, Faber published a new British edition of *Waiting for Godot*, the jacket copy of which reads as follows: 'The author has made a number of important revisions to the text of *Waiting for Godot* since it was first published and this new edition, complete and unexpurgated, has been authorised by Mr Beckett as definitive'. At first glance, our problem would appear to be solved; *for every single variation outlined above*, the definitive edition adopts the American reading. Thus, although the first British edition appeared two years after the American, it was presumably the inferior translation. Eleven years after its first publication, then, English readers on both sides of the Atlantic finally have the same text of *Waiting for Godot*.

Or do they? A closer examination reveals that there are still a number of discrepancies between the definitive British edition and the American, although considerably fewer than previously and none so obviously glaring as the 'Catullus' vs. 'Adam' readings.[6] In comparing the stage directions of the two editions, for example, one can detect certain slight variations. Sometimes it is simply the case of different words being used to express the same idea. Thus when Didi and Gogo race around the stage in terror in response to the '*terrible cry*' they hear (a cry heralding the entrance of Pozzo and Lucky), the British text directs that Estragon '*runs towards Vladimir*',[7] while the American text notes that Gogo '*runs to rejoin Vladimir*' [15]. Sometimes, however, the variations involve the actual presence or absence of a stage direction; in each case, it is the definitive British version that accords most closely with the original French text. For example, when Estragon protests that he is in great pain ('Hurts! He wants to know if it hurts!'), he does so '*angrily*' in the American edition [7B] but without stage direction in the British [10] or French [13]. Pozzo's lament 'I've lost my Kapp and Peterson!' is spoken, in the American text, '*on the point of tears*' [23B], although again there is no similar stage direction in either the British [35] or French [56]. And Pozzo's continuation of that speech ('You didn't by any chance see . . .')[8] is preceded, in the British and French texts, by the direction '*looking up*' [35] ('*levant la tête*' [56]), but not in the American.

The dialogue of the play likewise contains a host of (mostly minor) variations. In Act II of the British edition, Didi and Gogo support between them the blind and suffering Pozzo; Estragon, soon tiring of this burst of kindness, cries out, 'How much longer must we cart him round?' [86]. In the American edition, the line reads, 'How much longer are we to cart him around' [55] – cf. the French: 'Combien de temps va-t-il falloir le charrier encore?' [146]. The differences in the line are slight but instructive: there are shifts in punctuation, in syntax and in vocabulary. Such shifts are common, and the more important of them deserve comment. Punctuation in the two versions differs greatly, but the variations rarely affect the meaning of the play. More significant, perhaps, are the slight changes of syntax, if only because the rhythm of the text is subtly altered. Compare, for example, the British Vladimir's condemnation of Pozzo, 'He thinks of nothing but himself!' [82], with that of his American counterpart: 'He can think of nothing but himself!' [53]. (The original reads 'Il ne pense qu'à lui' [138].) Similarly, the British Estragon complains of being beaten regularly by a pack of ruffians: 'There were ten of them' [59], whereas his American counterpart is somewhat looser grammatically: 'There was ten of them' [38B] (Cf. the original: 'Ils étaient dix' [100].) And, in the ensuing lyrical passage, the British Vladimir flourishes a nice rhetorical balance ('The sun will set, the moon will rise . . .' [77]) with which the American partly dispenses: 'The sun will set, the moon rise . . .' [50]). (Cf. the original: 'Le soleil se couchera, la lune se lèvera . . .' [130].)

Changes in vocabulary are more numerous and more interesting. Some of these variations involve the presence of a word in the American text which does not appear in the British or French – the American edition is, as a result, slightly more wordy. Thus the British Estragon muses, 'I wonder if we wouldn't have been better off alone . . .' [53]), while his American counterpart confesses, 'I *sometimes* wonder if . . .' [35; my italics]). Similarly, whereas the British Vladimir comments of the word 'happy' that 'Perhaps it's not the right word' [59] to express his feelings, the American version reads: 'Perhaps it's not *quite* the right word' [38; my italics]. Other vocabulary changes simply represent alternative translations. Thus the French Vladimir notes of his youth 'On portait beau alors' [13]; in the British edition, the line reads, 'We were presentable in those days' [10], whereas the American version runs, 'We were respectable in those days' [7B].[9] Estragon's begging money from Pozzo, 'Même un louis serait le bienvenu' [63], becomes, in the British, 'Even ten francs would be welcome' [39], and in the American 'Even ten francs would be a help' [26]. And Didi's response to Gogo's question about how long they have been together is 'Fifty years perhaps' in the British [53], 'Fifty years maybe' in the American [35].

There is very little to choose, in terms of either aesthetics or thematic significance, between 'Fifty years perhaps' or 'Fifty years maybe'. If the former is to be preferred, it is only because Beckett appears to have given it his final blessing (assuming that we trust the British 'definitive' label, that is). But there are three instances of dialogue variation in which the British edition is clearly superior simply on the basis of textual evidence; the corresponding version in the American edition is evidently in error. The first of these instances, involving Estragon's taste in vegetables, is relatively minor. Vladimir has mistakenly handed Estragon a turnip instead of a carrot; when Gogo complains, Didi is suitably apologetic:

> Oh pardon! I could have sworn it was a carrot . . . (*He rummages.*) Wait, I have it. (*He brings out a carrot and gives it to Estragon.*) There, dear fellow. (*Estragon wipes the carrot on his sleeve and begins to eat it.*) Make it last, that's the end of them. [14]

The above quotation from the American edition glosses over a practical staging problem: what does Gogo do with the turnip he has rejected? He cannot simply hold it in his hand for the remainder of the act. The British edition solves the problem by restoring a line which was apparently lost in the earlier translations:[10]

> There, dear fellow. (*Estragon wipes the carrot on his sleeve and begins to eat it.*) Give

me the turnip. (*Estragon gives back the turnip which Vladimir puts in his pocket.*) Make it last, that's the end of them. [20]

Not only does this reading satisfy the practical requirements, it also accords exactly with the original French: 'Violà, mon cher. (*Estragon l'essuie sur sa manche et commence à la manger.*) Rends-moi le navet. (*Estragon lui rend le navet.*) Fais-la durer, il n'y en a plus' [31].

A more significant error occurs in Pozzo's chilling, climactic 'They give birth astride of a grave' speech. This is one of the most famous and oft-quoted passages in all of Beckett, yet the American version is incorrect. Here is the beginning of that speech in the Grove Press edition:

Have you not done tormenting me with your accursed time! It's abominable! When! When! One day, is that not enough for you, one day he went dumb, one day I went blind, one day we'll go deaf . . . [57B]

Presumably all those 'one day' repetitions confused the compositor (or perhaps Beckett himself), who accordingly skipped a phrase; in the definitive edition, the passage runs as follows:

Have you not done tormenting me with your accursed time! It's abominable! When! When! One day, is that not enough for you, *one day like any other day*, one day he went dumb, one day I went blind, one day we'll go deaf . . . [89; my italics]

The above reading also appeared in the 1956 Faber English translation [89] and, more conclusively, in the original French: 'Un jour, ça ne vous suffit pas, *un jour pareil aux autres* . . .' [154; my italics].

The third, and most extensive, instance of dialogue variation can be found in Lucky's celebrated 'think'. Most of these differences result from slight shifts in translation. Where the definitive edition refers to 'dead loss per caput since the death of Bishop Berkeley' [44], for example, the American edition reads 'the dead loss per head . . .' [29].[11] Similarly, the British Lucky notes that man, or his skull, 'is seen to waste and pine waste and pine' [43], 'to shrink and dwindle' [44], 'to shrink and waste' [44]; the corresponding words of the American Lucky are 'wastes and pines wastes and pines' [29], 'fades away' [29], 'fading fading fading' [29B]. Again, there is not much to choose here, beyond the fact the British version is supposedly definitive.[12] But there is one variation in Lucky's speech in which the British version is decidedly superior. Once more it would appear that the American compositor has become confused (in this case, not surprisingly) and has omitted some words. The definitive text reads:

in spite of the strides of physical culture . . . sports of all sorts autumn summer winter winter tennis of all kinds hockey of all sorts penicilline and succedanea in a word I resume *and concurrently simultaneously for reasons unknown to shrink and dwindle in spite of the tennis I resume* flying gliding . . .[13] [43–4; my italics]

The American compositor, or Beckett, skipped from the first 'I resume' to the second and left out all the intervening words (indicated above in italics), so that the Grove Press text reads: 'penicilline and succedanea in a word I resume flying gliding . . .' [29A].

Waiting for Godot is studied extensively in schools and universities on both sides of the Atlantic and is frequently performed. The fact remains, however, that an American student or theatre-goer reading or watching the play is dealing with a different text from that of his British counterpart. While the same might be said of a play by Chekhov, say, or Brecht, the situation is not really comparable. After all, English is Beckett's mother tongue, and he has himself prepared the English translation (or, better, adaptation) of the play. *Waiting for Godot* is thus, for all intents and purposes, an English play. Is it not bizarre, then, that this arguably most famous and significant work of the post-war English theatre – and certainly the most analysed in scholarly periodicals – should exist in one form for a British audience and in another, somewhat different form for an American one? At the risk of making the defensive offensive, let me repeat that those two forms are not so very different – but that there should be differences at all is startling and disturbing. Perhaps it is now time for Grove Press to bring the American edition of the play into line with the 1965 definitive Faber edition (particularly as there appears to be no reason for us to doubt that 'definitive' label). At the very least, the American text should restore those passages which it omitted presumably through error, whether that error was initially Beckett's or the compositor's. Since Beckett has approved a definitive edition, surely we ought to respect his wishes and have the play as he intended it – *Waiting for Godot* is too seminal, too important a work for us to settle for anything less.[14]

SOURCE: article, 'The Alterable Way of Words: The Texts of *Waiting for Godot*', in *Educational Theatre Journal* (March 1977), pp. 77–84.

NOTES

[Supplemented by the author for this Casebook – Ed.]

1. Samuel Beckett, *Waiting for Godot* (London, 1956), p. 14. All further references to this first British edition of the play (published by Faber) will be included within the body of my essay.

2. *Waiting for Godot* (New York, 1954), p. 10. For some inexplicable reason,

this American edition of the play (published by Grove Press) is wretchedly paginated, only the left-hand pages being numbered; I have therefore arrived at the awkward solution of assigning the letter 'B' to the facing, right-hand page. All further references to the American edition of the play will be included within the body of my essay.

3. *En attendant Godot* (Paris, 1952), p. 143. All further references to the French edition of the play (published by Les Editions de Minuit) will be included within the body of my essay.

4. Beckett, *Proust* (1931; rpt New York, 1970), p. 49.

5. Beckett, *Malone Dies* (1956: rpt New York, 1970), p. 67.

6. The principal reason for such discrepancies is that, while the definitive British edition adopts most of the American readings, it does not adopt all of them. In some cases, the definitive edition retains the readings of the 1956 Faber text, although that text is, on the whole, much inferior to the American; in other cases, it adopts readings which appear in *neither* of the previous two editions.

7. *Waiting for Godot*, 2nd edn (London, Faber, 1965), p. 21. All further references to this definitive edition of the play (published by Faber) will be included within the body of my essay.

8. There is also a slight variation in the wording of this line. In the British text, Pozzo wonders 'You didn't by any chance see . . .' [35]; the corresponding line in the American edition runs, 'You didn't see by any chance . . .' [23B].

9. 'We were respectable in those days' is also the reading of the 1956 Faber (first British) edition [10]. Here we have one of those rare instances in which the first British edition and the American edition offer an identical reading which the definitive edition of 1965 rejects.

10. The 1956 Faber edition likewise omitted this line [20].

11. The definitive (1965) and American editions may disagree about 'caput' vs. 'head', but at least they are in accord over 'Bishop Berkeley'. The 1956 Faber edition is off on its own on both scores: 'the dead loss per *capita* since the death of *Samuel Johnson*' [45; my italics]. Just to add to the confusion, compare with the French: 'la perte sèche par tête de pipe depuis la mort de Voltaire' [73].

12. It is obvious that Beckett had difficulty deciding on the proper translation of these particular phrases, since they are, for the most part, different still in the 1956 Faber edition: 'wastes and pines wastes and pines' [43]; 'to dwindle dwindle' [43]; and 'to shrink pine waste' [44].

13. This reading is supported by the original French: 'la pénicilline et succédanés bref je reprends *en même temps parallèlement de rapetisser on ne sait pas pourquoi malgré le tennis je reprends* l'aviation . . .' [73; my italics].

14. [Ed. Dr Zeifman has provided this additional note for our Casebook.] In the summer of 1986, as this anthology's selection plan was being finalised, Faber published a one-volume edition of Beckett's *Complete Dramatic Works*. Astonishingly, the text of *Godot* which appears therein is not the 'complete and unexpurgated' text of 1965, 'authorised by Mr Beckett as definitive', but rather the first Faber text of 1956! Since, in the words of Faber's own jacket

copy, that earlier text was clearly deemed inferior by Beckett, its inclusion in the *Complete Dramatic Works* is a serious error. The 1956 text of *Godot* contains not only lines which Beckett ultimately rejected and revised, but also all the changes demanded by the Lord Chamberlain's office. Most of this censorship is merely fatuous, as I pointed out briefly at the beginning of my article, but some of it directly affects our understanding of the text. Consider, for example, the scene in which Didi and Gogo contemplate hanging themselves from the tree. Here is the bowdlerised text as it appears in the *Complete Dramatic Works*:

ESTRAGON: What about hanging ourselves?
VLADIMIR *whispers to* ESTRAGON. ESTRAGON *highly excited.*
VLADIMIR: With all that follows. Where it falls mandrakes grow. That's why they shriek when you pull them up. Did you not know that? [17]

The passage as printed makes very little sense, since it primly requires Vladimir to '*whisper*' what needs to be spoken aloud if we are to understand his meaning. The text should read:

ESTRAGON: What about hanging ourselves?
VLADIMIR: Hmm. It'd give us an erection!
ESTRAGON: (*highly excited*). An erection!
VLADIMIR: With all that follows. . . . [1965 text, 17]

'Erection' was presumably considered too threatening a word to rear its ugly head in the British theatre of 1955–56. It is appalling that, in 1986, Faber should perpetuate such barbarism by publishing a *Complete Dramatic Works* in which Beckett's most famous play is mistakenly printed in a corrupt and censored text.

Anselm Atkins The Structure of Lucky's Speech (1966)

Lucky's torrent of words in *Waiting for Godot* is a carefully wrought poetic structure. It divides into three distinct parts. The first, which ends with the phrase 'better than nothing', is the unfinished protasis of a theological or philosophical argument presented in the rationalistic geometrical mode of Descartes and Spinoza. *Given* the existence of God, *then*. . . . Every word in this part, with the exception of the scholastic duck-quacks, is part of a coherent syntax – the skeleton of which has been identified by Ruby Cohn.

The second part, like the first, is an incomplete fragment of a rational argument. It is the last half of an *objection* – 'But not so fast!' – to the unfinished demonstration in the first. It begins in its own middle, but comes to a full period stop. Thus its syntax, though coherent, is not, as Cohn seems to suggest, continuous with that of the first part. The grammatical outline of the second part is

> . . . and considering, what is more, that, as a result of the labors left unfinished . . . of Testew and Cunard, it is established . . . that man, . . . in spite of the strides of alimentation and defecation, wastes and pines . . . and . . . in spite of the strides of physical culture . . . fades away, . . . the dead loss per head . . . being to the tune of one inch-four ounce . . . stark naked . . . in Connemara.
> [American edn, Act I]

Three subdivisions are discernible within this second part: 1. a self-repeating verbal trap reminiscent of the dog-song in Act II; 2. an enumeration of activities taking place in cycles of time ('autumn, summer, winter') and place ('Feckham, Peckham, Fulham, Clapham'); and 3. a collection of contradictions and malapropisms.

The third part begins as a second objection in parallel with the earlier one – '. . . and considering, what is more' – but after a half-hearted try at the self-repeating trap, it discards all syntax and lapses into complete aphasia. Its phrases are of two kinds: 1. those with elements repeated from or referring to the previous parts, and 2. poetic words introduced for the first time.

SOURCE: short article, 'A Note on the Structure of Lucky's Speech', *Modern Drama* (Dec. 1966), p. 309.

Harry Cockerham (1975) Bilingual Playwright

. . . The basic facts concerning Beckett's bilingualism are perhaps well enough known for it to be unnecessary any longer, even in Britain, to defend the view of him as at least as much a French as an Irish writer. A resident in France for most of his adult life, Beckett has written part of his output in French, part in English, subsequently translating the greater part of his work, either alone or in collaboration, into the other language. This bilingualism is a feature especially of his work since the Second World War, but it was an increasingly important factor even at a time when he was writing mainly in English. Indeed, the pattern of works composed in both French and English was established in the later 1930s: some of his French poems of that period strongly resemble poems in English of similar date, whilst others exist in both languages. Arguments over whether he is properly a French or an Irish writer are therefore necessarily sterile and it may indeed be that his example and the fact of his existence as a bilingual writer will do much to break down barriers between national cultures and encourage a trend towards comparativism in literary studies. We are faced, not with a writer who abandoned one language for another (a not infrequent occurrence), but with the possibly unique phenomenon of one who, throughout his career, has divided his efforts and his interests between two languages.

Amongst the questions raised by Beckett's bilingualism, that of his French style has given rise to even more disagreement amongst critics, if that were possible, than has the problem of the meanings to be found in his works. At one extreme, the more detailed type of study has provided guarded and even astringent judgements, stressing the limitations of Beckett's French and pointing to features which are directly attributable to his foreign origins.[1] Most commentators who broach the subject do so, however, only in the most general and frequently impressionistic fashion and tend to heap high praise on Beckett as a stylist. Thus for Jean-Louis Barrault, he is the modern writer who, by his concern for purity, simplicity, musicality, and careful selection in style, is most reminiscent of Racine. Jean-Jacques Mayoux's few reservations about Beckett's French are far outweighed by his enthusiasm for a style which he places above considerations of French or English. Beckett's voice and accents are seen as so characteristic as to rise above whichever language he writes in: they recall, not Racine, but Chateaubriand.[2] Similar disagreement is to be found amongst those who have compared the French and the English version of some of Beckett's plays. Again, most of these comparisons are brief and impressionistic and they often lead (for example on the question of whether Beckett is more amusing in French or in English) to conclusions radically opposed to one another but expressed all with equal passion. Even the one reasonably detailed study of the subject is at several points less than convincing, having perhaps suffered by appearing too early to be able to take into account the plays originally written in English.[3] Nevertheless, methodical comparison of the French and English versions of the five major stage plays at present available in both texts can shed much light on Beckett's bilingualism, some on his French style and a little even on the reasons for critical dissension on these subjects.

In translating his plays Beckett had a long experience to draw on. In 1952, Maurice Nadeau, one of the most aware of Paris critics, was able to say that until then Beckett had been known only to a small circle of friends and initiates, and then mainly as a translator. His career as a translator in fact stretched back at least to 1932, when he was rendering into English the poems of the French surrealists Breton and Éluard. Long practice does not, however, seem to have made him come to see translation as anything less than a highly demanding task. This much is borne out by one of his . . . reported remarks on the subject, made at a rehearsal of *Endgame* in London. On hearing his own translation of Clov's punning remark about his telescope (through which he has just scanned the audience and seen 'a multitude in transports of joy'): 'Ça alors, pour une longue-vue c'est une longue-vue' ('That's what I call a magnifier'), Beckett is said to have exclaimed: 'It's a rotten line. Bad translation. . . . The more I go on the more I think things are untranslatable.'[4] There are a number of lessons in that remark. It shows the seriousness with which Beckett approaches the task of translation, his meticulousness over details, the importance he attaches to humour and word-play in his plays and his irritated awareness of how a translation can fall short of the original. It also raises the fundamental question of why Beckett chooses to write each of his works in two languages: a question which has attracted surprisingly little critical attention and which is not satisfactorily answered by the fact of the wider audience this practice enables him to reach. It says much for Beckett's artistic zeal that he is concerned not to leave the translation of his works, into either language, to others but persists so earnestly in a task from which a lesser artist might have felt his success as a creative writer should have liberated him. More than that, it gives to the English and French translations of his works an authenticity not enjoyed by translations of other authors, and raises the question how far his translations are such and how far (since they come from the author himself) they become distinct works of art, fresh treatments of the original subject with their own qualities and characteristics. Such considerations make his translations worthy of the same attention as the original versions and justify, indeed make necessary, detailed comparisons between the two.

Between the French and the English versions of the plays[5] there exist, in the first place, certain types of difference which do not, however, provide a basis for making distinctions as to quality or character. Thus the English *Waiting for Godot* can occasionally be more wryly poetic than the French, as in the remarks of Estragon (not in the French) at the end of Act I about the moon: 'Pale for weariness . . . of climbing heaven and gazing on the likes of us.' Or indeed in Act II, where the haunting exchange between Estragon and Vladimir about their surroundings, an exchange already poetic in the French, is if anything more so in the English. . . . On the other hand, Beckett is not always so successful in rendering the poetry of the French. The alternating four and five syllable lines of the starkly poetic exchange about the tree, in Act I, lose much of their rhythm, and thus power, in translation –

ESTRAGON:	Qu'est-ce que c'est?	What is it?
VLADIMIR:	On dirait un saule.	I don't know. A willow.
ESTRAGON:	Où sont les feuilles?	Where are the leaves?
VLADIMIR:	Il doit être mort.	It must be dead.
ESTRAGON:	Finis les pleurs.	No more weeping.

– whilst the yearning of Estragon's vision of the benefits Godot will bring is lost in the English, where the passage is omitted: 'Ce soir on couchera peut-être chez lui, au chaud, au sec, le ventre plein, sur la paille. Ça vaut la peine qu'on attende, non?'

The same cancelling out of differences is to be found in the matter of passages in the one or the other language which throw light on meaning or appear to affect the interpretation of parts of the plays. In a question and answer omitted from the English *Waiting for Godot*, the French text explains what Pozzo means by the word 'knook' applied to Lucky:

VLADIMIR: Qu'est-ce que c'est, un knouk?
POZZO: Vous n'êtes pas d'ici. Etes-vous seulement du siècle? Autrefois on avait des bouffons. Maintenant on a des knouks. Ceux qui peuvent se le permettre.

. . . It is a much less straightforward matter to establish that the same balance exists, between the French and English versions, in regard to their comic quality, although this could be deduced from the fact that Beckett is pronounced funnier in each of the two languages by roughly equal numbers of commentators. Despite the fact that the French *Waiting for Godot* is described on the title-page as simply a 'pièce en deux actes', whilst the English is 'a tragicomedy in two acts', Ruby Cohn finds the French play more comic, because more colloquial, than the English one. But this is to ignore the impression created by an accumulation of increased comic emphases in relatively small details in the English translation. Many of these are in Estragon's responses to Vladimir, for example his formula for explaining why Vladimir should be the first to hang himself on the tree (French text: 'Qui peut le plus peut le moins'): 'If it hangs you it'll hang anything.' Or his extravagant reaction to Vladimir's mild reproach when he appears to lose interest in his comrade's musings on the crucifixion story ('J'écoute'): 'I find this really most extraordinarily interesting' – or again his reply to Vladimir's routine inquiry about the state of his foot ('Il enfle'): 'Swelling visibly.' Similarly, when Pozzo, having made grotesquely long-winded preparations to answer Estragon's question why Lucky doesn't put down his bags, at last arrives at his point, Vladimir's reaction in the French ('Attention') becomes much more openly sarcastic in the English (to Estragon): 'Make a note of this.' . . .

Moreover, whole categories of humour which are present in the French versions are either absent or much less noticeable in the English ones. A noteworthy example is that of the joke based on the foreigner's image of the Englishman, which Beckett, as an Irishman, was able to share with a French audience, but which he seems to have thought unlikely to amuse an English one. To Estragon's 'Calm . . . Calm . . . The English say cawm', the French text had added a joke about English phlegm: 'Ce sont des gens cââàms'. When Nagg tells his tale, in *Endgame*, about the Jewish tailor and his English client, a stage-direction in the French (but missing from the English) tells us that 'il prend un visage d'Anglais'. On the other hand, one joke about the English is preserved in the translation of *En attendant Godot*: Estragon's mimicking of their pronunciation of 'très bon'.

Although on occasion Beckett can produce a brilliant translation of French word-play – as when Clov's amusing mispronunciation of *coite* as *coïte* is rendered by a play on the English *lying* and *laying* – in general this is another kind of humour which, whether because of the sheer difficulty of translation or because punning is much more of a national sport in France than in English-speaking countries, is lost to the reader of the English versions. . . . Sometimes Beckett solves the problem by substituting humour of another kind. When Pozzo, suddenly noticing the absence of Vladimir, who has gone to the lavatory, reproaches Estragon for letting him go off ('Vous auriez dû le retenir'), Estragon, in a punning reply, jokes about his friend's kidney ailment: 'Il s'est retenu tout soul' (English text: 'He might have waited' – 'He would have burst'). . . .

. . . No doubt the most striking loss of this kind to the English reader is the humour Beckett derives from a mixture of real and invented proper names in Lucky's speech in the French *Waiting for Godot*, where the punning is dazzlingly rich. It is true that the crudeness of the names of two of the spurious authorities Lucky refers to – Fartov and Belcher – would be lost on a French audience (although they appear in the French text), but the infinitely more complicated humour of the other proper names used has been replaced by mere pale imitations in the English. Thus the English 'Acacacacademy of Anthropopopometry of Essy-in-Possy' had been that of Berne-en-Bresse in the French: an amusingly obscure or provincial-sounding town which in fact doesn't exist. It recalls Bourg-en-Bresse, a centre not of learning but of gastronomy, and Beckett's replacement of Bourg by the Swiss Berne is probably to be explained by the association with the verb *berner*, to hoodwink or hoax. Similar resonances are present in the names of most of the 'scholars' Lucky mentions. Puncher and Wattmann in the English text are a rather lacklustre Anglicisation of the French Poinçon et Wattmann – a *wattman* in French being a tramdriver, so that Poinçon (*poinçon* = ticket-punch) is his conductor. This helps to explain the 'public works' they are involved in, whilst both names are vaguely reminiscent of those of actual authorities such as James Watt or the French mathematician Louis Poinsot.

The range of suggestion of the English Testew and Cunard is limited when compared to the vistas opened up, for the amateur of puns, by the Rabelaisian French names they are derived from: Testu et Conard. The most obvious association here is with *têtu et conard*: mulish and (in coarse slang) stupid. There are also the echoes, given the context, of French words for testicle (*testicule*) and vagina (again in slang: *con*). Finally the names are also those of real people in the world of learning: Testu, author of an *Histoire universelle des théâtres de toutes les nations* (1779–81) or Jean-Léo Testut,[6] author of a standard medical textbook (*Précis d'anatomie descriptive*) which has appeared in many editions since 1926 – and Conard, the eminently respectable Paris publishing house responsible for standard editions of numerous French authors. Finally Steinweg et Petermann (Steinweg and Peterman in the English text) are slightly more recondite because of the German element. For an English audience familiar with underworld slang (peterman = cracksman), the second of these two names could seem absurdly humorous. For a French audience it would be amusing in a different way (*péter* = to fart). It seems likely, however, that the joke is even more intricate and characteristically Beckettian in that it brings in a knowledge of German and of elementary etymology: these two German authorites are as dry (or as dense?) as stone, since *stein* = stone and *Peter* = Greek petros = stone. This would also account for the fact that in the remainder of Lucky's speech stones are mentioned seven times.

One last type of humour present in French but less noticeable in English is that of Beckett's jokes about his French style, which reveal him as somewhat self-conscious in his use of French. Lucky's false start to his speech: 'D'autre part, pour ce qui est . . .' (in the English: 'On the other hand, with regard to – ') is a parody of learned prose and also a piece of self-parody by Beckett, since John Fletcher points out that the use of this expression is one of his mannerisms, for example in *Molloy*.[7] More striking still is the humour inspired by the intricacies of French grammar when, in Act II, Estragon and Vladimir argue over whether the tree was there the previous day. In asserting that it was, Vladimir uses a very complicated French construction and pauses in the middle of his argument to check that he has got the mood and tense of the verb right:

ESTRAGON: Il n'était pas là hier?
VLADIMIR: Mais si. Tu ne te rappelles pas. Il s'en est fallu d'un cheveu qu'on ne s'y soit pendu. (*Il réfléchit.*) Oui, Oui, c'est juste (*en détachant les mots*) qu'on-ne-s'y-soit-pendu. Mais tu n'as pas voulu. Tu ne te rappelles pas?

No translation of this has been attempted in the English version, but a rather unsuccessful one is offered for a similar joke a few moments later when Vladimir, agreeing with Estragon that it is difficult not to look at the skeletons around them, uses a very idiomatic French expression which Estragon, perhaps finding it amusing, perhaps not understanding it, makes him repeat:

ESTRAGON:	Il n'y a qu'à ne pas regarder.	You don't have to look.
VLADIMIR:	Ça tire l'oeil.	You can't help looking.
ESTRAGON:	C'est vrai.	True.
VLADIMIR:	Malgré qu'on en ait.	Try as one may.
ESTRAGON:	Comment?	I beg your pardon?
VLADIMIR:	Malgré qu'on en ait.	Try as one may.

Was Beckett aware of the inadequacy of this translation? An amusing exchange nine lines later in the English version, but not present in the French, sounds very much like an attempt at compensation, especially since it involves the use of a French expression:

ESTRAGON: Que voulez-vous?
VLADIMIR: I beg your pardon?
ESTRAGON: Que voulez-vous?
VLADIMIR: Ah! que voulez-vous. Exactly.

In view of all this there seems to be little justification for regarding either the French or the English versions of the plays as funnier. Scrutiny of the points at which the versions differ from each other significantly reveals the fact that, in translating his plays either way, Beckett takes great care to maintain the humour of the original whilst at the same time often varying its character.

On the evidence of the first two plays it has also been claimed that Beckett is more vigorously crude in French than in English. No doubt some of his word-play has helped to create this impression, but in *Waiting for Godot* alone there are many places where the English reinforces the vulgarity of the French. Estragon cuts short the discussion about the Gospels in Act I with an obscenity if anything stronger in English than in French ('Les gens sont des cons') – 'People are bloody ignorant apes'. When Estragon says of his carrot that the more he eats the worse it gets, Vladimir responds in rather refined French ('Je me fais au goût au fur et à mesure' – which becomes in English: 'I get used to the muck as I go along.' Vladimir's suggested name for Lucky's dance ('le cancer des vieillards') is infinitely cruder in the English, which Beckett has confirmed as scatological: 'The hard stool.' When Estragon and Vladimir are annoyed by Pozzo's pleas for help in Act II, their French (ESTRAGON: 'Casse-lui la gueule.' VLADIMIR: 'Vermine') is milder and less violent than their English: 'Kick him in the crotch' / 'Crablouse'. Finally, when the two decide to while away a few moments with an exchange of insults, these are specified in the English but not in the French: 'Moron! Vermin! Abortion! Morpion! Sewer-rat! Curate! Cretin! . . . Crritic!' . . .

Systematic comparison between the French and the English versions of the plays thus casts doubt on the notion that Beckett is more poetic, or comic, or crude, or economical, or less enigmatic in the one language than in the other. Instead it reveals in Beckett what might have been expected of one who from very early in his career was a professional translator as well as a creative writer: a high level of consciousness and conscientiousness in reproducing his works in a second language. If he gives in to the temptation to improve at certain points by additions or, more often, by abbreviation, he does so without altering the essential quality of the original. . . .

SOURCE: extracts from essay-chapter ('Bilingual Playwright'), in Katharine Worth (ed.), *Beckett the Shape Changer* (London, 1975), pp. 142–5, 146, 147–8, 148–51, 151–2.

NOTES

[Reorganised and renumbered from the original – Ed.]

1. See J. Fletcher, *Samuel Beckett's Art* (London, 1967), ch. 6.

2. See J.-J. Mayoux, 'Samuel Beckett and the Universal Parody', in Martin Esslin (ed.). *Samuel Beckett: A Collection of Critical Essays* (Englewood Cliffs, N.J., 1965), pp. 90–1.

3. Ruby Cohn, *Samuel Beckett: The Comic Gamut* (New Brunswick, N.J., 1962); ch. 12, 'Beckett Self-Translator'.

4. *Fin de partie*, ed. J. & B. S. Fletcher (London, 1970), p. 86.

5. Editions referred to here are: *Waiting for Godot* (London, 1965); *En*

attendant Godot, ed. C. Duckworth (London, 1966); *Endgame* (London, 1964); *Fin de partie* (Paris, 1957); *Krapp's Last Tape* (London, 1965); *La Dernière bande* (Paris, 1959); *Happy Days* (London, 1966); *Oh les beaux jours* (Paris, 1963); *Play* (London, 1968); *Comédie* (Paris, 1966).

6. I owe this observation to M. Jean-René Démoris.
7. Fletcher, op. cit., p. 99.

Bert O. States 'Plots' (1978)

. . . The two plots of *Godot* (Pozzo/Lucky and Vladimir/Estragon) bear the same dialectical relationship to each other as *kairos* and *chronos*. That is, they dramatise antithetical concepts of being-in-time. The drama of Pozzo and Lucky is a *tick-tock* (a half-hunter with deadbeat escapement) inserted into the undifferentiated flux of Vladimir's and Estragon's vigil.[1] This is what, among other things, gives the vigil its interest, relieves it of tedium, tells its time, much as a falling meteor 'tells' the emptiness of space. The accompanying diagram shows how we might visualise the scheme. The solid lines

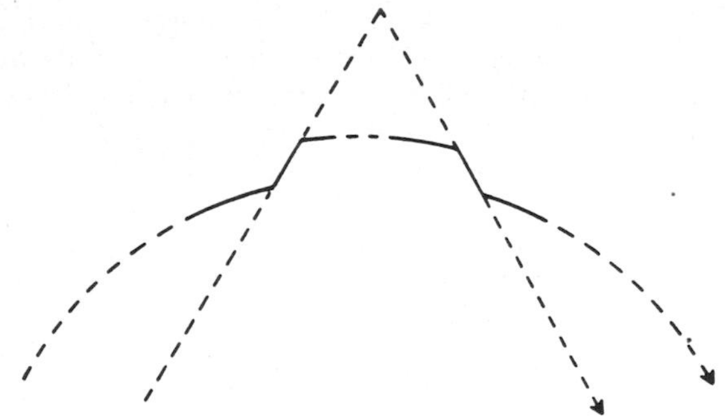

represent actual stage time, the dotted lines the trajectory of the characters' careers outside the play. The pyramid, as we have said, is the Pozzo/Lucky plot, marked at the apex by a peripety, or moment of reversal in which Pozzo is struck blind and Lucky dumb; the arc is the Vladimir/Estragon plot, a self-repeating circle, briefly displaced into linearity (on either slope) by the collision. In short, two opposed yet complementary geometries of experience – chronology versus chronicity – are brought into conjunction to form a single plot which, in effect, is a metaphorical tension of two deep structures, each carrying its own archetypal charge. . . .

. . . The distinction I would draw between our two plots – and of course there are other ways of putting them into relief – is quite close to Georg Lukács antithesis of tragic and modern drama on the principle of 'constructing the guilt' or 'building bridges between the deed and the doer'.[2] On one hand, the world represented by Pozzo and Lucky implies a concept of cause and effect, of sin and punishment, or at least of Fortune striking with some justification. The world of Vladimir and Estragon, on the other, is one in which Pride does not go before a Fall but before a vast silence. Hence the impression of an unchanging essential: of time without content, chronicity without chronology. Everything happens, as it were, at a distance and leaks through the surface of a diversionary routine which is the last refuge of the dying ego. There is only a vestige of the oppressive society in the form of thugs who administer unprovoked beatings under cover of night, and all that remains of the demanding god is a dim historical memory with barely enough gravitational pull to keep his 'subjects' in a vague orbit of supplication. But the Vladimir/Estragon plot is intelligible largely as a 'last bridge' in this whole burdensome history of obligation and ego-frustration. It is in this sense that Lukács's 'Sociology of Modern Drama', written in 1909, seems almost as valid as a prophecy of Samuel Beckett as it is an 'Aristotelian' commentary on the drama that had already been written. For instance, as a last bridge between deed and doer, consider *Godot* in the light of this passage:

> This is the [modern] dramatic conflict: man as merely the intersection point of great forces, and his deeds not even his own. Instead something independent of him mixes in, a hostile system which he senses as forever indifferent to him, thus shattering his will. And the why of his acts is likewise never wholly his own, and what he senses as his inner motivating energy also partakes of an aspect of the great complex which directs him toward his fall. The dialectical force comes to reside more exclusively in the idea, in the abstract. Men are but pawns, their will is but their possible moves, and it is what remains forever alien to them (the *abstractum*) which moves them. Man's significance consists only of this, that the game cannot be played without him, that men are the only possible hieroglyphs with which the mysterious inscription may be composed. . . . [p. 151]

This is such an umbrella passage that it effectively covers everything between Hebbel and Beckett; hence it is not very useful as a means of isolating subtraditions in modern drama. I cite it, however, because one can see how the structure of the imposed situation (that is, the protagonist as 'pawn') in modern drama is a variation of an indispensable plot-form dating back to the Greeks. Screen out certain peculiarly modern overtones, beginning with the nature of the *abstractum*, and the passage applies about as well to Orestes as it does to Marguérite in *La Dame aux camélias*.[3]

I would not insist on as clear a distinction between the two plots of *Godot* as I have drawn out rather severely here; for one thing, as we shall see, there is considerable blending of their energies in the second act. Nor is this the only way to view their differences. In fact, another, and more theological, perspective on what I have been saying is suggested by Kenneth Burke's essay on 'The First Three Chapters of Genesis' in *The Rhetoric of Religion*. Burke is here trying to demonstrate how biblical narrative style in Genesis expresses the idea of 'original' versus 'actual' sin. He distinguishes two styles which he calls the circular and the rectilinear. Another word for circular, he says, might be mythic in that myth 'is characteristically a terminology of quasi-narrative terms for the expressing of relationships that are not intrinsically narrative, but "circular" or "tautological"'.[4] Thus, the Vladimir/Estragon plot is tautological in that it tells the same story twice: the repetition of the structure of Act I in Act II serves, continually, to renew past time, in much the same way that the Cain/Abel story is renewed in the stories of Jacob and Esau and the two thieves. From the perspective of man's situation as a 'waiting' creature fallen from God this is the perfect form for expressing conclusively the fact that nothing has changed, that the original conditions still obtain, that man endlessly commits the sin of Adam and therefore endlessly enacts the Crucifixion.

The rectilinear style, on the other hand, is a narrative unfolding, a temporal progression that embodies the larger biblical premise of a Grand Dénouement of the world's drama ('a linear progression to end all linear progressions', as Burke says). To come back to my earlier point, we might think of Beckett's narrative problem in *Godot* as being essentially a biblical one: how to keep the Vladimir/Estragon situation from becoming a tautological bore; how, in short, to give this circularity enough linear drive to make it interesting without compromising the all-important theme that the essential doesn't change. To this end, Pozzo and Lucky give the play a considerable narrative boost: theirs is the drama of man's 'charge' through time; they are the personifications of historical motion and thrust, of becoming, of man burdened with the baggage of a sinful past and bound for a future which will come, like the Judgement, when they least expect it. Put side by side as purely temporal rhythms, these two plots also have something of the same relationship that tragedy has to the history play: tragedy (the isolation and death of the hero) completes its action, implying that everything that is important happens one fatal time; the history play (the trials of the nation, or race) implies a fresh beginning in every ending (often with a new trouble rising, like Richard Crookback, from the ashes of temporary victory), and assures us that what has been done will have to be done again and again.

I have perhaps put too much stress on the serious side of the play at the expense of the comic. In one connection [in an earlier section of this study – Ed.] I likened the Vladimir/Estragon plot to a vaudeville routine, a standard interpretation, and in another to the revenge drama of Orestes and [see note 3, below] Hamlet. I hope this is not the absurdity it seems, but the reader may wonder how he is supposed to get from the music hall to the palace. So some directions may be in order: in terms of pure organisational mechanics, the Vladimir/Estragon plot is a routine in every sense of the word; that is, it is built up out of improvisational 'numbers' which, if nothing else, at least entertain the comedians. . . . To come at the problem of the play's mixture of comedy and tragedy from still another angle, I might cite a passage from Schopenhauer as an inadvertent comment on *Godot*:

> The life of every individual, viewed as a whole and in general, and when only its most significant features are emphasised, is really a tragedy; but gone through in detail it has the character of a comedy. For the doings and worries of the day, the restless mockeries of the moment, the desires and fears of the week, the mishaps of every hour, are all brought about by chance that is always bent on some mischievous trick; they are nothing but scenes from a comedy. The never-fulfilled wishes, the frustrated efforts, the hopes mercilessly blighted by fate, the unfortunate mistakes of the whole life, with increasing suffering and death at the end, always give us a tragedy. Thus, as if fate wished to add mockery to the misery of our existence, our life must contain all the woes of tragedy, and yet we cannot even assert the dignity of tragic characters, but, in the broad detail of life, are inevitably the foolish characters of a comedy.[5]

. . . Even the comic part of life is not funny for Schopenhauer. But, looking at *Godot* 'as a whole', Pozzo's and Lucky's tragedy fades into the larger 'tragedy' of all humanity, represented by the unrewarded vigil of Vladimir and Estragon. It is not, of course, a tragedy in any technical sense, but it *is* serious: it takes up all those issues with which tragedy is concerned, even death itself (in the metaphor of the gravedigger-obstetrician). But if we go through the play 'in detail' this same general structure yields a series of 'scenes from a comedy' involving the doings and worries of the day, the mockeries of the moment, desires, fears and mishaps, all seemingly brought on by chance.

These seem to me the main structural dynamics of the two plots of *Godot*. Moving a step back, we might notice, in conclusion, that in the important respects the play is following the principles of good plot construction beneath all its modern liberties with form; for these two deep structures, in their rhythmic interplay, create (to recall Kermode's terms) an overall or synchronic *tick-tock*.[6] The 'waiting' of Vladimir and Estragon produces a 'lively expectation' of Pozzo and Lucky (an arrival of some sort) and they, in turn help to bestow upon the play both its duration (a closure of its openness) and its meaning. . . .

SOURCE: extracts from chapter ('The Imposed Situation') in *The Shape of Paradox* (Berkeley, California, 1978), pp. 74–5, 81–6, 88–9.

NOTES

[Reorganised and renumbered from the original – Ed.]

1. [Ed.] Immediately prior to this 'plots' enquiry, States has been considering 'the empty intervals between and around *tick* and *tock*', referring to Frank Kermode's celebrated discussion of the presence in imaginative literature of 'an overall of synchronic tick-tock' – cf. Kermode, *The Sense of An Ending* (London and New York, 1967), pp. 45–7.

2. Georg Lukács, 'The Sociology of Modern Drama', trans. Lee Baxandall, in *Tulane Drama Review*, 9, no. 4 (Summer 1965), p. 150.

3. Perhaps the play that most clearly lives up to this 'prophecy' is Tom Stoppard's *Rosencrantz and Guildenstern Are Dead* which is literally about what happens when 'the baser nature' becomes the 'intersection point' of mighty opposites. For illustration purposes, we might retitle it *Didi and Gogo Meet Hamlet*: not only does it lean heavily on *Godot's* characterisations and devices of style, but it brings into clear focus its structural underpinnings of a classical tragedy unfolding in the context of modern alienation. Here we see just where Hamlet, that great asker of modern questions, has led us – to a complete dissolution of the *act* as a statement of will. Quite apart from its own merits as a play, *Rosencrantz and Guildenstern* is also an astute piece of Existentialist criticism from the post-*Godot* era. It seems to say: 'This is what Beckett has shown us. This is how we would rewrite the Renaissance!'

4. Kenneth Burke, *The Rhetoric of Religion: Studies in Logology* (Berkeley and Los Angeles, 1970), p. 258. Burke repeatedly uses the word *style* in this essay, and as far as I can see he is not referring to literary style but to different 'logological' perspectives one might take on the same image or incident in the Bible, or on the Bible as a whole. For instance: 'Thus, where the Scofield Bible comments, "The history of Israel in the wilderness and in the land is one long record of the violation of the law", we should interpret this logologically to mean that the Biblical narrative is but continually restating the principle of circularity intrinsic to the idea of Order, continually coming upon this circular situation despite the rectilinearity of the narrative method' [p. 224].

In other words, it is not a question of the style of the *text* (in, for instance, Auerbach's use of the term *style*), but of one's perspective on the text. Maybe not. In any case, the point needs clarification inasmuch as I am adjusting Burke's idea to suit a more literary use of the word *style*. In fact, what I have said about the two plots of *Godot* more closely follows Burke's principles of style as set forth in *Counter-Statement*. That is, the 'cyclical' style is an exercise in Qualitative Progression, or maintaining the same principle (waiting) under different guises (Act II qualitatively repeats Act I); and the 'rectilinear' style is an exercise in Syllogistic Progression, which moves *from* something, *through* something, *to* something quite different (the 'drama' of Pozzo and Lucky). The idea would be that any story (say, Cain and Abel) would be a rectilinear narrative, but considered in the context of other stories of grace-given and grace-withheld (say, Jacob and Esau or the Two Thieves) it would be a circular tautology.

5. Arthur Schopenhauer, *The World as Will and Representation* (1819), trans. E. F. J. Payne (New York, 1966), I, p. 322.

6. [Ed.] See note 1, above.

Raymond Williams (1963) — 'A Modern Tragedy'

. . . It is clear that in certain respects *Waiting for Godot* belongs to the tradition we are tracing [in the general argument of Williams's book – Ed.]. It presents a total condition of man, and this belongs within the familiar structure of feeling:

> . . . one day we were born, one day we shall die, the same day, the same second, is that not enough for you? . . . They give birth astride of a grave, the light gleams an instant, then it's night once more. . . .
>
> . . . Astride of a grave and a difficult birth. Down in the hole, lingeringly, the grave-digger puts on the forceps. We have time to grow old. The air is full of our cries. . . . [Pozzo, echoed by Vladimir, Act II]

Yet the dramatic method is in fact unlike that of Chekhov and Pirandello, where the movement is normally a single action showing how the characters fit in with each other, sharing comparable illusions. The method of *Waiting for Godot* is older. The play is built around an unusually explicit set of contrasts: between the tramps, Vladimir and Estragon, and the travellers, Pozzo and Lucky; and the further contrasts within each pair.

This polar opposition of characters was used in early expressionism to present the conflicts of a single mind. But now the method has been developed to present the conflicts within a total human condition. It is an almost wholly static world, with very narrow limits set to any significant human action. Yet the struggles for significance, of each of the pairs, are sharply contrasted. The movement of the play is the action of waiting. In each of the two acts, the tramps come together to wait, meet the travellers, who pass on, and then the tramps are left waiting for an appointment that is not kept. But whereas in the travellers there is change between the acts, in the tramps there is no change. This follows from the different responses they have made. The simplest illustration can be taken from the two speeches quoted above: the first by Pozzo, the second by Vladimir. The sense of life in each is identical, but Pozzo's next word is 'On!', the command to movement, while Vladimir's next words are 'But habit is a great deadener', the patience and the suffering of waiting. Pozzo and Lucky belong to the world of effort and action; Vladimir and Estragon to the world of resignation and waiting. Neither response is more significant than the other, in any ultimate way: the travellers fall and the tramps wait on in disappointment.

Neither the way of progress nor the way of salvation leads out of this human condition. But the way chosen affects the human beings who choose it. The way of the travellers is marked by power and exploitation, which in the end consume themselves. Pozzo, the comfortable accommodated man, leads Lucky as a slave with a halter on his neck, but in the second act the same rope is that of the blind being led by the dumb. It is a way of domination and dependence: relationships which can only be reversed. The way of the tramps, on the other hand, is one of compassion in degradation. Irritation drives them apart, and the power of sympathy is always likely to fail. Hysterical cruelty waits at the edge for these break-downs. Yet, under pressure, the relationship holds, and within the tradition we have been tracing this is the main originality of the play. The compassion which was always present in Chekhov had virtually disappeared by the time of Pirandello and his successors. Their exposure of illusion (as indeed in Beckett's own other work) carried a mocking harshness which could not go beyond itself. The world and life had been 'seen through', and that was that. In the Pozzo-Lucky sequences, Beckett continues this tone, but he combines it with what had seemed to be lost: the possibility of human recognition, and of love, within a total condition still meaningless. Strangely, this answering life, at a point beyond the recognition of stalemate, is convincing and moving. . . .

The condition is absolute, and the response confirms it. But as they stay together, with nothing to go for and nothing but disappointment to wait for, yet staying together, an old and deep tragic rhythm is recovered.

SOURCE: extract from essay, 'Tragic Deadlock and Stalemate' (1963); reproduced in Williams's *Modern Tragedy* (London, 1979), pp. 153–5.

Richard Keller Simon Beckett, Comedy and the Critics (1987)

From the beginnings of Beckett scholarship in the late 1950s, and for more than a decade afterwards, critics regularly explained his work as a form of philosophically and theologically complex comedy, one that affirmed the values of humor, laughter and mockery against suffering and despair. Murphy and Molloy, Vladimir and Estragon, Hamm and Clov, all of Beckett's central characters were described as clowns, clochards and music hall comedians who demonstrated the clown's special ability to survive under the worst of circumstances. Among the earliest critics to take this position were Maurice Nadeau in France (1951) and Gunther Anders in Germany (1954). In England and the United States, the first major critics developed a comic interpretation, establishing the context in which Beckett would be read and understood by others – for example, Hugh Kenner in essays published in 1958 and 1959, then in *Samuel Beckett: A Critical Study* (1961) and *Flaubert, Joyce, and Beckett: The Stoic Comedians* (1962); Ruby Cohn, in essays published between 1959 and 1961, then in *Samuel Beckett: The Comic Gamut* (1962); and Martin Esslin, in essays on the modern theatre in 1959 and 1960, then in *The Theatre of the Absurd* (1961). Kenner called Beckett's techniques 'a unique comic repertoire, like a European clown's' [*Samuel Beckett*, p. 13]. Cohn wrote: 'As he moves from a baroque to a colloquial style, Beckett retains his comic vision. An analysis of his humor therefore traces an attitude that is pervasive in his work, at its complex core, and an understanding of that humor may elucidate the core' [*Comic Gamut*].

In *Godot* the worst insult Vladimir and Estragon have in their extensive repertoire of abuse is 'crritic', worse than moron or vermin, more devastating than curate or cretin. When Vladimir hears it he wilts. Beckett, of course, was a critic very early in his career, and it should not be surprising that he would write texts with such individuals consciously in mind. In *Godot*, Vladimir and Estragon are constantly commenting on and evaluating their own performances, explaining their possible meanings, playing the game of reviewer and critic in front of audiences of reviewers and critics. And in a curiously comic way *Godot* plays a game with its critics by anticipating their obvious responses, and confounding them.

The two most common critical interpretations of the play are as religious parable and as clown show, and yet both are little more than elaborations of statements contained within the play. There is an extensive discussion of the Bible early in Act I, but before the critic or reviewer can find a moment to think about this during intermission, as the act ends Vladimir and Estragon compare themselves to Christ. If he wishes to sound either intelligent or original, the critic should find something else to say about the play. In Act II there is the long piece of comic business, the hat trick, which would suggest the play is a clown show; but already, in Act I, before such explicit borrowings from comedy, Vladimir and Estragon have compared their performance with public entertainment: once to the musical hall, and *twice* to the circus. The play undercuts the critic by making its themes so explicitly obvious. Will he simply repeat what the characters tell him (and everybody else) the play means? No one should belabor the obvious – at least, not without examining the evidence carefully.

Yet it was into this particular trap that Beckett's first critics fell, looking for ways of explaining the obscurities of the play. Esslin used the lines to support his argument that the play was comic: 'And the parallel to the music hall and the circus is even explicitly stated' [*Theatre of the Absurd*, p. 14]. Kenner wrote: 'Thus a non-play comments on itself' [*Samuel Beckett*, p. 135]. Jacobsen and Mueller observed that it reminded them 'of the milieu in which, we must never forget, all takes place' [*The Testament of Samuel Beckett*, p. 14]. For John Fletcher, 'Beckett's characters never forget that they are present at their own spectacle' [*The Art of Samuel Beckett*, p. 66]. The lines about the music hall and circus were taken at face value – the characters were regarded as reliable guides by critics who did not consider that Vladimir and Estragon are not always the best of authorities, or, for that matter, that what a character says is not what an author says. About the relationship between Beckett and his critics, Esslin argued in 1965:

> Inevitably there exists an organic connection between his refusal to explain his meaning . . . . and the critics' massive urge to supply an explanation. Indeed, it might be argued that in that correlation between the author's and the critics' attitude lies one of the keys to the whole phenomenon of Samuel Beckett, his *oeuvre* and its impact. [*Samuel Beckett*, p. 1]

But there Esslin seems obviously wrong. At the beginning at least, the organic connection was rather between the meanings Beckett tossed out to the critics (much as Pozzo tossed out bones) and the ways in which the critics grasped hungrily at them, digesting without a second thought. Thus Beckett very obviously invites us to see *Godot* as religious parable and a circus performance – it is part of his complex playing. And no critic is necessary to provide us with these meanings. It was on evidence like Vladimir's and Estragon's blather about the music hall and the circus that critics built the case for Beckett as comedian.

The comic elements function much as they do in Shakespearean tragedy, as a kind of relief, momentary interruptions in the tedium and despair. In retrospect what we can now see is that they were simply the most recognisable elements, and the first critics seized upon them as a way of explicating Beckett's difficult texts. What was most obvious about them became what was most essential. But by no generally held definition can these texts be called comic – they do not celebrate the golden mean, integrate the individual into society, or show the victory of young lovers over blocking characters. Neither are they about rebirth, marriage, festivity, saturnalia or fertility of any sort. In fact, by most of these definitions, Beckett's texts are clearly *anti*-comic: precise inversions of the comic literature, being about death, sterility, disintegration of the individual.

Comedy has sometimes been defined as an inversion of the normal and the everyday, as the world turned upside down. Beckett's literature is an inversion of that inversion, a perversion of the comic. And therefore, the comic elements in plays like *Godot* and *Endgame* may not be incidental comic relief after all, but among the primary objects of the author's attack. By only one very general definition can the texts be called comic: they provoke audience laughter, and therefore are perceived as 'funny'. Yet such laughter is a notoriously unreliable guide to the generic meanings of a text. Forced somewhat awkwardly into problems of audience response, the first Anglo-American critics converted the subjective response into objective characteristics of the texts. By a sleight of hand, laughter became comedy. But Beckett was writing a form of literature that might be more appropriately called metacomedy: drama and fiction about comedy, humor and laughter.

SOURCE: rewritten for this Casebook by Dr Simon from an article originally published in 1979; a different version is in the press as part of his new volume, *Beckett Translating/Translating Beckett*.

David Bradby 'Beckett's Shapes' (1984)

Beckett's work for the theatre consists of a long refinement on the success of his initial achievement in *En attendant Godot*. If the model for his particular type of stage action was the clown, it is far less apparent in his later plays. It is possible to perform *Godot* as a warm, almost cheerful, piece about two people who preserve a dignity through tenderness for one another despite their decrepitude (though this is not Beckett's own choice of interpretation). But in *Fin de partie* the tone is altogether more savage and so it remains in all Beckett's subsequent plays. The single, inescapable defining context of the long wait for Godot by the tree, that made his first play so original, is also refined in the later plays, its stranglehold on the characters tightened. In *Godot*, some relief was provided simply by the appearance of the two new characters, Pozzo and Lucky. But in *Fin de partie* the action remains rigorously restricted to the one room in which Hamm lives with his servant Clov and his aging parents in their ashbins. All of Beckett's subsequent characters inhabit spaces that are hermetically sealed, into which only occasional memories can intrude, and their constant preoccupation is with finding a way to understand their situation, come to terms with themselves, find a language in which to express their sense of transience within stasis. . . .

All Beckett's characters are haunted by voices. Vladimir and Estragon talk of them:

ESTRAGON: All the dead voices.
VLADIMIR: They make a noise like wings.
ESTRAGON: Like leaves.
VLADIMIR: Like sand.
ESTRAGON: Like leaves. [*W.f.G.* (1965 edn) p. 62]

Krapp plays them back on his tape recorder; the characters in *Play* are reduced to the point where they are almost nothing but voices, and this process is taken one stage further in *Not I* where the only thing visible to the audience is a speaking mouth and a dim, barely perceived, listening presence.

The voices are there because they can never be silenced. Many of the characters in the plays attempt to end, to be quiet, to achieve silence, but none succeed. . . .

At the linguistic level . . . shaping devices range from the very simple to the very complex. At the simplest are devices like the song

Vladimir sings at the beginning of Act II of *Godot*. . . . The fact that Beckett particularly enjoyed this song is shown by its reappearance in *The Unnamable* . . ., a rare case of Beckett quoting himself. This song is not used because of any meaning enshrined in it, but because it embodies, in a peculiarly vivid form (not without a certain mystery), a particular shape or structure: the shape of the endless cycle. A similar effect is achieved by the repetition that is a feature of Vladimir and Estragon's reflections. . . .

Similar in their function to jokes are the vividly paradoxical statements that Beckett makes his characters utter at moments of extreme tension. Vladimir, filled with anguish at seeing Estragon asleep while the boy once again comes to announce that Godot will not appear that day, summarises existence in the words 'Down in the hole, lingeringly, the grave-digger puts on his forceps'. . . . This paradoxical image, bringing together in one brutal phrase the birth that marks the beginning of a life and the death that ends it, is a striking example of one particular shape perhaps best described as the antithetical paradox. . . .

Most complex of all, as linguistic shaping devices, are those speeches on which Beckett has imprinted the form of a disintegrating intellect. Attempts to decode the meaning of Lucky's 'think' or of the mouth's monologue in *Not I* will fail, since they are written in the discursive rational mode. But the overall shape of their disjointed fragments conveys, in the case of Lucky's monologue, the shape of a mind that shrinks, pines and dies as a result of the failure of the world as perceived to meet the demands of the enquiring mind. In the case of *Not I* the monologue's structure is one of a constant attempt at evasion but an attempt that constantly fails. The suggestion is of a confession, reinforced by the dimly perceived presence of a hooded figure listening to the babbling of the mouth. But the repeated breaking off on the phrase 'not I' suggests a failure to evade the responsibility that is the original motive force behind the confession.

At the scenic level, Beckett constructs shapes that are strikingly expressive of confinement and endless sameness. During early performances of *Godot*, it was most frequently after the curtain had gone up on the second act, revealing the same deserted road, that spectators walked out. They could no longer bear the tension of hoping something would happen and finding that nothing did. The physical positions into which Beckett puts his characters have a vivid, condensed quality that is present at every level of his dramaturgy, but perhaps most clearly evident here. . . .

As well as language and scenic elements, the things done on stage in Beckett's plays need to be approached with an eye to their shape. The obsessive quality with which Vladimir and Estragon return again and again to the same phrase, image or joke, finds its counterpart in action, with Estragon's obsessive pulling at his boot, or the endless changing of hats in Act II. . . .

One of the most interesting features of these shapes and structures is that in so many of Beckett's plays the characters accept and confess their status as characters in a play: that is, people whose function it is to entertain an audience for a couple of hours. This is particularly true of Vladimir and Estragon whose dialogue, as has frequently been pointed out, owes much to the tradition of the music-hall cross-talk acts that Beckett had appreciated in the Dublin of his youth. The salient feature of the cross-talk act is that it elevates the aside to the level of structural principle: its humour derives from the fact that either one of the two characters can, at any moment, step outside his assumed role in order to comment upon it.

So we find that Beckett presents his audiences with a shape that is not just endlessly cyclical (like Vladimir's song) or paradoxical (like the grave-digger/midwife image) or condensed (like the grandparents in ashbins), but also a shape that is self-conscious, that comments upon itself – and that is the shape of a performance. To ask Why? What does it mean? is to commit the same error as the people to whom Winnie so scornfully refers: 'What does it mean? he says – What's it meant to mean – and so on – lot more stuff like that – normal drivel'. . . . The reason why the plays call attention to their own shape is that this is another, more concrete way of warning the audience not to look for meanings behind or beyond the work, but to consider it for what it is: simply a play. Beckett himself, normally so unwilling to comment on his work, has made this plain by saying, 'My work is a matter of fundamental sounds (no joke intended) made as fully as possible, and I accept responsibility for nothing else'. . . .

By using the means so far described, Beckett presents an image of existence as endless expectation. The dominant impression of someone who waits is of time passing slowly or coming to a standstill. Beckett exploits this experience of time. It was the *nouveau romancier* Robbe-Grillet who drew attention to this in a commentary on the question put to Pozzo by Vladimir and Estragon on two occasions in the course of Act I: 'Why doesn't he put down his bags?' Robbe-Grillet commented:

This is indeed the question that was asked a few minutes earlier. But in the meantime Lucky has put down the bags; Didi is able to convince everyone with the argument that 'Since he has put down his bags it is impossible that we should have asked why he did not do so.' Logic itself. In this universe where time stands still, the words *before* and *after* have no meaning; all that counts is the present: the bags *are* down and so it is as if they had always been. . . .

There is a contrast between the audience's perception of minute changes, such as bags being picked up or put down, and the characters' feeling that nothing changes. It is by exploiting this contrast that Beckett achieves the dynamic force needed to give the plays their minimum necessary forward movement so as to prevent them becoming paralysed in total stasis. . . .

SOURCE: extracts from chapter ('The Parisian Theatre II: The New Theatre') in *Modern French Drama* (Cambridge, 1984), pp. 66, 67, 68, 69, 70–1.

David H. Hesla (1982) 'Beckett's Philosophy'

. . . It is a little odd that [Cormier and Pallister][1] are so hard on Beckett for his want of optimism. Christians such as Pascal found little in man to praise. Here is Pascal in the *Pensées* on Didi and Gogo as they are waiting:

> Nothing is so insufferable to man as to be completely at rest, without passions, without business, without diversion . . . He then feels his nothingness, his forlornness, his insufficiency, his dependence, his weakness, his emptiness. There will immediately arise from the depth of his heart weariness, gloom, sadness, fretfulness, vexation, despair. [PP: II, 131, p. 38]

And here he is on Godot and his offer as the 'foundation' on which the two tramps mean to build their lives:

> Nothing stays for us. This is our natural condition, and yet most contrary to our inclinations; we burn with desire to find solid ground and an ultimate sure foundation whereon to build a tower reaching to the Infinite. But our whole groundwork cracks, and the earth opens to abysses. [PP: II, 72, p. 19]

In Pascal's view man is miserable because he is without God. In Schopenhauer's he is miserable because he is will – the will to live:

> This great intensity of will is in itself and directly a constant source of suffering. In the first place, because all volition as such arises from want; that is, suffering . . . Secondly, because, through the causal connection of things, most of our desires must remain unfulfilled, and the will is oftener crossed than satisfied. [PS: 65, p. 293]

Schopenhauer has no time for God, but that does not mean he cannot establish a moral code and distinguish wrong from right. In the interaction of two human beings – that is, two wills –

> the will of the first breaks through the limits of the assertion of will of another, because the individual either destroys or injures this other body itself, or else because it compels the powers of the other body to serve *its own* will . . . This breaking through the limits of the assertion of will of another has always been distinctly recognised, and its concept denoted by the word *wrong*.
>
> [PS: 62, p. 279]

Wrong shows itself in acts of cannibalism, murder, the mutilation or injury of another body, in the 'subjugation of another individual, in forcing him into slavery', and in the seizure of another's goods [PS: 62, pp. 279–80].

In presenting his concept of the right or good, Schopenhauer takes pains to distinguish his position from Kant's. Kant differentiated between actions resulting from 'inclination' and those resulting 'from duty'. The former include all such acts as arise out of man's nature or instinct or temperament; the latter includes only those acts done freely and in obedience to the categorical imperative, which in one formulation reads, 'Act only according to that maxim by which you can at the same time will that it should become a universal law' [FMM: 39]. Such a maxim, however, can be determined only by the application to a given situation of the faculty of reason.

Kant supplies an interesting example of the difference between inclination and duty. Suppose, he says, you have someone who is by disposition or inclination a friend to mankind, someone who finds an inner satisfaction in spreading joy and rejoicing in the contentment of others. For such a person to be kind to another would have no moral worth, for his act would be merely natural or instinctive. But now suppose that

> the mind of that friend to mankind was clouded by a sorrow of his own which extinguished all sympathy with the lot of others and that he still had the power to benefit others in distress, but that their need left him untouched because he was preoccupied with his own need. And now suppose him to tear himself, unsolicited by inclination, out of this dead insensibility and to perform this action only from duty and without any inclination – then for the first time his action has genuine moral worth. [FMM: 14]

This is the distinction Didi makes when he discourses on the possibility of helping Pozzo get up. 'All mankind is us', he declares. 'Let us represent worthily for once the foul brood to which a cruel fate consigned us!' [*Godot*, p. 51]. He and Gogo do indeed represent all mankind, for the action they are about to take is an expression of their will that that act should become a universal law. They do not immediately help Pozzo up, however, for Didi's resolution is paralysed by Kant's distinction between inclination and duty, the tiger representing the former: 'It is true that when with folded arms we weigh the pros and cons we are no less a credit to our species. The tiger bounds to the help of his congeners without the least reflection . . .' [*Godot*, pp. 51–51b]. In the Kantian frame of things Didi and Gogo cannot represent worthily their species by leaping to Pozzo's aid, for that would be an act arising out of inclination and so of no moral worth. They act 'humanly' and 'morally' only if they think about what they are doing, and then act 'from duty'.

Schopenhauer rejects Kant's rationality and the idea of a categorical imperative. For him 'no genuine virtue can be produced through moral theory or abstract knowledge'; such virtue must rather 'spring from that intuitive knowledge which recognises in the individuality of others the same nature as our own' [PS: 66, p. 299]. Real goodness then does not proceed from abstract knowledge but from 'a direct intuitive knowledge . . . which cannot be communicated, but must arise in each for himself, which therefore finds its real and adequate expression not in words, but only in deeds . . .' [PS: 66, p. 320]. that 'intuitive knowledge' is nothing other than sympathy, and sympathy is simply the knowledge of the suffering of others [PS: 67, p. 303].

So it is only when Didi and Gogo have fallen down that Didi can accurately name himself and his fellow: 'We are men'. And being down, they can sympathise with the suffering of the fallen Pozzo. (Pozzo's other miseries were of a sort the two tramps could not understand and so sympathise with.) The tableau that is then presented to us – 'They get him up again. Pozzo sags between them, his arms round their necks' – is as explicit as Beckett allows himself to get in telling us what to do, how to live.

Schopenhauer also explains why Beckett calls the play a 'tragicomedy':

> The life of every individual, if we survey it as a whole and in general, and only lay stress upon its most significant features, is really always a tragedy, but gone through in detail, it has the character of a comedy. For the deeds and vexations of the day, the restless irritation of the moment, the desires and fears of the week, the mishaps of every hour, are all through chance, which is ever bent upon some jest, scenes of a comedy. But the never-satisfied wishes, the frustrated efforts, the hopes unmercifully crushed by fate, the unfortunate errors of the whole life, with increasing suffering and death at the end, are always a tragedy. Thus, as if fate would add derision to the misery of existence, our life must contain all the woes of tragedy, and yet we cannot

even assert the dignity of tragic characters, but in the broad detail of life must inevitably be the foolish characters of a comedy. [PS: 58, p. 261]

The point I am trying to make is that Beckett – does this still need to be said? – is no more a nihilist than he is a Marxist, a Pyrrhonist or a Christian. But he is a moralist, if by that term one means simply that there is in *Godot*, as in all his work, an explicit difference between right and wrong. It is wrong for Pozzo to treat Lucky as he does. It is wrong for Gogo to kick the fallen Lucky, even though the moral significance of his action is immediately obscured by the comic effect of Gogo's hurting himself and calling Lucky a brute. All such Punch-and-Judy antics are fundamentally sadistic; but as Nell says, echoing Schopenhauer, 'Nothing is funnier than unhappiness' [*Endgame*, p. 18].

In all of *Godot* there are only two actions that are right: Didi's covering with his own coat the sleeping Gogo [p. 45a], and the two of them helping Pozzo to stand. Both proceed from sympathy, for Didi knows it is preferable to be warm rather than cold, and both know that it is preferable to be up rather than down. These acts of kindness are few and transient, unearned and without effect; but they establish the moral principle in terms of which all other actions are to be assessed. If we do not understand this, it is because we are too decadent to receive it.

Beckett is no more pessimistic than his predecessors in the tradition of despondency – Schopenhauer, Leopardi, Calderon, the Abderite.[3] He is no grimmer than Pascal: 'The last act is tragic, however happy all the rest of the play is; at the last a little earth is thrown upon our head, and that is the end for ever' [PP: III, p. 210]. No grimmer, for that matter, than Koheleth, the Preacher: 'So I returned and considered all the oppressions that are done under the sun: and behold the tears of such as were oppressed, and they had no comforter; and on the side of their oppressors there was power; but they had no comforter' [Eccl. 4:1]. Yet Koheleth, like Schopenhauer and Beckett, sees a comfort, albeit a small one, in sympathy; for two are better than one:

> Two are better than one; because they have a good reward for their labour. For if they fall, the one will lift up his fellow; but woe to him that is alone when he falleth; for he hath not another to help him up. [Eccl. 4:9–10]

SOURCE: extract from review article in *Journal of Beckett Studies*, 7 (1982), pp. 140–3.

NOTES

[Reorganised and renumbered from the original – Ed.]

1. [Ed.] Ramona Cormier and Janis L. Pallister, authors of *Waiting for Death: The Philosophical Significance of Beckett's 'Waiting for Godot'* (Montgomery, Alabama, 1979) – the book under review by Hesla.

2. References for *Godot* and *Endgame* are to the Grove Press editions; for Pascal [PP] to section, paragraph and page of *Pascal's Pensées*, trans. W. F. Trotter (New York, 1958); for Schopenhauer [PS] to section and page of *The Philosophy of Schopenhauer*, ed. Irwin Edmon (New York, 1928); and for Kant [FMM] to *Foundations of the Metaphysics of Morals*, trans. Lewis White Beck (Indianopolis, 1959).

3. [Ed.] By 'the Abderite', Hesla alludes to Democritus (460–370 BC), born at Abdera in Thrace; his philosophy denied immortality, holding that the soul died with the body.

Jacques Dubois Beckett and Ionesco (1966)

Beckett's *Waiting for Godot* and Ionesco's *The Chairs* opened in Paris within the same year; they are perhaps the two most outstanding and significant works of the avant-garde theatre. It is therefore surprising that scarcely any attention has been paid to similarities so striking that both plays might have been constructed from the same outline.

Let me explain. From their openings, *The Chairs* and *Godot* place the spectator in very similar situations; we are in the presence of a couple who will not leave before the end of the play – in the one case, husband and wife, in the other, two inseparable friends. In both plays, we find two aged beings, two social outcasts – in the one case, two miserable tramps, in the other, two old people ending their mediocre existence in a kind of dotage. The two members of the couple cannot do without each other, not so much because of real affection as because of habit and fear of solitude. Their outbursts of friendship are ridiculous because they are rarely in the same emotional key. These miserable beings are trapped, prisoners; the one pair in a house on a lonely island, the other in a deserted place on a nameless road to which they seem riveted, despite their repetitions of 'Let's go'. They have been in other places, but their memories are vague, confused, challenged as soon as evoked. Their conception of time has become uncertain.

Everything suggests that these people are cast-offs of a humanity which is disintegrating and on the point of disappearance. The Old Man says this to his imaginary public: 'To you, ladies and gentlemen, and dear comrades, who are all that is left from humanity, but with such left-overs one can still make a very good soup' (Donald Allen translation). Vladimir does not go quite so far when he declares: 'at this place, at this moment of time, all mankind is us, whether we like it or not'. 'This place', 'this moment' limit his affirmation, making it more banal. Nevertheless, *this* place, *this* moment, so isolated and empty in their monotonous repetition, inhabited only by these grotesque creatures – are they not a parabolic designation of a whole universe running down? In both *The Chairs* and *Godot*, this microcosm is a reduced image of the macrocosm which is our universe.

In this vast emptiness, human absurdity becomes extremely sharp. Alone in the face of time, man has few resources by which to endow things with meaning. There remains one solution: to fill time in the most gratuitous fashion, to try in any possible way to stuff all the holes, to indulge in a parody of existence, hoping perhaps that the Meaning will emerge from it. A game, an entertainment – but a game and entertainment which will be largely verbal, in view of man's logorrheal tendency and also because one is in the theatre. There will therefore be a game of speech, though one knows that such exertions are futile. Compare these passages from the two plays (in each case, the line from *Godot* precedes the one from *The Chairs*):

Say you are, even if it's not true.
Let's amuse ourselves by making believe, the way you did the other evening.

Suppose we repented.
Come on now, imitate the month of February.

You know the story of the Englishman in the brothel?
Tell me the story, you know *the* story.

Say anything at all!
Ah! Yes, go on . . . tell me. . . .

It is easy to predict the direction of such word-games – towards a mechanisation of language. The machine will occasionally run out of energy; it will misfire or repeat. However, in Beckett's play, such repetition can become poetic synonymity – the same meaning in other words. But often, Vladimir alone supplies the variations in these exercises, whereas Estragon repeats the exact phrase. In Ionesco's play, the phonograph needle falls in the same rut. Towards the end of *The Chairs*, the voice of the Old Woman is reduced to an echo of the voice of the Old Man. This is a powerful presentation of man alone before the world's nothingness: he hears only his own voice in answer to his repeated cries.

This universe of empty words would remain at a level of formless magma, were it not for the narrative direction and the dramatic meaning which structure the plays. On the one hand, the four pitiful characters are hampered, threatened, assaulted by the world of objects; and on the other, their waiting and faith depend upon hope in a spiritual force which would free them from nothingness, and compensate for their failure.

Physical Menace. Beckett and Ionescu both show us man as a prey of the world of objects. Ionesco gives us a clear image, and its pattern is famous: the Old Couple assemble chairs on stage for guests who exist only in their imagination, and the multiplication of chairs finally separates the two characters from one another, forcing them to opposite ends of the stage, from which they will throw themselves out of their respective windows. This is a concrete and violent representation of man conquered by the proliferation of the objects he has created, of man overwhelmed and alienated by things. And the author has no fear of exaggerating the image and placing it at the heart of his action. (Sartre was far more timid with his symbolic flies.) But whereas Ionesco works through multiplying objects – a kind of cancer! – Beckett seems to prefer the opposite – rarifying them. Carrots and turnips, nourishment of the tramps, grow rarer and rarer. *Godot* is permeated by an atmosphere of scarcity. But this difference between the two authors is more apparent than real. Beckett sees man caught in a basic contradiction,; he suffers both from a particular cause and from its contrary, from one contingency and its opposite. Thus, man is crushed as much by the presence as by the absence of material goods. On the one hand, the two tramps suffer from their lack of comfort and possessions; nevertheless, they are burdened, overcome, tortured by their wretched clothes – the shoes of the one and the hat of the other. Like the playing with chairs in Ionesco's drama, the tramps' playing with hats represents the futile agitation of man among things; each play proclaims the absurdity of human actions.

Spiritual Hope. This is the major similarity between the two plays, but it may not be immediately evident in the complex structure. In both cases, the 'heroes' await the arrival of someone, whether the celebrated but indefinite Godot or the Orator who is supposed to deliver the Old Man's message. In each play, this wait is the guiding thread which seems to lead us towards a single goal. One cannot overestimate the importance of this goal, for it alone appears capable of giving life a meaning, and, in a parallel fashion, of giving the play a direction. As Vladimir says, 'In this immense confusion one thing alone is clear. We are waiting for Godot to come –'. Similarly, after having looked back on the past of the Old Man as an 'old black drain', the Old Woman declares, 'all is not lost, all is not spoiled, you'll tell them everything, you will explain, you have a message. . . .'

But what does Godot represent? What does the message contain? In each case, the same mystery but also a comparable hope of salvation. But alas! Godot will continue to postpone his visit; and when the Orator appears, he proves to be deaf and dumb. Hope was deceptive. And yet, the characters remain deceived: the Old Couple commit suicide, satisfied that they have fulfilled their mission even before the Orator tries to speak; the two tramps continue to believe the young messenger who appears each time to announce that Godot will come not today but tomorrow. The image of the human being, always deceived in his dreams and ideals, nevertheless perseveres in his illusions and utopias.

One might object that the two cases are different, or even opposed to each other. Whereas the tramps await something from outside themselves, the Old Man wishes to offer something to others. But the Old Man will save himself in saving others. Moreover, his message is outside himself since he is incapable of formulating it, and he gives the task to another. Finally, the Godot of Estragon and Vladimir might not be so far outside themselves, but rather a projection of their deepest hope. On the whole, the same concept of redemption dominates the two plays; what is more important than either Godot or the message of the Orator is the waiting itself.

We have now reached the very heart of the two plays, and it will be interesting to back off and see how the roles are distributed – or, rather, to see the functions of the characters in these two strange actions. *Grosso modo*, Estragon and the Old Woman are 'doubles' of Vladimir and the Old Man. Let us concern ourselves only with the latter. Vladimir and the Old Man are Man, a fallen and miserable creature, who nevertheless retains hope of salvation. The one places his hope in Godot, that person or power whose existence is proven *ex absentia*;[1] the other places his hope in himself, only to transfer it to the Orator who alone is capable of expressing the message. Unfortunately, this specialist of thought and language is revealed as powerless. Beckett has provided a similar character, a thinker – Lucky. And, curiously enough, this character who performs an exercise of knowledge, already incoherent in Act I, is dumb by Act II! Not only does Lucky stand for the Intellectual but, with his master Pozzo, he embodies the dialectic of Master and Slave. With extraordinary economy, the couple stands for the essence of social relationships. Ionesco does not neglect man's social make-up, but rather than evoke it through a definite couple, he suggests it more diffusely and spectrally through the imaginary characters of the

Lady, the Belle, the Photo-engrave, the Colonel, the Emperor, etc.

Thus we see that in the two plays, the cast of characters breaks up into the same functions: existential man, saviour or prophet, thinker, social man. But the division is not exactly symmetrical, operating with a regular displacement suggested in the following diagram:

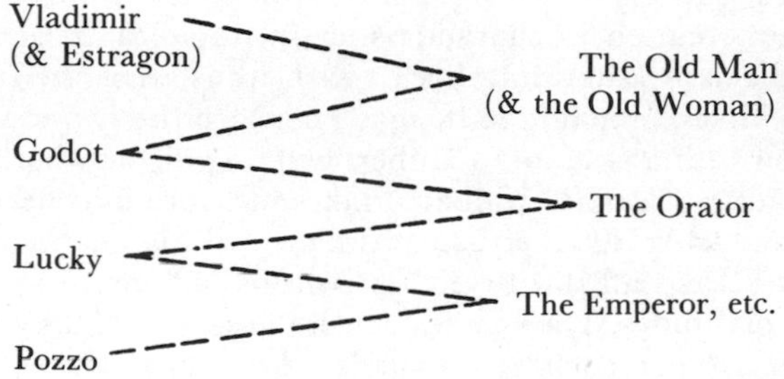

In their most polished plays, our two dramatists seem to have been forced to a convergence of ways, towards the same dramatic outline, towards a similar basic structure. In other words, the comparison of the two works reveals a kind of invariant structure that is doubly interesting: 1. we can grasp the quintessence of the image of the absurd, which the two works share; and 2. we can see how each author has worked upon the basic plan, giving it his personal variation. Nor are we concerned with variations of detail, but major variations of that region where art and thought dissolve into one another – *world vision*. Critics of French literature such as Lucien Goldmann and René Girard have insisted upon the sociological implications of this phrase. And such implications will be discernible in Beckett and Ionesco, precisely at the point where their ways cease to converge, and where each will affirm his own originality.

In comparing the central images of the two works, the wait for Godot and the proliferation of the chairs, we can see that, though both authors oppose physical menace to spiritual hope, they emphasize different aspects of this pair of ideas. Beckett, who highlights spiritual hope, expresses the absurd at its highest, purest point – a tragic summit beyond which is nothing. Ionesco, who accents the physical menace, is more closely tied to concrete reality; he provides a more familiar criticism of manners, and he seems to offer man the possibility of improvement in a better balance between the spiritual and material. From this springs the more purely dramatic quality of his parable, as confirmed by the end of *The Chairs*. As in a newspaper item, the Old Couple end by a ridiculous suicide, thus proving that there is at least one solution to the problem of life – refuse it. Furthermore, the questionable aspect of their suicide gives a hint of possibilities of more sensible conduct, of going beyond it. There is nothing of that in Beckett. Vladimir and Estragon are continually torn between a wish for death and the wait for a saviour, for both exits are blocked: suicide seems impossible, and Godot continues not to come. The situation is characteristically tragic, and Beckett has recognised this by subtitling his English translation '*tragi*comedy'. This is the first distinction to be made between the two visions, and comparison with Pascal and Flaubert will provide another.

Like Flaubert, Ionesco probably takes pleasure in collecting *idées reçues*. Exactly like Flaubert, he likes to give his characters lines, tirades, speeches stuffed with clichés, truisms, stereotyped phrases or bourgeois platitudes. Therein lies one of the secrets of his comic gift. Flaubert, carrying such ready-made ideas into novels, is more discreet and satiric. However, on at least one occasion, he showed his keen sense of the explosive power ready to burst forth from bourgeois language. This takes place in the great scene of the *Comices* in *Madame Bovary*. In a long section, Flaubert alternates the speeches of an agricultural councillor and Rodolophe's courting of Emma. Even separately, the official eloquence and the seductive eloquence betray their own inflation and conventionality, but their ridiculous vanity emerges all the more powerfully from their juxtaposition, their collision that yields a hollow sound. As the two discourses approach their end, the rhythm accelerates, and the two threads interpenetrate by phrases, forming a burlesque dialogue in which language is swallowed by nonsense. At this point, Flaubert is very close to the parodic techniques of Ionesco.

We are therefore intrigued by a few lines preceding this section, beginning with certain words of Rodolphe:

> 'My friends! What friends! Have I any? Who cares about me?' And he followed up the last words with a kind of hissing whistle.
>
> They were obliged to separate because of a great pile of chairs that a man was carrying behind them. He was so overladen that one could only see the tips of his wooden shoes and the ends of his two outstretched arms. It was Lestiboudois, the grave-digger, who was carrying the church chairs about amongst the people. [Paul De Man translation]

A couple preoccupied with love, a romantic duet, is temporarily separated, interrupted by the passage of a third person completely absorbed in his petty duties. Flaubert traces a sketch through the meaningful juxtaposition. The novelist did not want Lestiboudois himself to be the obstacle for the couple; Flaubert has him disappear behind his scaffolding of chairs, and it is the chairs themselves that break the couple up. Isn't this an abridged version of the main image of *The Chairs*? Objects that reduce social man to a thing, and isolate the idealist?

The comparison may be tenuous, since the Lestiboudois episode is brief, anecdotic, without influence on either action or characters. Nevertheless, the curious coincidence remains that this episode takes place in a scene that prefigures Ionesco's criticism of language through theatrical means. Moreover, everything is organically related by Flaubert, and the chairs of Lestiboudois are the cause of another kind of interruption. The noise that they make, along with that of the animals, drowns the voice of the councillor, and makes it seem as though the public at the *Comices* also has its dumb or aphasic orator.

These parallels between *The Chairs* and the *Comices* show us the close relationship between the vision of Flaubert and Ionesco, entirely aside from any question of influence. The art of Flaubert seems to us to consist essentially in the ironic criticism of two kinds of behaviour: 1. those who, in their stupidity, dedicate themselves to material things to such an extent that they swiftly and absurdly merge with them; and 2. those who, in order to escape from the mediocre world of the first group, project their unfulfilled desires towards deceptive goals. A 'metaphysical desire' operates in this second group as René Girard has defined it in *Mensonge romantique et vérité romanesque*; this is an illness of bourgeois, democratic society, in which the individual no longer draws his desires from an authentic and personal source, but borrows them by imitating an envied model. Reification of people by things, metaphysical desire, and above all an ironic criticism through a satire which engenders an absurd drama – this is also the vision that Ionesco offers us in *The Chairs*. The dream of the Old Couple seems to me particularly Bovaryst, for their ideal (the message) is based upon aspirations of egotistical vanity. After having played the comedy of those who rise in the world, who distinguish themselves, the Old Couple will commit suicide, and this is Emma's ultimate act of romanticism. They too cease to *exist*, because they have never *been*. The vision is Flaubertian; this is seen in the basically ironic tone – Girard would call it *romanesque* – the increasingly swift passage from a satire on manners to an existential, Bovaryst drama. The difference lies in the fact that Ionesco uses a more slender spring-board than Flaubert (perhaps borrowed from him); and in order to give that tiny image a wide meaning, he exaggerates it, deforms it, pulverises it.

Like the characters of Flaubert and Ionesco, those of Beckett entertain illusions, but they can correct their great naïveté by humour towards themselves, their situation, and above all by a lucid perception of the vanity of man's behaviour, and the essential tragedy of his destiny. Even though their consciousness works only through brief flashes in the darkness, that consciousness is reminiscent of the terrible clairvoyance of Pascal in *Les Pensées*.[2]

The theme of two infinites may be discerned in *Godot*, worked in filigree, especially towards the end of the play. At very tense moments, Pozzo and Vladimir sketch a paradoxical conception of lived time, with superb metaphors of birth and death. For Pozzo, human existence is like the fleeting instant, the infinitely small: 'They give birth astride of a grave, the light gleams an instant, then it's night once more.' But Vladimir, who takes up the image, counters that life is long, long, and infinitely large because there is too much time to grow old and suffer: 'Astride of a grave and a difficult birth. Down in the hole, lingeringly, the grave-digger puts on the forceps. We have time to grow old. The air is full of our cries.'

Beckettian man, like Pascalian man, is torn between two infinites: a very short life in view of his appetite for living, and a very long life because of his suffering; neither nothingness nor eternity; an elusive situation, forever illusory, tragic because impossible. This tragic vision was suggested to me by Lucien Goldmann's fine analysis in *Le Dieu caché*; there is a double basis for this vision: 1. man is torn between two infinites, two absolutes; 2. he feels everywhere the presence of a hidden god, invisible god, who does not act in the theatre of the world, nor reply to human questions:

> For the tragic mind, in fact, every moment in life mingles with one single moment, that of death. 'Death is an immanent reality, indissolubly linked with all the events of his existence', writes Lukács of the tragic hero, and Pascal expresses the same idea in a different and more powerful way when he writes: 'Christ will be suffering the torments of death to the very end of the world; for all that time we must not sleep.'
>
> In this eternal and intemporal moment which lasts to the very end of the world, tragic man remains alone, doomed to be misunderstood by sleeping men and exposed to the anger of a hidden and an absent God. But he finds, in his very loneliness and suffering, the only values which he can still have and which will be enough to make him great: the absolute and rigorous nature of his own awareness and his own ethical demands, his question for absolute justice and absolute truth, and his refusal to accept any illusions or compromise.[3]

One may see with some surprise that this analysis of *Les Pensées* would serve for *Godot*, especially for the last passages quoted. In both works, life is reduced to a single instant, that of death. In both works, suffering man is opposed to sleeping man, Beckett suggesting that each man thinks that he alone is awake while others sleep. Finally, each work is dominated by the image of a hidden God, *deus absconditus*, of which Godot is a perfect representation, however concretised and vulgarised. Godot is an ever-present God, since all action and hope emanate from him, the awaited one; but he is also ever-absent because he never appears and gives no clue as to his intentions. Can one then be surprised to find in *Les Pensées* a passage that seems to foreshadow the famous theme of *Waiting for Godot*? One should be all the less surprised, since this passage follows three famous fragments (in the Lafuma edition of Pascal) – the two infinites, the thinking reed and the eternal silence, which are all relevant to *Godot*: 'Take comfort; it is not from yourself that you should await [him or it], but on the contrary, in waiting for nothing from yourself that you should await [him or it].'[4]

What else do Didi and Gogo do? They wait, and wait (notice how Pascal insists upon the verb) for an ill-defined figure, without giving anything of themselves, convinced as they are of their great misery and of their complete lack of power in the middle of the infinite spaces. The wait itself is the only good, the only hope remaining to these two 'thinking reeds' of pitiable appearance. Beckett's genius lies in these two achievements: giving the tragic dimension to two tramps, and taking a simple phrase literally – Pascal's 'You should wait for him'. It is in the development that Beckett has rendered them powerful, deploying them so that two acts emerge from two lines, and a vast metaphor of situation from a metaphor of style. In developing *The Chairs* from a detail of *Madame Bovary*, Ionesco works similarly, structuring his work through elaboration of an image and extension of its particulars.

In this analysis, we have sought to show the common kernel of the two plays, the better to call attention to the distinctive quality of each work and the striking originality of each author, which nothing but a thorough structural study could define accurately. In juxtaposing Beckett and Pascal, Ionesco and Flaubert, we hope to open the path to a sociological study of the avant-garde theatre. Agreeing with Goldmann and Girard, we believe that certain world visions can be seen at different periods of history, in works of very different subject-matter, genre and tone. Thus, the basic tragedy of Beckett and the romantic irony of Ionesco are not new visions; on the other hand, they arise again in different forms in the social climate of our time and the contemporary state of literature and the theatre.

Source: article, 'Beckett and Ionesco: The Tragic Awareness of Pascal and the Ironic Awareness of Flaubert', *Modern Drama* (Dec. 1966), pp. 283–91.

NOTES

1. Günther Anders, 'Being Without Time', in Martin Esslin (ed.), *Samuel Beckett* (Englewood Cliffs, N.J., 1965), p. 145.
2. Beckett was early linked to Pascal, by Jean Anouilh who called *Godot* 'a music-hall sketch of Pascal's *Pensées*, played by the Fratellini clowns'.
3. Lucien Goldmann, *The Hidden God*, trans. Philip Thody (London, 1964), pp. 80–1.
4. Blaise Pascal, *Pensées*, ed. L. Lafuma (Paris, 1951), p. 142. (Translated to emphasise waiting, by Ruby Cohn.)

Hans Mayer Brecht's *Drums*, A Dog and *Godot* (1972)

Ein Hund ging in die Küche
Und stahl dem Koch ein Ei
Da nahm der Koch sein Hackebeil
Und schlug den Hund entzwei.

Da kamen die andern Hunde
Und gruben dem Hund das Grab
Und setzten ihm einen Grabstein
Der folgende Inschrift hat:
Ein Hund ging in die Küche . . .
[Brecht, *Drums in the Night*][1]

Un chien vint dans l'office
Et prit une andouillette.
Alors à coups de louche
Le chef le mit en miettes.

Les autres chiens ce voyant
Vite vite l'ensevelirent
Au pied d'une croix en bois blanc
Où le passant pouvait lire:
Un chien vint dans l'office. . . .
[*En attendant Godot*, II]

A dog came in the kitchen
And stole a crust of bread.
The cook picked up a ladle
And beat him till he was dead.

Then all the dogs came running
And dug the dog a tomb
And wrote upon the tombstone
For the eyes of dogs to come:
A dog came in the kitchen. . . .
[*Waiting for Godot*, II]

Every child in Germany knows the roundelay about the unfortunate fate of the dog who went into the kitchen and stole an egg from the cook. You can repeat it endlessly, and children love this because their aesthetic principle obeys an impulse to repeat things, not an impulse to create things eternally anew. Moreover, children are not disturbed by the light touch of obscenity in the horror story, whereas Brecht made conscious use of it: the stolen *Ei* ('egg') means much more than the simple product of a hen and rooster in German.

This story haunted Brecht his entire life. In the first version of *Drums in the Night* (Munich, 1923) the dog is already present in the text. . . .

In March 1954, Brecht finally allowed his early dramas to be reprinted, and he contributed a preface entitled 'On Looking Through My First Plays', which revealed his distance from the early texts and also had a distancing effect. In this essay he expressed special irritation about his re-encounter with *Drums in the Night*: 'In *Drums in the Night* the soldier Kragler gets his woman back, even though she is "damaged", and he turns his back on the revolution. This appears to be just about the shabbiest of all possible alternatives, especially since there is still a faint hint of approval on the part of the playwright.'[2]

As a result, Brecht attempted to eliminate the political 'shabbiness' of the original text by carefully retouching it. Kragler's proletarian counterpart, the nephew of the gin mill owner Glubb, who is merely mentioned and never appears, is nevertheless alluded to, and thus becomes the alternative to the petit bourgeois misery of Kragler and his kind. Aside from this, Brecht is more thoroughgoing as an adapter in Act IV of this new version where the dog originally appeared in a short quotation. Now, Kragler, drunk and malicious, sings the entire lamentable story through to the eternal repetition. In doing so, he demonstrates his petit bourgeois and fatalistic viewpoint – just as his author and adapter would have it.

When Brecht began work on the new version of his early drama, most likely during 1953, Samuel Beckett's *Waiting for Godot* was already extant. In fact, the German translation by Elmar Tophoven had been published, and Brecht had read it. An edition of the Beckett play with textual changes in Brecht's handwriting was discovered in his posthumous papers.[3] Originally Brecht had hoped to adapt the play by Beckett for himself and possibly for a production at the Berliner Ensemble. The notes and rough drafts allow us to see the direction that the adaptation was to take – toward social concreteness. The sham abstraction of the clowns in Beckett's play displeased the Marxist *Dramaturg* Brecht. He makes an 'intellectual' out of Vladimir and a 'proletarian' out of Estragon so that the play would have reverted to the Brechtian *Conversations of Refugees* between the proletarian Kalle and the intellectual Ziffel. The relationship between the master and his servant was also placed more exactly in its proper sociological context. Lucky was to be an 'ass or policeman', while Brecht thought he could make an aristocratic landowner out of Pozzo, hence a new Herr Puntila.

As a consequence, the plans for a Beckett adaptation would have basically found their own natural ending. This projected reutilisation (*Umfunktionierung*) of Beckett would not have produced anything new for Brecht, merely a repetition of *Herr Puntila* and *Conversations of Refugees*. However, in his attempt to adapt Beckett, Brecht once again came across his favourite story of the dog and the cook at the beginning of Act II; except this time he encountered it from the perspective of 'negative infinity', to use Hegel's words. Didi is waiting for Gogo and tries hard to remember the story. Beckett took great pains to record this children's ditty as accurately as possible, first in the French version and then in his own English version. In the original French text, the sausage (*l'andouillette*) still suggests the obscene word play of the *Ei* in German. The English version has apparently abandoned this association.

It is evident that Beckett was familiar with the story about the dog and was not introduced to it by Brecht. On the other hand, Brecht was probably drawn to the dog, the cook, and the repetition once again as he *simultaneously* began adapting his own early dramas and Beckett's play. Of course, this cannot be proved, and on the surface it would seem to have significance only for philologists that Brecht was influenced by Beckett to include the entire children's song in his new version of *Drums in the Night* where it had originally been used only as a quotation and a fragment of memory. Yet, there is more to this than meets the eye.

Brecht was aware of the potential and meaning of the ballad from the very beginning. However, it was probably Beckett's conscious, metaphysical use of it that caused Brecht to adopt the same story with all its metaphysics and to use it for presenting a new interpretation of Andreas Kragler – as extreme alienation. If one compares the two plays, *Godot* and the final version of *Drums in the Night*, from such a vantage point, then the dog becomes an important symbol in both cases. In fact, thanks to the dog, we can more readily gain insight into the differences of the dramaturgy of Beckett and the late Brecht. . . .

What remains when one transforms the story about the dog and the cook into praxis is the posthumous fate of the dead dog who once dared to take a bite. His fame runs through the history of all times, but as 'negative infinity'. Eternal, but boring. This is the way that the petit bourgeois Kragler wants to look at it. And because he found this interpretation of the ballad rather dubious, Brecht distanced himself completely from Kragler in the new version of this early drama. Kragler sings about the negative infinity and Nietzsche's 'eternal recurrence of the same'. However, the Marxist Brecht knows exactly just what to make out of all this.

The only reference to the dualism of the ballad about the dog in Brecht and Beckett is in the dissertation 'The Dialectic and the Early Brecht: An Interpretative Study of *Trommeln in der Nacht*' by David Bathrick,[4] who has elaborated upon the meanings of the songs as ideological commentaries. In speaking about the dog and the cook, he states: 'It is interesting that Act II of *Waiting for Godot* opens with the recitation of this same ditty. Beckett was obviously interested in the circularity of its structure (the last line of the second stanza introduces the first line of the first stanza like a round) as well as the horror of its message. Both are important for *Trommeln in der Nacht* as well.'[5]

Of course, this reference seems to indicate that Brecht and Beckett take the same position in regard to that circular movement and negative infinity. In reality, it is right here – in *the contrasting function of the ballad* in Brecht and Beckett – that the *ideological antagonism* between the two playwrights becomes especially evident. Brecht's opposition to Beckett becomes even more explicit when one reads in his 'Practice Scenes for Actors' how he wanted the stanzas about the dog employed. Brecht was of the opinion that these roundelays were a good exercise for actors of the epic theatre. This is why he recommended that 'the lines . . . be said in a different gesture, each time by different characters in different situations. The exercise can also be used for learning how to fix the manner of delivery.' The actors of his Berliner Ensemble worked this out in the production of the dramatised version of Brecht's dramaturgy – *The Purchase of Brass*.

The playwright Brecht recommends extreme gestic and mimetic activity in the presentation of a text which must explain all that happens as senseless. For Brecht the roundelay is an artistic device for learning the estrangement technique. Whereas the other exercises for actors posed the technical task of developing famous dramatic scenes from Shakespeare or Schiller for the epic theatre, the actor here is supposed to learn from the roundelay how to 'dramatise' an epic report. This must and is supposed to produce a comic effect. The impotent infinity of the roundelay fits perfectly into the dialectical concept. Also, the spectator learns something in the process, as Brecht assumed, namely the difference between real and theatrical 'praxis'.

In Beckett's *Waiting for Godot* the dog already has a prominent position in the dramaturgical structure. The first words at the beginning of Act II are 'A dog came in. . .'. To be sure, there is also the important, silent activity by Vladimir after his entrance which preceded this. As is well known, this play is marked by its *repetition* – dramatically as well as dramaturgically. The angry and disturbed audiences at the first performances who were accustomed to traditional spectacles felt this to be an imposition: to be forced to continue to experience after the intermission what was seemingly only a reproduction of what had already been produced on the stage. This is why the stage directions for Act II begin with the words: 'Next day. Same time. Same place'. Didi is extremely active. He runs, stands, investigates, is ready for action and begins to sing loudly upon reaching the high point of his desire for action. Then there is the conventional misfortune of the clown who starts in too high a voice and must learn to control his artistic expression. Didi now lets loose with the song about the dog, cook, death and burial. Here he falters for the first time, becomes contemplative, and begins once again. He recalls the solidarity of the other dogs and the burial. Again he runs straight through the story to the end. Didi is not disturbed by the fact that he now *reproduces* the story just as actively and smoothly as at the beginning, a story that he had already presented and sung. Obviously he does not distinguish between a first-hand report and a report about a report. For him, everything is on a single level.

Of course, he returns to the story of the tomb and the burial in the repetition. Once again it is the repetition of the repetition – contemplation and then a new beginning. However, this time it does not continue. He tries it once again but now sings 'somewhat more softly'. Yet, it will not go any further. The ending is the tomb, not the tombstone. He becomes quiet, stands immobile. Then he runs wildly and feverishly around the stage again. Act II is already reproduction in that the clown Vladimir begins it. He sets both the form and essence of this act to tune with a roundelay of endless reproduction according to Beckett's intention – and in the process, he sets the tune for the structure of the entire play. Activity is confronted everywhere by frozen situations – the same scenery, time and place, whether it be product or reproduction. In the end it is always the same – the tomb. Only Didi is capable of disturbing it. He remains a man of action and an idealist to the end. He constantly has new hopes and is ready to wait for Godot. Nothing seems to lead him astray. Only sometimes he becomes contemplative again, and this is when he is struck by the thought that the dog is now dead and buried. The roundelay was for him merely a form of activity, production of art, and aesthetic superstructure up to that fateful sentence. He sang loudly because of his desire for activity. But the 'work of art' had attached itself to reality. Didi surrendered himself too easily to empathy. Suddenly art spoke about death and the tomb and took on a disturbing element in 'life'.

It is clear that Beckett is once more concerned here with the opposition between an ahistorical view of history on the one hand and a subjective, affirmative view on the other. It could also be demonstrated that he may even have similar philosophical conceptions as those of the humanitarian Andreas Kragler. More important, in regard to the remarkable similarity between Brecht's and Beckett's use of the symbolical dog, is the remarkable way in which they differed in their use. Whereas Beckett ironically employed the roundelay about the dog, the cook and the tomb to serve his dramaturgy of *empathy*, Brecht felt it to be an especially good example for demonstrating the dramatics and dramaturgy of *Verfremdung*.

SOURCE: extracts from 'Brecht, Beckett und ein Hund', *Theater Heute* (June 1972); translated by Jack Zipes (with slight revisions) as 'Brecht's *Drums*, A Dog and Beckett's *Godot*', in Siegfried Meurs and Hubert Khust (eds), *Essays on Brecht: Theater and Politics* (Chapel Hill, N.C., 1974), pp. 71–2, 73–4, 76–8.

NOTES

[Reorganised and renumbered from the original – Ed.]

1. Brecht, *GW*, I, pp. 112–13. 2. Ibid., XVII, p. 945.

3. For details, see Werner Hecht, *Aufsätze über Brecht* (Berlin, 1970), pp. 118ff.

4. David Bathrick, dissertation of 1970 (University of Chicago).

5. Cf. also David Bathrick, '"Anschauungsmaterial" for Marx: Brecht Returns to *Trommeln in der Nacht*', *Theater Heute*, 2 (1972), pp. 136–48.

Katharine Worth 'Irish Beckett' (1974)

Many lines of the European imagination meet in Beckett, but as playwright he is above all the heir of Yeats and the Irish/French drama. . . . He strides from Dublin into France like the modern man of Synge's imagining whose role it would be to 'take Ireland into Europe'. In himself he seems the epitome of that union. With almost uncanny appropriateness he takes his place among those Irish predecessors who felt so strongly the lure of France, sometimes even to the extent of turning themselves into Frenchmen – Wilde writing

Salomé in French; bilingual Synge, one foot in Aran, the other in Paris; Yeats so receptive to the flow of experience and ideas from European art and drama. Beckett seems to sum all this up: an Irishman who lives in France, writes with equal facility in French and English, regularly translates himself from one to the other and always keeps in his English an Irish lilt, whether his characters are called Rooney and grope their way down a road near Dublin or Estragon and Vladimir who might be travelling on any road in Europe.

Modernism arrives in the popular theatre with Beckett. 'Popular' may seem an unlikely word, but must be the appropriate one for plays which, for all their strangeness, have become known all over the world, and are continually being revived by the professional as well as the amateur theatre. It was hardly fortuitous that the repertoire of the National Theatre for its opening season in its new South Bank home should include *Happy Days*. Beckett now occupies a position in the English theatre where it is natural to turn to his plays for such great occasions; they have become our 'modern classics'. And yet he has drawn these international audiences for a theatre which is intensely inward, the complete fulfilment of Yeats's idea of a drama of 'most interior being'. Such a drama was confined to corners of Dublin and of London in Yeats's day; it is a measure of Beckett's virtuoso skill and also of his humaneness that he has been able to give it this great extension into the public domain and in doing so change the course of modern theatre, for nothing has been the same since *Waiting for Godot*.

Beckett's theatre has always startled and impressed by its bareness, his 'void' effect, but the final impression the plays leave is not bare but rich; they spark off such a host of associations, images, echoes, it seems one would never come to the end of them. In the intricate web he weaves the Irish strands are strong. It would be a futile labour to pull apart and try to identify the separate threads, but it is possible to distinguish shades of colour and perhaps in so doing illuminate the subtle synthesis.

We do not have to strain to catch in Beckett's theatre echoes from the drama I have been discussing. He himself has drawn attention to his feeling for his Irish inheritance. He has spoken of the plays he saw at the Abbey Theatre – 'the Yeats *Sophocles*, most of Synge, O'Casey's three'[1] – and made very clear the value he sets on them. When asked by Cyril Cusack for a contribution to a centenary programme on Shaw, he replied: 'I wouldn't suggest that G.B.S. is not a great playwright, whatever that is when it's at home. What I would do is give the whole unupsettable apple-cart for a sup of the Hawk's Well, or the Saints', or a whiff of Juno, to go no further.'[2]

The plays themselves tell us of this allegiance. It is easy to hear behind Hamm's stories or Winnie's romancing the tale-telling of the Douls, behind the knockabout turn of Hamm and Clov, O'Casey's sad, sardonic and farcical double acts – the blind and paralysed pair in *The Silver Tassie*, the neatly afflicted Chair Attendants in *Within the Gates* – as behind them those other blind and lame beggars of *The Cat and the Moon*.

To think of the importance blindness has on Beckett's stage is . . . to be reminded of *The Sightless* . . . and those other symbolist plays of Maeterlinck which fascinated Beckett's Irish predecessors, notably Yeats and Synge, and which have striking affinities with his own drama. . . .

Unsettling intuitions of some other order of existence . . . often take the Maeterlinckian form of half memories or a haunting sense of *déja vu*. A large part of the experience of Estragon and Vladimir cannot be brought over the threshold of consciousness. Vladimir questions Estragon anxiously and lovingly about his nightly misery – 'Who beat you? Tell me' – and like Mélisande shrinking from Golaud's so similar questioning ('Who was it that hurt you?'), Estragon can only turn away with an evasive 'Another day done with'. The line between memory and dream is blurred. 'You dreamt it', says Estragon of Vladimir's 'yesterday' which for the audience is still to come, the moment when they nearly hang themselves from the tree.

Of course in Beckett's world we are able to laugh at these lapses and assertions of memory. . ., as at everything else, including the eccentricities of his afflicted characters. Blindness, for instance, is almost as prominent on his stage as on Maeterlinck's and carries many similar associations with perception and insight. Hamm and Pozzo when blind strike vatic notes and indulge in apocalyptic brooding, like the statuesque figures in *The Sightless*. But Beckett's wise-cracking pair are not statuesque: their thorough immersion in the comic element prevents us from taking them too seriously as Tiresias figures, much though they might like us to. They are not allowed to stand on their dignity or make too sustained a bid for pathos. In place of the blind people solemnly feeling for each other's cold hands to locate themselves, comes Hamm feeling his way into the dead centre of his room with much identical clowning, irritating Clov with his pernickety 'I feel a little too far'. The absurd pomposity of Pozzo invites laughter even after he has been stricken blind and acquired some new insights. 'The blind have no notion of time. The things of time are hidden from them too', he says, and we listen seriously; but Vladimir still comes in to undercut him 'Well just fancy that! I could have sworn it was just the opposite'. . . .

In his love of music and passionate sense of the value of silence,

Beckett is again close to Maeterlinck. The musical phrasing of his dialogue, with its changes of rhythm, long pauses and silences, can produce hypnotic, ritualistic effects strikingly like the murmurings of the blind characters in *The Sightless*:

ESTRAGON: All the dead voices.
VLADIMIR: They make a noise like wings.
ESTRAGON: Like leaves.
VLADIMIR: Like sand.
ESTRAGON: Like leaves. *Silence*

In these incantations the dream deepens, we go further into the nebulous region where it is hard to distinguish between the dead and the living. That passage is highly finished, performed with conscious musicality, but of course Beckett excels also in suggesting stumbling, hesitating words, coming mysteriously, not expected or planned. It would be misleading to talk of 'inarticulacies' where his witty people are concerned, but although they are so good at finding just the right word, Beckett manages to get them into Maeterlinckian positions all the same, through their bad memories, their inconsistencies, their difficulty, as in *Words and Music*, in finding the right tone, and through the undermining of their words by silent visual contradictions, as in the most famous of all, the 'Let's go' of Estragon and Vladimir, never to be followed by their going.

We cannot but think of Beckett as Maeterlinckian in these musical orchestrations of little words, laconic phrases, pauses and silences. So too in his extraordinary ability to give dramatic life to seemingly deadly negatives, go so far into the 'blank' experience of death and birth, make silence and immobility so active, draw from blindness and darkness such strange light.

But of course within the sombre Maeterlinckian outlines there is a drama of quite another sort, richly humorous, dense with human interest, less 'passive', to use Yeats's term. Where Maeterlinck's emphasis was on the fragility and helplessness of human life, Beckett's is on its resourcefulness and resilience – and its humour. Winnie sunk in the earth can still keep her head above ground with her jokes, and death itself is cut down to size in *Endgame* when Hamm and Clov go into their knockabout turns and Clov comes out with laughter-raising lines like 'If I don't kill that rat he'll die'. The echoes we hear now are Irish, the gallows humour of Synge, O'Casey's gusty farce with its black undertones. As with everything he touches, Beckett takes that humour to its furthest limit: hanging is a harsh conversational joke in *The Playboy of the Western World*: in *Waiting for Godot* it provides the climactic situation when Estragon and Vladimir try to hang themselves from the tree and are let down by the rope. . . . The scene is serious all right – I think especially of the German production Beckett directed at the Royal Court Theatre in 1976 which was heavy with moonlit sadness and the sense of mind at the end of its tether. But in the cool 'That's what you think' we sense an irresistible energy as well, an energy that changes things, anything – even the brute fact of death – by changing the angle of vision, insinuating its wry, droll view which is so friendly to life.

Energy was what Yeats thought missing from Maeterlinck and admired so much in Synge. It was Synge above all . . . who showed Yeats the way out of the more passive symbolist world, and it is Synge who can be sensed in the background of Beckett's drama especially when his characters are engaged in their energetic creation of a dynamic universe out of unpromising dead-looking materials.[3] *The Well of the Saints* was one of the plays that came naturally to Beckett's mind, to drive out the unwanted image of Shaw. No wonder – for the blind, physically unprepossessing Douls are unmistakable prototypes for all those characters with sore feet, kidney trouble, poor sight, failing memory and mobility who dominate Beckett's stage, marvellously opening it up by the force of their imagination.

Again, as ever, Beckett gives us the situation in its most intense and condensed form. Loneliness in Synge's drama is modified by its setting in a real world. On Beckett's stage the isolation is complete; ordinary life is always outside, somewhere else; the Pyrenees might be there, but all that is uncertain. . . .

. . . In his use of farce and caricature Beckett's affinity with another of his Irish predecessors, O'Casey, becomes very apparent. . . . Rather sadly, O'Casey never came to know Beckett properly and was antagonistic to what he took to be his pessimism [see excerpt in Part Three, below – Ed.] . . . he was wrong all the same, for he is certainly in Beckett even if he thought Beckett wasn't in him. Beckett himself is in no doubt about this, to judge from his inclusion of *Juno and the Paycock* in a rare tribute. . . . He showed his sympathy with O'Casey in a practical way by withdrawing his mime plays from the Dublin Festival of 1958 when *The Drums of Father Ned* was banned from performance there. And he reveals his understanding and feeling for O'Casey's comedy in the review he wrote in 1934 of the two one-act farces, *The End of the Beginning* and *A Pound on Demand*. O'Casey is, says Beckett, a 'master of knock-about' who 'discerns the principle of disintegration in even the most complacent solidities and activates it to their explosion': so that we end with 'the triumph of the principle of knockabout in situation, in all its elements and on all its planes, from the furniture to the higher centres'.[4]

As this suggests, Beckett and O'Casey share a very similar sense of fun. Beckett is equally fascinated by the special relationship with intractable matter enjoyed by clowns, loves the release of knockabout and often draws from the same music-hall and musical comedy repertoire. Articles of clothing – boots and hats in *Godot*, handbag and umbrella in *Happy Days* – figure on his stage with the same absurd seriousness as on O'Casey's. Like the top hat in *Cock-a-Doodle Dandy*, which leads the characters such a dance, the hats in *Godot* acquire a life of their own; are solemnly passed round, knocked off, jumped on. Beckett's stage abounds with grotesquely afflicted pseudo-couples who are blood brothers to O'Casey's Barrys and Darrys and limping Chair Attendants, and sometimes indeed, seem to speak for all of them. . . .

And yet, despite all these likenesses, Beckett's characters are a long way from the largely unselfconscious dramatising of Synge's and O'Casey's. For always, in the very act of building up a drama, Hamm, Winnie and the rest are scrutinising it, puzzling about its source, registering the bewilderment, amusement or torment they undergo in the process of playmaking.

In his sardonic self-consciousness, as in so many other ways, Beckett is supremely Yeats's heir. His is above all a drama of 'moments' ('an action . . . taken out of all other actions') or 'briefs', to use his own word. Beckett indeed has done more than anyone to acclimatise the theatre to the idea of such a drama. At a time when audiences were still geared to the three or even four act play, he gave them the two acts of *Waiting for Godot* followed by one act *Endgame* (cut down from the two of an early draft) and by the many ruthlessly concentrated short plays, where, if there is a division, it is only a means to intensification, as in *Happy Days* and *Play*.

Beckett's 'interior' has many Yeatsian features. *Waiting for Godot* especially recalls *At the Hawk's Well*, one of Beckett's favourite plays. The ironic repetition of the 'luck' motif in Yeats's play is echoed in the bizarre figure who bears the name Lucky in Beckett's and who performs the dance of the Net, Hard Stool or Scapegoat's Agony, that grim parody of man's freedom of movement. 'The wind in the reeds' is one of the sounds Estragon and Vladimir hear (an affectionate Yeatsian allusion here)[5] and above all there is the situation of waiting by the bare tree for the events that will always elude them – both Vladimir who gets as far as speaking with Godot's messenger and Estragon who always sleeps when he appears, like the Old Man mesmerised by the Hawk Woman's unmoistened eye.

Above all Beckett is close to Yeats in his achievement of a remarkable 'double' effect: the self-conscious and unconscious elements in his drama are kept in a delicate state of equilibrium so that the incessant activity of the conscious, scrutinising, probing self leaves untouched the integrity of the spontaneous, intuitive, irrational self. Along with this goes the striking doubleness which makes the drama seem at once real and dream-like, the reflection of an outer and an inner world, an engagement of recognisable personalities and at the same time something more impersonal, as if these pseudo-couples were interlocking elements of a complex psychic organisation. As in Yeats's world, everything depends on the pull between opposites – life drifting between a fool and a blind man to its end – and on the ability of the opposites to complement one another. . . .

. . . I have been stressing likenesses and have shown, I hope, that they are indeed real. Beckett's affinity with Yeats, with Synge and O'Casey and – although there is no direct influence here – with Maeterlinck, stands out from the page and asserts itself in production. To feel the closeness of these relationships we need only imagine a programme made up, say, of *Interior*, *At the Hawk's Well* and *Endgame*, or *Purgatory* and *Play*, *Purple Dust* and *All that Fall* or *The Sightless*, *The Well of the Saints* and *Waiting for Godot*. But of course Beckett works within this 'modern tradition' as a great original, and . . . it is he who has launched the Irish drama in Europe into the centre of world theatre. There are many reasons for his fuller appeal – fuller, at least, than any Maeterlinck or Yeats has yet commended – and I have been trying to keep these in mind throughout the comparison.

His humour is entirely his own and a great source of his universal appeal. Not separate from that, but crucially bound up with it is the sense of spiritual achievement coming out of the strange and painful experiences his characters endure. Always there is a movement, however faint or obscure, towards a closer truth, a clearer perspective, and it is this, I feel sure, that has given him his special position in the modern movement. For he goes as far as anyone and further than most, into a modern universe which is terribly empty and accidental looking, without losing the sense that man's aspiration to truth is serious; it is not what it might sometimes seem (and often seems to his characters) simply one of nature's crueller jokes.

SOURCE: extracts from ch. 10 (on Beckett), in *The Irish Drama of Europe from Yeats to Beckett* (London, 1974), pp. 241–2, 243–4, 248–5, 257–60.

NOTES

[Reorganised and renumbered from the original – Ed.]

1. Letter to J. Knowlson (17 Dec. 1970), in Professor Knowlson's catalogue (1971) for 'Samuel Beckett: An Exhibition' (held at Reading University Library, May–July 1971).

2. In the programme for the 'Shaw Centenary', Gaeity Theatre, Dublin, 1956; quoted in the Reading Exhibition catalogue, op. cit.

3. Critics who have felt this include Alec Reid, 'Comedy in Synge and Beckett', *Yeats Studies*, 2 (1972); and J. Knowlson, 'Beckett and John Millington Synge', *Gambit*, 28 (1976).

4. Beckett's article, 'The Essential and the Incidental', *The Bookman*, 86 (1934), p. 111.

5. Yeats's collection of early poems, *The Wind among the Reeds* was published in 1899. Another poem, 'The Tower' (in the collection of the same titling, 1928), which ends 'Among the deepening shades', provides the title and some quotations for Beckett's . . . *but the clouds* . . . .

Yasunari Takahashi Qu'est-ce qui arrive?: Beckett and Noh (1983)

'Beckett and Noh' may sound a far-fetched subject, for unlike Yeats or Claudel or Brecht, Samuel Beckett is, on his own evidence, quite unfamiliar with Noh; much less has he ever tried to imitate or steal the riches of this ancient theatre form of the East. The absence of actual influence, however, would be all the more significant if it could be shown that the two theatre forms, with a vast temporal and spatial distance between them, do share some fundamental characteristics.

'Nothing happens, nobody comes', complains Estragon. This would remind any 'Japanalogist' of Claudel's famous dictum: 'Le drame, c'est quelque chose qui arrive, le Nô, c'est quelqu'un qui arrive.' One is almost tempted to suspect that Beckett is here making a conscious allusion to the insight of the French playwright-diplomat. But the allusion, if conscious, should be surprising for its wry obliqueness. For if one can claim that *Waiting for Godot* is a negation of the European notion of drama wherein some action *must* take place, one can also claim that the play is at the same time a negation of the essential dramaturgy of Noh in so far as Claudel is right in the second half of his dictum and in so far as Estragon is right in the second half of his complaint.

Or maybe *negation* is not exactly the word. For something does happen, or indeed many things do happen, on this place dubiously called 'The Board' (the stage): businesses with hats and shoes, gestural mimicries, dances, games, quarrels, even an attempt at suicide. But none of them is a 'real' dramatic action: they are all 'pseudo-actions' performed simply to kill time, all 'non-events' tending toward no logically climactic moment. Similarly, someone does come if you count Pozzo or Lucky or the boy. But they are obviously not that 'someone' who, by 'arriving', is supposed to make Noh what it is, any more than they are Godot himself.

Here some remarks on the origin and the structure of Noh would be in order. Noh is closely connected with the ancient Japanese belief in the unpacified spirit of the dead. The unquenched passion of love, grief or hatred endows the dead with a sort of immortality, and the ghost is compelled from time to time to emerge out of the Buddhist purgatory in a corporeal form that was his or hers in life and visit the world of the living in order to gain a partial relief from present torments by telling someone the story of his or her agony, somewhat in the manner of Coleridge's Ancient Mariner. In the typical structure of a so-called Fukushiki Mugen-Noh (dream-noh in two parts), the Shite (protagonist) first appears as an ordinary village woman and then, after an exit, reappears as a veritable ghost to enact her life story before the eye of the Waki (secondary character), a travelling priest, who finally manages to pacify her agonised soul by the power of his prayer. Noh in this light could be regarded as theatrical transformation of a ritual of exorcism of the demonic power of the dead.

But in a slightly different though related light, the protagonist of Noh could also be taken for a specimen of what Japanese anthropologists call 'mare-bito', literally, a 'guest', but a special kind of sacred guest. This 'epiphanic' stranger was entertained by the villagers with sumptuous hospitality in the hope that he would turn himself into a benevolent spirit and sanctify the village with his holy blessing. One might think of the *Oresteia*, in which the Erynies (the Furies) are transformed into the Eumenides (the Kindly Ones), who the Athenians hoped would bless the city of Athens. Of course, Zeami's theater is conceived in a scale that is anything but Aeschylean; it is far less epic and totally apolitical, far more refined in its private lyricism – so much so that you could almost call it a 'minimalist' art. Nonetheless, it is important to see in Noh a form of 'holy theatre' whose ultimate aim lies in making an epiphany possible, that is, in preparing a space, a kind of 'void', so that this empty space may be filled in by the arrival of a strange guest, a sacred spirit in a human form, a god incarnate.

What is to be stressed in this connection is the importance of the Waki, for it is he who actually does the preparing for the epiphany. Much more than a simple traveller, he is a priest possessed with a shamanic power to perceive (or indeed evoke) a supernatural presence (one notices here a curious reversal: he, a stranger from elsewhere, meets an indigenous spirit, a ghostly inhabitant of the place). He is a medium requisite for the supernatural hero to take flesh momentarily. It is even possible to argue that the central action of a Noh play, the 'coming' of the Shite in the second part, really takes place in a dream of the Waki, which is why it is called a 'dream-noh'. In any case, the audience finds itself at one with the Waki in an atmosphere taut with tension, waits for the apparition, watches the Shite dance out his or her undying fire of passion, and finally experiences a certain catharsis, be it Aristotelian or not, of fear and pity.

Now some of the structural peculiarities of *Waiting for Godot* would seem to be illuminated by the light shed by the above observations on Noh. Didi and Gogo are seen to be not so much the real protagonists (Shites) as the secondary players (Wakis) who wait for the Shite to arrive. Of course they are far from resembling the serious-looking priest of Noh; they are much more like the comedians of Kyogen, a genre of farce usually performed as an interlude between two pieces of Noh plays. As for Pozzo, his arrival in the first act gives the Wakis an illusion that he might be the awaited Shite, which, however, is quickly proved to be false. And although his reappearance in the second act, much transformed and probably revealing his true identity, does remind us of the Shite in the second part of Noh, he is after all a 'pseudo-Shite', a miserable caricature of the true Shite, who is supposedly none other than Godot. Thus Didi and Gogo have to go on waiting for a true epiphany, and Godot's failure or refusal to come must leave the space, the stage, empty and unblessed with the visit of a ghostly guest. No transformation of reality, no communion of the sacred and the profane, takes place. No catharsis is allowed to the audience.

It may indeed be doubted if the coming of Godot, should it take place, would be of any help to Didi and Gogo, for the fact that his name itself sounds like a parody of God might imply that all they can hope for is an endless sequence of 'pseudo-epiphanies' of 'pseudo-Gods'. One almost wonders if that is not precisely the state of modern man as envisaged by Beckett and if that is not precisely the state of Western theater as embodied in the structure of *Godot*. I would submit that both situations are made poignantly conspicuous by the very absence of those elements that constitute the vision of the dramaturgy of Noh. Perhaps it is not so frivolous as it may seem to call *Godot* a kind of 'anti-Mugen-Noh'.

Another aspect in which *Godot* sharply contrasts itself with Mugen-Noh is its attitude toward the past. The Shite in Noh is an apparition from the past, often a very distant time; he or she is dead, but the past is not; the presence of the Shite, which is as it were the time past made flesh and voice, is even more potently present than that of any human being alive. In contrast, everything in *Godot* is here and now (though 'here' and 'now' in this play are admittedly ambiguous enough in comparison with the unitary time-space scheme of a realistic play). The 'dark backward and abysm of time' whose memory might torment the characters is deliberately dismissed; there is an almost hysterical revulsion against the 'remembrance of things past' whenever the characters are faced with questions concerning the past. All this, of course, may be a paradoxical testimony to their obsession with time, and it is true that Didi and Gogo listen to the voices of the dead in the air, but there is no such encounter of the living and the dead, of the time present and the time past, as we find in Noh. . . .

SOURCE: extract from essay-chapter ('Qu'est-ce qui arrive? Some structural comparisons of Beckett's Plays and Noh'), in Morris Beja, S. E. Gontarski and Pierre Astier (eds), *Samuel Beckett: Humanistic Perspectives* (Columbus, Ohio, 1983), pp. 98–102.

Dina Sherzer (1978) — De-Construction in *Godot*

. . . Beckett is . . . a writer who is preoccupied with sounds, but he is also interested in and plays with verbal behavior, so much so that in *Waiting for Godot* it is possible to establish a typology of the different ways in which rules of language and speech are manipulated: 1. the discourse of speech acts and events, that is, the communication established between characters in particular contexts; 2. the manipulation of the rules of semantic association; 3. the use of different registers of language; 4. the use of semantic paradigms and synonyms; 5. the use of common expressions and clichés; 6. the exploitation of the different meanings of a single word; and 7. the use of sounds and sequences of sounds. . . .

Play with the Rules of Discourse

In order to understand the ways Beckett manipulates rules of discourse, it is necessary to view language in the context of its use. To do so I will make use of the components of the speech event described by Jakobson [1960] and elaborated by Hymes [1972]: *participant* (addressor-addressee), *key* (the way the message is to be taken – seriously, mockingly, etc), and *topic of discourse*.

Manipulation of the relationship between participants and discourse. Pozzo is talking to Vladimir and Estragon and also to his servant Lucky: 'Gentlemen, I am happy to have met you. Yes, yes, sincerely happy. *Closer! Stop!* Yes the road seems long when one journeys all along for . . . yes . . . yes, six hours. That's right six hours on end, and never a soul in sight. *Coat! Hold that! Coat!* Touch of autumn in the air this evening. *Whip!* Yes, gentlemen, I cannot go for long without the society of my likes even when the likeness is an imperfect one. *Stool!*' This speech has one addressor – Pozzo – and two sets of addressees: Vladimir and Estragon form one set and Lucky alone forms the other. To Vladimir and Estragon, Pozzo comments on his recent meeting with them, talks about his situation as a traveller, and makes remarks about the weather. He establishes contact by means of an ordinary, superficial conversation. On the other hand, when he addresses himself to Lucky he gives orders. Pozzo is thus involved in two speech events which are mingled and overlapped within a single discourse. The result is a verbal pattern analogous to juggling, and it recalls the technique of a clown.

Play with the key. Another interesting example of manipulation of the relationship between the participants and the discourse is provided in the scene where Vladimir and Estragon look at Lucky. . . . Vladimir and Estragon talk about Lucky in his presence; they are very close to him and in fact are inspecting his neck. Furthermore, Vladimir and Estragon express their private thoughts about Lucky; they make remarks that ordinarily would not be uttered in front of the person that is talked about, unless done in a humorous way, in which case both the addressor and the addressee are aware of it. But the conversation about Lucky is carried on very seriously, and it can therefore be taken as a playing with what Hymes calls the key. In other words, the serious (rather than humorous) key used by Vladimir and Estragon is that appropriate to talk about children, animals and other 'non-persons' in their presence. . . .

Play with the topic. Vladimir and Estragon are always looking for things to do or say to make time go by, and at one point Estragon suggests, 'What about hanging ourselves?' After the two characters have agreed to hang themselves, the following exchange takes place:

VLADIMIR: Go ahead.
ESTRAGON: After you.
VLADIMIR: No, no, you first.

Such formulas of politeness are quite common and can be heard in a bus or in front of a door: they refer to such insignificant actions as taking a seat or going through a door. But here this everyday ritual is used by characters talking about hanging themselves. It is not the structure of the interaction that is played with, but the relationship between the topic and the discourse. This distortion creates a comic and a disturbing effect at the same time, because a banal subject is replaced by a serious one and because the characters can talk about hanging themselves in a very matter of fact fashion, as if it were a subject of no more importance than who goes through a door first. . . .

Play with the relationship between the meaning of individual elements of an utterance and its total meaning. When Vladimir first sees Estragon at the beginning of the play he says to him: 'So there you are again.' And Estragon answers: 'Am I?' Vladimir's utterance is a speech act of greeting and has to be understood as a whole; instead Estragon interprets it at a more superficial syntactic level and focuses on the literal meaning of the verb *to be*. Further in the play Vladimir, referring to Godot, says to Pozzo: 'Oh he's a . . . he's a kind of acquaintance.' And Estragon adds: 'Nothing of the kind, we hardly know him.' The ambiguity is created by the word 'acquaintance' which means 'somebody one knows'. Estragon thinks that Vladimir has not said the truth, and wants to correct him, because for him acquaintance means 'somebody one knows well', when in fact Vladimir tells Pozzo they do not know Godot intimately.

In this section of the play the manipulation of the rules of discourse has two results. First, the characters do not use language according to commonly held rules but rather in incongruous ways. Second, language does not establish communication between the characters; thus these devices present them as absurd. At the linguistic level, Beckett shows an awareness of discourse structure. By his manipulations he creates not deviant structures but deflective ones [Halliday, 1971] which always point back to the basic structure. Thus the reader and the spectator are able to understand how he is modifying this structure.

Play with the Logic of Semantic Association

In the following examples a certain semantic expectation is built up at the beginning of the sentence but by the end of the sentence what was expected logically is not said; instead the sentence changes direction.

Estragon asks Pozzo to sit down: 'Come come, take a seat I beseech you, you'll get pneumonia.' One expects that Pozzo should take a seat not to get tired or to rest; but instead Estragon says it is to avoid pneumonia. . . .

Play with Registers

Registers are the different types or styles or language used in different situations – language of sport, familiar language, formal language of lecture or conference, poetical language, child language, and so forth [Halliday 1968]. Pozzo, for instance, speaks in very lyrical terms of the night, of torrents of red and white lights, of the sky which loses its effulgence, of a veil of gentleness and peace; and then adds, 'That's how it is on this bitch of an earth.' . . .

Spiralling of Semantic Paradigms

A recurrent device employed by Beckett is the use of series of words that are related to each other in one way or the other. When these series appear in the text it seems that a spring is uncoiling. Pozzo has lost his pipe, and we hear:

> What have I done with my *pipe*?
> What can I have done with that *briar*?
> He has lost his *dudeen*.
> I have lost my *Kapp and Peterson*. [my italics]

The italicised words are all ways to refer to the same object, and they form a kind of paradigm. *Pipe* is the neutral, basic word; *briar* is a metonymy which insists on the quality and is slightly slang; *dudeen* is an Irish word for a type of pipe; and *Kapp and Peterson* is a brand name that would be used in a pipe store or by a specialist. Here a paradigm, namely the different ways to name a pipe, is exploited in order to create a verbal pattern. . . .

. . . When Vladimir and Estragon exchange insults:

VLADIMIR: Moron!
ESTRAGON: Vermin!
VLADIMIR: Abortion!
ESTRAGON: Morpion!
VLADIMIR: Sewer-rat!
ESTRAGON: Curate!
VLADIMIR: Cretin!
ESTRAGON: Crritic!

One insult calls for another one, and again it is a verbal juggling where juggling has to be taken literally, since the characters face each other and throw words at each other. The characters did decide to abuse each other, so all the words of the series are intended as insults. Yet nouns that are not necessarily considered insulting are used; they become insulting terms by association with the others. Furthermore, their presence is justified phonetically since the sounds in these words answer each other: moron/abortion, sewer-rat/curate, cretin/critic. Thus the words form both a semantic and a phonic set; to call such a verbal pattern a mere deviation would be to miss Beckett's ability to exploit the potentialities of language. . . .

Play with the Various Meanings of a Single Word

The various meanings of a particular word as it shifts context are also exploited to create puns, as in this example which appears in the French version – 'Vladimir: En effet nous sommes sur *un plateau*. Aucun doute nous sommes servis sur un *plateau*' [my italics]. During the whole play the characters give indications that this is in fact a play [Cohn, 1962a], and the word plateau means first a stage. Then the characters say they are on a plateau from which they can look down in the valley, so plateau is the geographical term. And finally, 'être servi sur un plateau' means to be served, to have everything brought to you as you desire, on a tray. The characters do not have to disturb themselves since Pozzo and Lucky are coming right where Estragon and Vladimir are – that is, as if they were being catered to.

Play with Sounds and Sequences of Sounds

On reading or on watching the play one cannot but notice that very careful attention has been paid to the sounds of words and that several types of phonic manipulation are deployed.

All through the play the sounds '*o*' and '*i*' reappear in the names (Godot, Gogo, Pozzo; and Didi, Lucky). In addition the play is punctuated several times by the same exchange between Vladimir and Estragon:

ESTRAGON: Let's go.
VLADIMIR: We can't.
ESTRAGON: Why not?
VLADIMIR: We're waiting for Godot.

These four lines . . . repeat the principal idea of the play, that of waiting, and in each case the same words are in the same position so that the same phonic exchange takes place, similar to a refrain. . . .

Variations on proper names allow the characters to play with sounds also. The name Pozzo clicks off a series of other names with similar sounds: Pozzo, Bozzo, Gozzo. Pozzo (not remembering the name of the person Vladimir and Estragon are waiting for) suggests Godet, Godot, Godin; then, a little further, he inverts the order: Godin, Godet, Godot. Lucky fills silence with the piling up of Feckham, Peckham, Fulham, Clapham.

The repetition of sounds and expressions is a comic device because it confers a machine-like rigidity to the speech of the characters; but at the same time it attracts attention to the phonic properties of language.

The different types of manipulation of language that I have discussed have several consequences. The accumulation of synonyms, the repetition and bouncing of sounds, the juggling with words, expressions, or speech acts, and the misunderstanding of certain expressions, are all comic devices. They function together with the play with hats, the pratfalls, the costumes and the grotesque behavior of the grotesque characters. That is, various communicative systems converge to make the play a comedy. . . .

SOURCE: extracts from ch. 4 ('De-construction in *Waiting for Godot*'), in Barbara A. Babcock (ed.), *The Reversible World: Symbolic Inversion in Art and Society* (Ithaca, N.Y., 1978), pp. 130, 131–2, 134–6, 137–8, 139–40, 141–2, 143–4.

Maria Minich Brewer (1985) A Semiosis of Waiting

Beckett has said of *Waiting for Godot* that it is 'a play striving to avoid definition'. It is certainly a play that problematises the definition of terms and limits as well the closure of stable symbolic meaning. The play's evasion or avoidance of definition appears, for instance, in the impossibility of defining Godot so as to represent him. The characters have received the message, 'wait', an imperative injunction, the speech act of ordering. Unlike Beckett's interpreters, who are anxious to discover what Godot *means*, Vladimir and Estragon's anxiety stems from their fear of not responding properly to the law of his performative discourse and failing to be present at the appointed time and place. The play is therefore not structured as a progressive unveiling of the meaning of Godot, but rather as a process of waiting for and a waiting on a further injunction or convocation.

It may seem paradoxical to offer yet another interpretation of *Waiting for Godot*, a play that eludes the ruses of interpretation's need to define meaning. Yet *Godot* exposes the lures of a structure of expectation that characterises a tradition of theatricality. Godot continues to be a void that interpreters (readers and performers alike) attempt to fill. God, Death, Humanity, Crisis of Consciousness, Waiting, Object of Desire – the list of overlapping definitions for Godot is as interminable as Beckett's characters' wait. In a structural sense, Godot is the absent Signified of Beckett's play, the proper name that language gives to Meaning. All the activities and exertions, games and exchanges between the characters are subordinated to Godot's 'coming'. Since their language and actions cannot be legitimated until his coming, the play displays a structure of expectation, a horizon of absence that devalorises the *mise-en-scène* or performance.

It is in this sense that Derrida's reading of Artaud may be taken to articulate the ways in which Beckett designates the end of a certain history of theatrical representation: 'The stage is theological . . . as long as it is dominated by speech, by a will to speech, by the designs of a primary logos which does not belong to the theatrical set and governs it from a distance.'[1] Artaud challenges classical representation, Derrida suggests, by replacing it with a 'closed space, that is to say a space produced from within himself and no longer organised from the vantage point of another absent life, an illocality, an alibi or invisible utopia'.[2] The alibi in Beckett is Godot, for he occupies the absent space outside of the performance space, organising it from afar through his discourse of mastery or theology. In this respect, Beckett's play is an exemplary semiotic text, structured by a clearly apparent system of oppositions: self/other, slave/master, inside/outside, day/night, discourse/meaning, signifier/signified. *Godot* radically foregrounds the semiological structure of opposition between presence and absence, signs and their meaning; furthermore, it stages the semiological as a structure of expectation in which signs are marked by their separation from an absent Signified. Yet Beckett's semiology goes beyond the mere presentation of these concepts. He exacerbates the very notion of stable oppositions by exploring the underlying system to which they belong. The semiological alibi, figured allegorically by Godot as Signified, is revealed to be shared by both a theatrical aesthetic and a structure of domination – that is, the theatrical *as* the scene of mastery. The question remains, however, as to whether Beckett's play enacts only the moment of a semiological crisis, which is also a crisis of values and beliefs, or whether it also stages the aftermath of such a radical turning inside out of the system of representation? In other words, what is left to do once the machinery of representation has been exposed? Is the answer Estragon's 'nothing to be done', the opening words of the play?

Godot involves the spectators in a process of waiting that doubles and repeats the waiting of the characters themselves. In other words, the structures of expectation, spectatorship and semiology are governed by the same alibi (figured by Godot) that grounds their theatricality. Beckett plays on the very limits of a metaphysics of absence, bringing to the stage the oppositions that ground it. Characters' bodies, minds and possessions are involved in a series of impairments; signs degenerate and fall apart in space and time because their signification, which is assigned to Godot, is lacking, Beckett uses every element of the theatre to distend to the breaking point the opposition between the materiality of the signifier and the absent signified for which it supposedly stands. In the process, the play brands its every element with the figure of its materiality. The dialogue between characters fails to assure communication because its language, instead of allowing passage from word to meaning, hovers between literal and metaphorical meaning. Godot's absence is the absence of a center (a signified) that would guarantee that a character's speech could coincide with the actions he performs. Beckett's stage directions as well as his performance notes insist on the disjunction between action and speech.[3] The effect is to undermine the traditional hierarchy between speech and gesture, materialising them both just as the play as a whole drifts toward materiality. When Pozzo is asked for money, what he offers instead is Lucky's performances (Pozzo: 'What do you prefer? Shall we have him dance, or sing, or recite, or think, or –'). Pozzo includes thinking in a series of performances – dance, song, recitation. His words equate these performances with the *act* of thinking, flattening out the distinction between the material and the spiritual, the physical and the cognitive. By making thinking yet another theatrical gesture involving the body and the voice, he deprives it of its metaphysical privilege as cognition. Voiced thinking, thinking as an act, thinking as recitation, thinking qualified as performance, all make thought essentially theatrical. Drawn to the side of the signifier rather than the signified (though as immaterial meaning), the hybrid 'thought-performance' breaks down the distinction between words and their meaning. The disjunction between characters' actions and their speech is here repeated in the disjunction between discourse as a performance and its cognitive content.

The breakdown of Lucky's syntax, together with his disruptive semiotic confusion of the body and the mind, the perceptible and the intelligible, proves to be unbearable for the other characters. They seek to silence Lucky's performance because, in exacerbating their own discursive dilemma, it drives home the fact that they, too, are on the brink of 'losing it'. His speech undermines language as communication since it lacks the minimal signs of identity (I/You) that ground the situation of utterance. (*I* occurs only as repetition and as citation in 'I resume', or as an anonymous *we*.) Lucky has been dispossessed of his freedom and humanity; he has also been dispossessed of his capacity to situate himself as an 'I', a linguistic subject in a dialogical relation to a 'you'. Thus, the semiotic relationship, which presumes that the speaking subject is present to control the functioning of the sign system, has been doubly decentered. The coherency of the transcendental signified is linked to the stability of the subject of discourse. When the speaking subject has 'lost it', as in Lucky's case, the entire machinery of representation is threatened with collapse.

Beckett's characters wait for the script that will define their roles. In the meantime, however, they create their own varied repertoire in a *bricolage* that assembles different types of theatrical genres, cultural, philosophical and religious references, and modes of language play. Thus, on the other hand, Beckett has indeed pushed the semiological or theological structure of theatre to its limits, and on the other he has also shown how the overall semiological *frame* may malfunction, how it can be subverted, and how the characters invent plays and games to undo the authority and limiting effect of theatre's frames of meaning. The principal medium of such inventions is language, the same language that is assigned to semiological ends. Yet it is 'the paradoxical Beckettian attack on language through the use of language'[4] that allows for the remarkable number and variety of plays and linguistic inventions to be performed. Repetition, contradiction, phatic refrains, rhythms, slippages and word-series – the play with sounds and rhythms, forms and syntax – are extraordinarily rich in their diversity, despite the edge of irony which is there to remind us that these language games have been irretrievably devalorised by Godot's absence. Desire marked by the lack of its Object is combined in Beckett with what desire presupposes – that is, plays and performances enacted for their own sake. Jean-François Lyotard, referring to the place of desire in modern art, writes 'it was no longer a question of fulfilling desire by entrapping it, but of disappointing it methodically by exposing its machinery'.[5] The machinery of theatrical desire is indeed turned inside out in *Godot*, which explores the semiotic underpinnings of the structure of desire as lack.

Vladimir and Estragon attempt to understand the metaphorical tie that binds them to each other and to Godot. Their bondage is literalised in the rope with which Pozzo binds Lucky and his other possessions to himself. Belonging to a figural chain that includes the rope that Vladimir and Estragon want so as to hang themselves, and the 'Net', the name of Lucky's dance figuring his entrapment, these references function as the rope (or umbilical cord) that, with Lucky and Pozzo's every entrance and exit, ties the stage to the off-stage and narrative space.[6] Extending beyond the visible stage space, both on and off stage, the rope has the effect of drawing the outside space into the inside space, and vice-versa. An important instance of Beckett's turning theatrically inside out, the rope is a concrete scenic figure foregrounding the link between inside and outside, between signs and their absent meaning. Godot's space is situated in the outside, narrative space, but the scenic image of the rope works to undo any purely symbolic relation between the material sign and its abstract meaning. Once the tie that binds is rendered as a visual metaphor on the stage, the figural 'bonding' of characters to Godot also undergoes a certain detachment. Forgetting, repetitions, discontinuities and breaks in the exchanges between characters succeed in suspending the power and authority of any singular semiotic structure of waiting *for*. *While* they wait (the sense of the French title *En attendant Godot*), they proceed to experiment with the whole gamut of language games and performances. Their words and gestures, rhythms and movements are not anchored in any absent Signified. The passing of time, the passing of hats, the passing around of words, all these are designed to *mark* time by speech, gesture and aborted narratives. Time in Beckett's play no longer obeys the pull of a linear, continuous narrative whose *telos* or narrative end would reside in Godot and all that he signifies. The time of play, as repetition and difference, is invented.

Beckett's characters invent plays and performances, experimenting with them for themselves and for each other as spectators. For example, Vladimir tells Godot's messenger boy, 'You must tell him you saw us', and Pozzo makes certain he has spectators before he performs ('Are you looking?'). The play does not seek to transcend the limit between stage acts and spectatorship. Instead, it disseminates the relation of performance by reinscribing it in every act, gesture and verbal game. In other words, Godot no longer occupies the privileged position of Grand Spectator to whom all performances are directed, to whom all speech is addressed. That position is fragmented and distributed among all the characters, in a variety of performance situations which the play stages. Whereas Godot's demand for the characters' presence frames their acts, their performances cannot be reduced to being a programmed response to that demand. . . .

SOURCE: extract from section ('A Semiosis of Waiting') of article, 'Performing Theory', *Theatre Journal* (March 1985), pp. 20–4.

NOTES

[Reorganised and renumbered from the original – Ed.]

1. Jacques Derrida, 'The Theater of Cruelty and the Closure of Representation', in *Writing and Difference*, p. 235. 2. Ibid., p. 238.
3. Ruby Cohn, *Just Play: Beckett's Theater* (Princeton, N.J., 1980), pp. 231ff.
4. Angela Moorjani, *Abysmal Games in the Novels of Samuel Beckett* (Chapel Hill, N.C., 1982), p. 38. See also Dina Sherzer. 'De-construction in *Waiting for Godot*', in Barbara Babcock (ed.), *The Reversible World: Symbolic Inversion in Art and Society* (Ithaca, N.Y., 1978), pp. 129–46. [Excerpted in this Part Two above – Ed.].
5. Jean-François Lyotard, *Des dispositifs pulsionnels*, p. 76.
6. Michael Issacharoff analyses 'mimetic' space (stage) and 'diegetic' space (narrative and off-stage) in 'Space and Reference in Drama', *Poetics Today*, 2 (Spring 1981) pp. 211–24. I am grateful to Sarah Bryant-Bertail for pointing out that the rope serves to tie the spaces together.

Peter Gidal (1986) 'Dialogue and Dialectic in *Godot*'

. . . The process of a dialogue [of duets] leads to the voiding of desire. The running down and out of motivated feelings, the evacuation of desire, the (constant) ending of dialogue, is what such process *is*. There is a materiality to such language-*use* which is outside of anything prior or predestined. It is language as language, used towards a position, situation, in language. The 'dialogue' has its specific ways of working, . . . and those specific workings are not 'about' something described, some event prior or in the future, but rather a material language process 'between' two ciphers. In the language they are situating themselves *vis à vis* one another, and the running down and out of language . . . is the effecting of *dialectic* nothingness. The nothingness towards which language takes one, that running down and out, the nihilism of the process, is not 'about' nihilism. It is not 'about' the evacuation of desire in language. It is the production of language as endless attempt to ward off the end. The dialectic strategies towards this in language in *Godot* are precisely such a process.

In all this there is much denial. There is, here, a hilariousness in denial, which functions both as denial *per se* and as reflexively about denial and its processes and strategies. Humour has no little sadism. Denial as hilarious, as in the *screamed*, and screeched, repetitions of NO NO NO NO NO NO NO NO. The attempted banishment of a phobia, or an idea, or simply any content, via the NO NO NO NO NO NO NO! Analogous to this, the *content* of the statement (in the *Godot* dialogue), 'You let me go!', could only be taken in a straightforward manner, without any break in identification, if accepted within a strictly Calvinist tradition or a Jewish tradition of guilt. The structure of Judaeo-Calvinist guilt's lack of hilarity is precisely *there*. The masochistic desire for the law, articulated through the word STOP or NO or DON'T GO, the ritual game's mythic, *real*, seriousness, points to nothing but the structure of immersion in self-pity, the butt of Beckett's humour.

Whilst a reflexiveness, a reflexive consciousness, is produced in the listener–viewer–audience, this is not given as such for Estragon. Thus, for the audience, his speaking does not function as some kind of 'successful' mimesis. The more 'successful' (i.e., the more dramatically precise) his shrieking mimesis, the *less* mimetic the performance and the less the words allow the identificatory process to take place for the viewer–listener–audience. This is a formalising of a structure of speech and a content of speech via its articulation as *extreme*. Unambiguous position in the content, 'you let me go', pared down form, extremity of technique in the shriek. The precision of Didi's and Gogo's mimesis forces the viewer to *not* identify-with. The fourth-wall naturalism in Beckettian theatrics foregrounds the structure, and produces the kind of constantly reflexive distanciation process which *opposes* the theatrical convention of fourth-wall naturalism: 'Play it *as* fourth-wall naturalism' (Beckett, directing *Endgame*). . . .

The inability [in the Vladimir/Estragon duets] to structure the one (Vladimir or Estragon) as dominant, forces an equation. Thus any codification, here, onto type, is a neat fiction and an impossibility. These dialogues go against the construction of archetype: in the production of *Godot* by Beckett the body's archness is supported by what Beckett called 'the text's ability to claw'. The quote pertained to *Endgame*, and for *Godot* the clawing is of a more subtle kind: the inability of the text's clawing to let go of the characters. They are never unbound from the text, never become realistic free-agents; they are always arch. The verbal text's speaking is, in fact, a *being-spoken* by each, by Didi and Gogo. And it is that which does not allow for a biological–characterological *type* to be produced. They speak it, it speaks them, no emanation other than the holding of the characters to the text's needs. In that sense they are marionettes without the characterological characterisational parameters that critics need to invent. Thus Didi not other of Gogo, neither are they a fusion. The need to find words, find something to say, say it, let that saying produce effects of speech, i.e., the other's speech, till it runs out and down – and the whole thing may or may not start again. Speech is therefore precisely not used as a ladder which one can utilise in order to then pull it (the ladder!) away. No vehicular notions for speech here.

Object-choice can be based on sameness, not denying 'difference' but not having to be an object-choice of such difference as to make finally of the choice a representation of manifest self-dislike.

This not a matter of moral categories, narcissism as somehow 'good' or 'bad' – simply that choosing an other on the basis of self-dislike, such masochistic narcissism, may feed short-term self-lacerating needs towards a long-term bind which in its self-piteous indulgence produces what can only be a redundancy. The ideology here is of the return of the same, outside history (one's own, for example). As opposed to what? A different kind of contract: Nagg's and Nell's, Didi's and Gogo's, Speaker's with Voice (in *Company*), 1st person and 3rd person (in *A Piece of Monologue*). The contract is for the Real, the choice of necessity a neurosis but not a representation, not a characterisation of a fabled *then*; *then* is nothing other than fable, duration annihilated to seamless ends. Instead: no end, constant end, just means, meanings, meaningless, means, the words in constant material and political process. 'Lick thy neighbour as thyself' (Beckett, 1931).

The constant demands of Estragon and Vladimir are monological materialisations of the impossibility of knowing the other, of 'insight'. Didi/Gogo monologues function as constant materialisations of the projection-mechanism (even!) in their constant disavowals. Non-knower, non-can-er, not non-doer. Always an act: an act of language and an act of the body in the *use* of language and the *use* of the body.

The impossibility of knowing is never anything but a political battle against the illusion of such (knowing), the smug humanistic satisfactions inducing no little catharsis, whose function is the forward-projected idealisation/sentimentalisation of a mythical past in the interests of 'less is more' or 'more is less', instead of the horrendous, and revolutionary, insight that less is less.

There are various problems with the understanding of such images. A *single* close-up, or even a single longshot, of this image can operate as a fragment-of something *else*, it can be taken as part for whole. The other possibility is that the series functions as a singular totality, 'series' being merely a manner by which to form a larger unit, collapsed into a single 'meaning'. One other possibility, neither part-for-whole, nor singular-totality, could be a series of differences, deferring singularity. The constant rearresting of an image, against a previous and future one. The latter structure's function would be without teleology, no retrospective good-conscience rationalising of means to ends. Thus each 'to end' would not be co-optable but would be, each time, each sight, each moment, a cessation against each previous and future cessation. There would be no annihilating time towards some metaphysic of finality (and attendant transcendences).

The third possibility outlined is the one inculcated by the theatre-*performance* itself. The series of differences function on the viewer as the force to take position. The act works thereby as never separable from the force to re-enact/re-act, thus a non-wholistic series of gestural acts. No en-actment, done thus, covers *other* moments, other gestures, prior, subsequent, or 'in the real world'. And no enactment, done thus, functions as metaphor.

SOURCE: extract from *Understanding Beckett* (London and Basingstoke, 1986), pp. 53–5, 70–1, 73.

James Mays (1987) Allusion and Echo in *Godot*

The myth of Echo and Narcissus structures Beckett's volume, *Echo's Bones*, and is to be taken seriously. It is important that Beckett chose to articulate a crucial stage in the freeing of his own voice by a myth in which subjectivity drowns in self-consciousness, and voice is condemned to an attenuated existence, distracting itself with complaint beyond the grave. Though the game myth is not overt in Beckett's subsequent writing, it is buried in the overall narrative of

More Pricks Than Kicks and may be disinterred from *Murphy* and the later trilogy. It also continues its half-life in the purgatorial situation of *Waiting for Godot*, in which movement has shrunk to stones and bones, and as a technique of echoes of many kinds. The play is filled with reverberations which generate levels of meaning which are related to, but distinct from, other kinds of allusion.

The distinction is basic. There are several kinds of allusion in *Godot* – non-verbal and verbal, idiomatic and literary, quotations and proper names, allusions on a broad scale and specific parody, even frustrated or reversed references – but what is common to the list is that all such kinds are contrived, or appeal to the conscious mind. Echo, on the other hand, has a life of its own and its workings are less predictable. It can rebound on its origins to change their appearance; it can develop differently from its beginnings, and exert power even when its beginnings have been lost; it can magnify small traces, just as it can diminish epics to a whisper ('like leaves'). Echoes can interfere with other echoes, and their disembodied life is different in kind, more ghostly, than connections that can be tagged and which are relatively stable. They multiply in a void, where the things alluded to are both there and not there.

Godot differs from Beckett's other writing by the nature of its echoic technique. It is structured by balanced patterns of internal allusions, and it contains allusions to writing and occasions outside of itself, both of which are quite usual; but the way in which these consciously-manipulated allusions operate is different because of their relation to the echoes in the play. In addition, one might begin by thinking that allusions are distinct and identifiable, but increasingly they come to exist as echoes. The uncertain relation between deliberate and adventitious aspects of the allusions – what in the previous paragraph I have called simply allusion and echo – in this way gives the play its unique quality. A kind of ghostly lyricism haunts the text with echoes of other texts, as well as with echoes of itself, which is sometimes unsettling and at other times reinforcing. There is, finally, reason to connect the kind of allusions which distinguish the play with the special conditions under which it was written, and even with Beckett's distaste for it.

The most obvious kind of allusion that *Godot* makes is non-verbal. The play even draws attention to the use it makes of traditions drawn from circus, vaudeville, commedia dell'arte and film, and these have been written about at length. Some non-verbal allusions are specific and apparently deliberate, such as to *Duck Soup* in the circulation of the three hats for two heads. Other equally specific non-verbal allusions appear to be fortuitous – for instance, the striking coincidences of detail and larger movement between *Godot* and the tradition of Nō Drama – or unconscious: for instance, the close parallel with the situation in Lord Dunsany's *The Glittering Gate* (a play often to be seen on the Dublin stage at the time Beckett was a regular theatre-goer).

The internal consistency of *Godot* depends on a network of cross-references of a similarly non-verbal kind. An elaborate patterning of visual correspondences weds characters to each other, overlaps pairs of characters, and matches event against event. There may be uncertainty about specific allusions or scope for disagreement about the balance of, say, circus and filmic elements, but such uncertainty is not confusing. Likewise, the internal workings of the play leave no doubt that Pozzo is genuinely blind in Act II, or that he is both meant to be associated with but is quite separate from the character of Godot. The interior system of correspondences and contraries makes these things clear to analysis, even while the other possibilities are re-awakened at every performance.

The primary effect of verbal echoes within the play is to reinforce the sense of two-ness. Vaudeville dialogue is employed as an echoic technique, and differences in character between Vladimir and Estragon are less important than their interdependence. 'Come on, Gogo, return the ball, can't you, once in a way?' It matters less that different tendencies of character can be distinguished, or that each occasionally acts out of such character as has been established, than that they are wedded like alternations of a pendulum. The characters live among words; their alternations lean phrase against phrase, and come to echo hollowly, or rebound with leaden inevitability. And the verbal allusions to texts outside the play are clearly designed to participate in the same design.

The allusions contained in Lucky's and Pozzo's speeches have an air of deliberateness, which in its turn serves a purpose. Pozzo as he says was taught all he knows by Lucky, and the range of his reference is smaller. Whereas Lucky refers to Verlaine and Hölderlin, as well as perhaps to Joyce and Shakespeare, Pozzo's derived eloquence is more ponderous, pretentious and restricted. He alludes to Classical mythology; he echoes Virgil and repeats Latin tags.[1] A similar relation, and differentiation, is made at the level of syntax, and the models this supposes.

Vladimir and Estragon's range of allusion is more random, and, most importantly, is less under control. Tags of conventional reading surface – such as when Estragon quotes Shelley or recalls Heraclitus – but adventitiously. 'Pale for weariness. . . . Of climbing heaven and gazing on the likes of us.' 'Everything oozes. . . . It's never the same pus from one second to the next.' They are tags from an imperfectly remembered prior existence. When they together recall Calderón's 'Man's greatest sin is to have been born' – a phrase Beckett himself quoted in *Proust*, deriving from Schopenhauer – they are characteristically unconscious that they are doing so.

One range of allusions in the play is drawn from a common source and works towards a shared effect. This comprehends the allusions to the two thieves, the crucifixion, the sheep and the goats, Cain and Abel.[2] The sequence of such allusions is deliberately introduced and thereafter manipulated so as to steer the theme of two-ness in a particular direction. It adds a dimension to the vaudeville clowning, from early on in the play, which brings into question the arbitrariness of moral and theological claims. So, for example, the visual polarity of tree and stone between which Vladimir and Estragon move is complicated to the extent that the tree becomes assimilated to the cross. Again, the two friends prop up first Lucky and then Pozzo in visual tableaux which are powerfully symbolic. The fact that the authorities – the Gospels – do not agree among themselves adds a further dimension. To the extent that Pozzo is confused with, associated with, Godot, a critique of religion is made an aspect of the critique of political power.

A characteristic aspect of these allusions is that they are negative or frustrated. Parallels are set up in ways which connect situations or verbal contexts, which nonetheless insist on their separateness. The method is a kind of parody, in which the thing alluded to is invoked and cancelled at the same time. The tree is the cross yet it is also the tree; Vladimir and Estragon are the two thieves and yet they are solely themselves; Godot is God but he is just as likely to be Pozzo or a cyclist or someone else. Frequently, what we see is contradicted by what we hear; 'let's go', they say, and they do not move. Inverted clichés are the verbal equivalent of pratfalls. When Estragon, for instance, says 'We are all born mad. Some remain so' or 'strike the iron before it freezes', he situates a commonplace world in an absurd perspective. As the sense of internal repetition accumulates, so the silence grows in which the repetition takes place. The silence becomes so strong, by the end, that it empties phrases of their meaning. Words are heard as echoes, not as what gave those echoes cause; action appears as self-deception or as merely consolation.

What I have said so far should not cause any argument, except that I have described *Waiting for Godot* as it must have been intended to work, and its actual working-out is slightly different. All the evidence suggests that it was written as a dramatic variation on the theme of two-ness which, at the time, preoccupied Beckett in his trilogy of novels. That is, to represent a world in which body and mind move in separate ways towards a condition of entropy. The admixture of a coherent skein of Christian allusion qualifies the humour of criticising pretension and questioning hope. As Beckett told Colin Duckworth, 'Christianity is a mythology with which I am perfectly familiar. So naturally I use it.'[3] The matters I have rehearsed are less simple in the working-out of the play mainly because of the admixture of Christian allusion. The way in which it distracted the first English audiences and prompted them to take the play as some kind of moral allegory is indeed part of cultural history.

What is significant about Beckett's use of Christian materials – and this is apparent in his remark to Colin Duckworth quoted above – is that the use is opportunist: the allusions do not cohere in a sequential way, they merely add a dimension to the presented situation. The method of allusion is not unlike the use of the cruciform lobster in 'Dante and the Lobster', or the cruciform blind-alley Molloy finds himself in after leaving Lousse. The presented situation is in each case the primary one; Beckett is not interested in salvation or in souls, except metaphorically; his Christian allusions are deflating only. Put another way, the added references are not substantive and not continuous, and the characters who act or speak them do not comprehend their significance. The allusions hover in the air for us, audience or readers, to grasp, but they are not understood in the same way by those who speak or act them, and therefore they are only partly embodied by the characters and action.

Thus released into a world of allusion, which we ourselves discover, it is often not clear where to stop. I refer not just to the tedious debates over the connotations of the word Godot, but to other echoes which may or may not be adventitious. For instance, is Stan Smith correct to see an echo of Lenin's 1902 pamphlet *What is to be done?* in the opening words?[4] If he is, who is to say there is not an echo of either Clifford Odets's *Waiting for Lefty* or Tom Kromer's *Waiting for Nothing* in Beckett's title? Or that the Hegelian master/slave relationship embodied by Pozzo and Lucky is not absolutely central to a socially-oriented play, as some Eastern European critics have argued? After all, it has been suggested that even Lucky's name might derive from the unity of contradiction Hegel calls 'das unglückliche Bewusstsein'.[5] Because the most coherent sequence of allusions in the play – to the crucifixion, Cain and Abel and so forth – is detached from the awareness of the characters, other possible allusions are unsettled and further unintended allusions come crowding in.

A number of commentators – notably Vivian Mercier and Hugh Kenner – have written on this aspect of the play, from which it comes to exist as a kind of Rorshach test. Others – particularly Bert O. States – have attempted to define how its latent meanings coalesce.[6] States notes the high incidence of proper names and particular references – far more than in Chekhov or Ibsen, for instance – which are specific yet arbitrary. Pozzo's Kapp and Peterson and the references to the Vaucluse are almost private, yet nothing is gained by sharing in that privacy. The changes between the French, American and early and late English texts – from Voltaire, to Bishop Berkeley, to Samuel Johnson, and then to Berkeley again, in Lucky's speech – are improvements of a kind that does not disturb the meaning, even though the historical personages are quite distinct. The text tolerates such changes because such references do not have a transitive life, and, as States says, other names would have served as well.[7] It does not matter whether Pozzo's references to 'The Board' are to the theatre in general or the governing body of Trinity College, Dublin, different or not so different as these may be in real life. They are like his word 'knook' in as much as they possess specific form and indeterminate import.

What is interesting, given Beckett's judgement that the play is 'messy' and 'not well thought out',[8] is that he attempted to give it shape not by intervening in the text but by non-verbal means. His own production for the Schillertheater in 1975 left the words relatively unchanged and instead concentrated on reinforcing patterns of visual correspondence, clarifying and emphasising the containing form of the play, de-realising individual parts and giving a greater determinacy to the whole ensemble. In the 1975 production, the play as a whole seeks to contain the aspects which threaten to sabotage it. Symbolic resonances are muted to the extent that more references can be contained, and the additions even have a clarifying function. Thus Beckett added a direction for Vladimir to hum 'Death and the Maiden' as he walks Estragon up and down, and for the two of them afterwards to hum 'The Merry Widow'.

I also find it interesting that Beckett's most comprehensive attempt to discover stability in the dramatic situation he had created is in German. Of course, quite adventitious reasons were probably the most pressing; that is, because he had been invited, because he knew the company, because German stage conventions suit his manner of working. One has nonetheless to recognise that the English text introduces allusions which are not present in the original French, and which the German can again screen out. I refer to the Irishisms which characterise the English version. They are not entirely innocent in the sense that they are largely literary and self-conscious, an Irish version of English which is part of an act. In other words, by means of phrasing like 'Get up till I embrace you' and 'I'd like well to hear him think' or words like 'dudeen' and 'ballocksed', or distinctive usages like 'cod' and 'crucify', peculiar mixture of talk and inaction can come to appear all too Irish, and difficult to imagine as anything more. So that, just as the play is difficult to do in England in a way which restrains audiences from imposing allegorical or symbolic explanations on it, so productions in Ireland find it difficult to escape another kind of false definition. They too often decline into too much entertainment of what is known as 'good crack', which is at worst a form of self-congratulation.

Allusion is still present in an ideal production, such as Beckett's German one of 1975, but it is under control. It continues as a set of determinants which suffuse the text of the play with a characteristic quality. Perhaps because the play was written in a mood of relative relaxation, to stand outside the 'awful prose' Beckett was writing at the time, the range of unfocussed allusion is very wide. It is quite different in quality from the allusions and references I have so far discussed – whether of the kind which distinguish Pozzo from Lucky, or Vladimir and Estragon from either of them, or of the biblical-religious kind referring to the crucifixion and the two thieves – which are all of the sort that can be tagged with a footnote. This other kind of allusion is made up of ghostly verbal echoes which often do not depend on a reader's full possession of the source-texts, and which may or may not be deliberate. The play would be different without this admixture, indeed it would be very thin. Such echoes are often only vaguely related to the play's themes, but they are essential to its quality.

A large proportion of allusions and echoes of the kind I am now talking about appear to have entered the play on the coat-tails of the crucifixion–two thieves motif. The play is filled with scraps and rhythms of biblical prose. They encompass phrases like 'the little cloud' [I Kings 18:44] and 'the wind in the reeds' [Matthew 11:7] – though the first might derive from Joyce's *Dubliners* story and the second from the title of Yeats's volume of poems, equally. They encompass scraps of hymns ('night is drawing nigh', by Sabine Baring-Gould, which Krapp also quotes) Sunday school remonstrances ('To every man his little cross': cf. 'Take up your cross', or 'No cross, no crown'), devotional reading ('All my life I've compared myself to him': cf. Thomas À Kempis). One is often hard put to identify a scriptural or related source for a word or phrase that is strongly reminiscent, and indeed many phrases work in the same way whether a source can be traced or not. For instance, Estragon's 'Another will come, just as . . . as . . . as me', and Pozzo's 'The things of time are hidden from them too'. Neither character can be reckoned to be aware of the scriptural connotations and most members of most audiences will not be able to identify their source (just as most will not be clear about the different Gospel accounts of the crucifixion which are referred to). But no sensitive person would not be aware of the distinctive cadence of what Pozzo says and of the eschatological promise behind Estragon's broken words.

I repeat what I have said about the importance of non-verbal allusion in *Godot*, because it provides a context in which these echoes proliferate. For instance, the first reference to Estragon's having been beaten, in the opening dialogue, is received straightforwardly as an unexplained event. But when the reference is repeated in the opening of the second act, it is against a background complicated by other scriptural references, verbal and non-verbal. The phrase in this way comes to be understood in a different way, which is associated with a biblical context and somehow connected with falling among thieves [Luke 10: 30–7]. It is characteristic of the manner of allusion that one would be quite misled if one identified Vladimir with the Good Samaritan. And it is characteristic that overtones of the first occasion are retrieved only as echoes to the second. The association is primarily verbal and largely opportunist. The associative links radically select from all the possible links. To take another example: the suggestion that the action of the play takes place on a Saturday is, to begin with, one that is passed over. If it is seized on, it has no significance. In retrospect, however, by association, the entire action is situated in the limbo period between Good Friday and Christ's resurrection.

Ruby Cohn has made a list of the Shakespearean echoes she finds in the play.[9] What I find interesting is that they are exactly the same sort of echoes as the biblical ones I have been describing. They shadow the dialogue in a kind of ghostly way; often the only prototype one can offer at once appears inadequate because, one supposes, it has blended with other sources at some deep level. They are the sort of echoes that John Hollander describes as resonating within a contextual cave, pieces of voice as small as single words and as elusive as particular cadences, frequently combining sources and kinds of allusion in ways that are no less strong because they cannot be footnoted.[10] I am indebted to Professor Hollander's book for suggestions and indeed many echoing phrases throughout his essay, but the kinds of echo in *Godot* differ from the kinds he surveys in that they are also dramatic, that is, situational. The blind Pozzo being led by Lucky might strongly recall the situation of *King Lear*, and this in turn works to prompt the mind to discover further echoes from the same play. In this light, as Ruby Cohn says, it is difficult to dismiss a resemblance between Edmund's 'An admirable evasion of whoremaster man, to lay his goatish disposition to the charge of a star!' and Vladimir's 'There's man all over for you, blaming on his boots the faults of his feet'.

So *Godot* varies in the texture of its allusions, from the relative simplicity of a canter between Vladimir and Estragon in the earlier part of the play, which might seem pure vaudeville, to a later passage which is very much more complicated in this respect. Take Vladimir's soliloquy, while Estragon is sleeping, late in Act II. It might remind one person of Hamlet's graveyard scene; or the phrase 'let him sleep on' might remind another of Christ at Gethsemene [Mark 14:41]; while the sentence 'We have time to grow old' might remind someone else again of Prufrock's 'I grow old . . . I grow old . . .'. Allusions accumulate from widely different backgrounds and cast a retrospective illumination over earlier passages, investing them with more than they intrinsically contain. Thus, in the same soliloquy of Vladimir's, the sentence 'The air is full of our cries' seems to me to combine Caliban's 'isle is full of noises' speech in *The Tempest* [III ii] with the liturgical response 'And let our cry come unto thee'. The same sentence also repeats the rhythm and thereby recalls the imagery of the earlier sequence beginning 'All the dead voices', which in turn associates our cries with the rustling voices of Dante's damned, among others. It is almost as if echoes from outside the text are generated by echoes which empty it from within, creating a space in which secondary meanings sound. The parallels between Vladimir's soliloquy and Pozzo's are only the obvious beginning of the reverberative process.

The way such processes modify both dramatic values and their intellectual significance can be demonstrated with reference to the way in which the English dialogue echoes Irish rhythms and idioms. As I have said, the effect is not to reduce the dialogue to blarney, but to invest it with certain expectations, in part deriving from Irish culture and in part from the literature of the Anglo-Irish renaissance. Vladimir and Estragon will be greeted, at least by Irish audiences, in a way that distorts many other expectations; the pleasure of recognition, simply, offers too much easy gratification, and when it palls, as inevitably it must, the tension of the second act is diminished. Pozzo cannot avoid being placed on an Irish stage as an Anglo-Irish landowner, of the kind met in Boucicault, so that his relation to Lucky will be obscured. Lucky, for whom there is little place in this scheme of things, unless as some kind of nineteenth-century retainer, will find his speech hurried or severely curtailed, and certainly played almost entirely for laughs. A recent Irish production at the Focus Theatre (Dublin, July 1985) was notable for playing the boy as a tinker. The idea was an inspiration in that it at once made available the cringing persistence of the child, but it was almost too immediate, too coloured. The opportunity the play offered proved to be like an echo that one is glad one has heard but which is otherwise distracting. . . .

Godot is continuous with Beckett's lifelong concerns, but not urgently so. A piece like *Krapp's Last Tape* is more directly autobiographical, *Endgame* is more representative of Beckett's effort to confront certain central dilemmas, both are consciously more trenchant. *Godot* differs in drawing on shared concerns to which everyone can respond – poverty, salvation and the like – and in leaving them more or less as we live with them, in a state of irresolution. Perhaps the allusions remain elusive in the play just because they were prompted by instincts the more spontaneous for not being deep. Such an echoing kind of allusion requires an amount of free play (*lusus*). It is not always manifest, that is, in hand; it is to an extent always out of control, the product of an unbuttoned mood. Ghostly echoes haunt the play, among which actors and audiences can get lost, for good and ill.

SOURCE: specially written by Dr Mays for this Casebook.

NOTES

1. The source of these references are conveniently given by Beryl S. & John Fletcher, *A Student's Guide to the Plays of Samuel Beckett* (London, and Boston, Mass.: 2nd, enlarged, edn, 1985).
2. Specific references are again given in the *Student's Guide*, op. cit., and a significant number is added by Kristin Morrison in 'Neglected Biblical Allusions in Beckett's Plays: "Mother Pegg" Once More', in Morris Beja, S. E. Gontarski and Pierre Astier (eds), *Samuel Beckett: Humanistic Perspectives* (Columbus, Ohio, 1983), pp. 91–8, and in her *Canters and Chronicles* (Chicago and London, 1983), pp. 13–27.
3. Colin Duckworth, *Angels of Darkness* (London, 1972), p. 18.
4. Stan Smith, 'Historians and Magicians: Ireland Between Fantasy and History', in Peter Connolly (ed.), *Literature and the Changing Ireland* (Gerrard's Cross, Bucks, and Totowa, N.J., 1982), pp. 135–6.
5. By David H. Hesla, *The Shape of Chaos* (Minneapolis, 1971), p. 198.
6. Bert O. States, *The Shape of Paradox* (Berkeley, California, 1978).
7. Ibid., pp. 36–7.
8. Beckett, quoted by Ruby Cohn, *Just Play: Beckett's Theater* (Princeton, N.J., 1980), p. 258.
9. John Hollander, *The Figure of Echo: A Mode of Allusion in Milton and After* (Berkeley, California, 1981), p. 88.

PART THREE

At Large

Martin Esslin The Universal Image (1987)

On 19 November 1957, a group of worried actors were preparing to face their audience. The actors were members of the company of the San Francisco Actors' Workshop. The audience consisted of fourteen hundred convicts at the San Quentin penitentiary. No live play had been performed at San Quentin since Sarah Bernhardt appeared there in 1913. Now, forty-four years later, the play that had been chosen, largely because no woman appeared in it, was Samuel Beckett's *Waiting for Godot.*

No wonder the actors and Herbert Blau, the director, were apprehensive. How were they to face one of the toughest audiences in the world with a highly obscure, intellectual play that had produced near riots among a good many highly sophisticated audiences in Western Europe? Herbert Blau decided to prepare the San Quentin audience for what was to come. He stepped on to the stage and addressed that packed, darkened North Dining Hall – a sea of flickering matches that the convicts tossed over their shoulders after lighting their cigarettes. Blau compared the play to a piece of jazz music 'to which one must listen for whatever one may find in it'. In the same way, he hoped, there would be some meaning, some personal significance for each member of the audience in *Waiting for Godot.*

The curtain parted. The play began. And what had bewildered the sophisticated audiences of Paris, London and New York was immediately grasped by an audience of convicts. As the writer of 'Memos of a first-nighter' put it in the columns of the prison paper, the *San Quentin News:*

> The trio of muscle-men, biceps overflowing, . . . parked all 642 lbs on the aisle and waited for the girls and funny stuff. When this didn't appear they audibly fumed and audibly decided to wait until the house lights dimmed before escaping. They made one error. They listened and looked two minutes too long – and stayed. Left at the end. All shook. . . .[1]

Or as the writer of the lead story of the same paper reported, under the headline, 'San Francisco Group Leaves S.Q. Audience Waiting for Godot':

> From the moment Robin Wagner's thoughtful and limbo-like set was dressed with light, until the last futile and expectant handclasp was hesitantly activated between the two searching vagrants, the San Francisco company had its audience of captives in its collective hand. . . . Those that had felt a

less controversial vehicle should be attempted as a first play here had their fears allayed a short five minutes after the Samuel Beckett piece began to unfold.[2]

A reporter from the San Francisco *Chronicle* who was present noted that the convicts did not find it difficult to understand the play. One prisoner told him, 'Godot is society'. Said another: 'He's the outside.'[3] A teacher at the prison was quoted as saying, 'They know what is meant by waiting . . . and they knew if Godot finally came, he would only be a disappointment.'[4] The leading article of the prison paper showed how clearly the writer had understood the meaning of the play:

> It was an expression, symbolic in order to avoid all personal error, by an author who expected each member of his audience to draw his own conclusions, make his own errors. It asked nothing in point, it forced no dramatised moral on the viewer, it held out no specific hope. . . . We're still waiting for Godot, and shall continue to wait. When the scenery gets too drab and the action too slow, we'll call each other names and swear to part forever – but then, there's no place to go![5]

It is said that Godot himself, as well as turns of phrase and characters from the play, have since become a permanent part of the private language, the institutional mythology of San Quentin.

When, during one of the periods of relative 'thaw' in Poland in the early 1960s, *Waiting for Godot* was allowed to be performed there, the audience, we are assured by a number of very competent observers, had no doubt whatever, that the Godot the two men were waiting for stood for national liberation. When Algeria was still under French colonial rule, performances of the play for audiences of landless peasants were, as Jean Duvignaud has reported, immediately understood as dealing with the endless and seemingly fruitless wait for land-reform. And, of course, audiences of European intellectuals have, in their time, regarded, and still regard *Waiting for Godot* as a statement about metaphysical anguish, the 'anxiety of being', the nature of time, the absurdity of the human condition.

How can a single text fit such a protean variety of mundane, political and philosophical interpretations? What is Beckett's play really about?

The answer is simple enough. It is not about Godot. It is about *Waiting*: the act of waiting for something that may or may not come, with the latter possibility becoming more and more overwhelmingly likely, as the action – or in-action – proceeds. It has become a commonplace in discussing *Waiting for Godot* that it is a play in which 'nothing happens', that its author has achieved the paradoxical feat of writing 'drama' (which means action) without any action actually taking place, of having written a play that may present character but has no real plot, does not really 'tell a story' – lacks, as Brecht would have put it, a 'fable'.

That certainly is true. And it is the measure of Beckett's innovative power. *Waiting for Godot* does not dramatise a story, it dramatises a *state of mind*, an emotion. In that sense Beckett's innovation is an exact parallel to Brecht's endeavours. Brecht wanted to write an 'epic' type of drama – concentrating on action rather than character, as cool and detached from the events it depicts as the novel is from what it describes as having happened in the past. Beckett's attempt, to dramatise an emotional state, the feel of an experience, is, strictly speaking 'lyrical theatre' – for emotional states, feelings, are precisely what lyrical poetry deals with. Except that, Beckett (as always, intent on going for the essentials of the human condition), is not just dramatising a fleeting emotion like the elation of seeing nature in springtime, or being in love, or lonely or unhappy – the subject matter of lyrical poetry – he is trying to capture the basic experience of being 'in the world', having been thrust into it without a by-your-leave, and having, somehow, to come to terms with 'being there', *Dasein* itself, in Heidegger's sense.

All art, ultimately, tends in that direction: towards capturing and communicating 'what it feels like' to be Orestes, Othello, Lear, Hedda Gabler; what it feels like to see the world with the eyes of Van Gogh or Michelangelo; to experience it with the emotions of Beethoven or Schubert. The ultimate subject of all art is the communication of such an 'Existenzgefühl' (an existential 'feel' or 'existential experience'). But in the visual and verbal arts, that communication takes place indirectly, mediated through the personal story of the dramatic characters, the look of the wheatfields or beautiful human beings. It is only music which, as Schopenhauer has pointed out, directly communicates an existential experience, pure emotion.

What Beckett has done in *Waiting for Godot* is, precisely, a daring attempt to write a piece of drama, with all its verbal and conceptual content, that would nevertheless approximate to the direct existential communication of music – the creation, in the audience, of an equivalent 'Existenzegefühl', which, by the presence of the verbal and conceptual element, would be more stimulating of thought about the emotion portrayed than a purely musical work of art could ever be.

What he has done here is to invent a method by which the paradox of an actionless drama can be achieved: namely, the breaking up of the *ultimately* actionless action into segments of actions that mutually cancel each other out, thereby always returning to a state of nothing's having happened, simply by making each momentary segment undo the positive movement of the previous segment. Thus each segment may in itself generate suspense and amusement without advancing the overall movement of the play beyond the point from which it started. Only by making each moment as amusing and riveting as possible can an audience be made to enjoy an action that goes no-where.

The analogy with music goes deep. Like a musical piece, which shapes the amorphous flow of time through rhythm, pace, variation and thus gives form to the formless, the ultimate statement of *Waiting for Godot* is made not verbally, but through the articulation of time.

The full meaning of the play emerges only at the final moment, when the audience realises that the shape of the second act exactly mirrors that of the first, and that, by implication, we have seen a fragment of a process that may be repeated over an endless series of days of waiting. This establishes the basic metaphor of the play as an image of the human condition – which, from the first day to the last, is the experience of something which we feel ought to have meaning, ought to reveal its meaning, but which, from one day to another, always fails to produce that meaning. The prisoner in his jail, the oppressed nation in its servitude, the landless peasant in his landlessness, concentrate on those aspects of their condition to an extent which makes that particular objective appear as the ultimate objective of their existence. Once they achieve that objective, they must realise that this was not so, that existence itself remains as mysterious and its goal as impenetrable as ever.

That is why Beckett's play is felt to be about every individual's, every community's, particular problems. It is a dramatised metaphor for the most general existential experience of humanity.

SOURCE: expanded into a wider context for this Casebook by Mr Esslin from a segment (pp. 19–20) of his *The Theatre of the Absurd* (1961; rev. edn, Harmondsworth, 1968).

NOTES

1. *San Quentin News*, San Quentin, Calif., 28 November 1957. 2. Ibid.
3. *Theatre Arts*, New York, July 1958. 4. Ibid.

Stanley E. Gontarski 'War Experiences and *Godot*' (1985)

. . . War is latent in much of Beckett's work, sitting as part of the subtext, the unstated. One interpretation of *Waiting for Godot* sees the play as an autobiographical account of Beckett's and Susanne's flight from Paris to the Vaucluse, where they slept by day in haystacks and walked at night, tired, hungry and without food. This autobiographical reading is plausible, since *Godot* contains at least one allusion to the Roussillon exile, a man called Bonnelley, from whom Beckett occasionally got food, but the play is fundamentally about stasis, not an arduous journey. Some of the dialogue and the stress may have been borrowed from the escape to unoccupied France and the strains of hiding from the Nazis, but the core of the play – the stasis, the uncertainty, the emptiness, the difficulty of filling time, indeed the waiting – must have come from another source. A more plausible suggestion is offered by Beckett's close friend and English producer, John Calder. Despite his fluent French, Beckett would easily be identified as an alien during his exile because of his Irish accent, and even if Beckett had little to fear from the local representatives of the Pétain government, Hitler violated his agreement with the Vichy government in order to help protect his southern flank from Allied invasion and ordered the seizure of unoccupied France on 10 November 1942. From then until the Americans entered Roussillon on 24 August 1944, Beckett was in considerable danger. The threat of German patrols passing through sent Beckett and perhaps Susanne – or more probably another alien like Henri Hayden, a Polish Jew who would be in danger even from local collaborators sympathetic to Hitler's Jewish policies – to hide in the forest and wait, sometimes for days, for word to return. Hiding in the woods and fields, they never knew, when they heard someone approach, whether it would be a Nazi patrol or friendly villagers.

The play is doubtless a conflation of incidents from the war period, and a similar composite of war experiences provides some of the origins of *Fin de partie*. What seems fairly plausible is that, despite very little direct reference to the war itself, *Waiting for Godot* grew out of Beckett's war experiences, not so much disguised, although disguise may have been part of Beckett's intention, as universalised. The war was certainly one of the most formative experiences in Beckett's life, but for his art it became simply another example of the human predicament, that most immediate and literal emblem of 'humanity in ruins'. The war background is finally not indispensable to the play precisely because of Beckett's successful transformation of his material, his undoing of his creative origins. . . .

SOURCE: extract from chapter ('Preliminary Versions of *Fin de partie*') in *The Intent of Undoing in Samuel Beckett's Texts* (Bloomington, Ind., 1985), pp. 35–6.

Kay Boyle All Mankind is Us (1975)

> It is not every day that we are needed. Not indeed that we are personally needed. Others would meet the case equally well, if not better. To all mankind they were addressed, those cries for help still ringing in our ears! But at this place, at this moment of time, all mankind is us, whether we like it or not. – Vladimir in *Waiting for Godot*.

Sam Beckett and I met in 1930. All I knew of him then was that he was a close friend of the Joyce family, and I was acquainted with the Joyces – in particular with Lucia, for we both danced with Elizabeth Duncan's group – and I had heard the family speak of Sam. The night I met him I had not read his poem 'For Future Reference' (published that same year in *transition*), which he dedicated to his 'cherished chemist friend' who had managed to lure him 'down from the cornice/into the basement/and there/drew bottles of acid and alkali out of his breast'. Also, I did not know that Beckett had just won the Hours Press prize for his poem *Whoroscope* in a contest Nancy Cunard and Richard Aldington had sponsored. The Beckett of that time (and he has changed little) Nancy Cunard accurately and perceptively described as 'tall and slim to leanness, of handsome aquiline features . . . a man of stone, you think until he speaks, and then all is warmth if he is with someone sympathetic to him. He is fair, with a direct gaze at times coming to pinpoint precision in his light blue eyes. . . . If you think he is looking slightly severe, this may be because he is assessing what has just been said, and his laughter and ease of manner are frank and swift. . . . He is very self-assured in a deep, quiet way, unassuming in manner and interested in mankind.'

Sam Beckett has since told me that it was in the Paris apartment of the poet Walter Lowenfels that we met. But whose-ever temporary stopping place it was, I cannot recall the faces or voices of any of the voluble people crowded into the room. It is as if they were simply not there at all. But Sam's face and the sound of his voice have never left me, for we must have talked for hours, sitting on a rather fragile sofa, upholstered in striped yellow and black velour, like a hornet's hide. Sam says that he tried to tell me about Machiavelli's *Mandragola*, which he had seen a night or two before, but that I showed no interest in it. He wanted to make me understand that it was the most powerful play in the Italian language, the language with which he was so much in love. This part of our talk has gone from my mind for, the very evening we met, a friend we both cherished had been committed to 'a place', an institution, a madhouse, and I was obsessed with my outrage over the human dilemma men call insanity.

The truth was that I didn't believe in madness, not for a minute and not under any guise. Even if I had been locked up in a ward with the allegedly demented, I would not have believed in that cynical appraisal of their ailment. I was of the simplistic opinion that love was the missing element, and it had not come into my head until Sam Beckett talked his good sense to me that love can be the heaviest of all burdens man is asked to bear. I had, until that evening in 1930, seen madness as an outside force, an actual sinister alien who moved slyly into the bodies and spirit of the lonely and unloved, into the grief and longing of those who were no more than innocent bystanders. I saw madness as a despoiler who forced his way in on the artless and the defenceless, and began hanging up in their closets his various diguises, then shifted around the furniture to his own perverted liking in the rooms of houses that had never been his. Finally, he rid himself of the books that were there on the shelves, and put in their place his own demented library.

I believed this until Sam Beckett described to me the true topography of the scene. I did not know then that behind him lived the irrefutable knowledge and the anguish experienced in his visits to the Bethlehem Royal Hospital in Kent, a mental hospital where a friend of his was a doctor. I did not know (and still do not know except for the revelations in *Murphy*) anything at all about the faces and voices he knew there, or the eternal rocking of a body bound to a rocker by seven scarves, that he could never forget. He explained to me that night in Paris that madness is a geographical location inside the self. As he talked, it was almost as if we moved through purgatory together, and he was quite modestly showing me the way out for the condemned, saying that just as there are deep, seemingly impassible crevasses in the static ice of a glacier which mountain climbers cannot cross, so between sanity and insanity lies a fathomless abyss that it is not possible to traverse either by emotion (love) or by choice (the free will). 'Once one has crossed over', Sam said, 'there is no way back unless a bridge can be constructed for the return.'

It was doubtless that same night in 1930 that Sam made reference to the two poets, Virgil and Dante, who passed together into Hell's antechamber and found themselves surrounded by the troubled who had in their lives pursued neither good nor evil and were therefore displeasing alike to God and to the Devil. That was easy enough to understand, but what the structure of the bridge for the return would be was not so simple to visualise. Some pilings or masonry of its foundations were perhaps to be found in the third canto of Dante's "Inferno," but I couldn't be sure about that although it was certainly Sam (become Virgil for the moment) who was saying:

> Here all misgiving must thy mind reject.
> Here cowardice must die and be no more.
> We are come to the place I told thee to expect,
> Where thou shouldst see the people whom pain stings
> And who have lost the high good of the intellect.

In that far century, Dante had asked of Virgil: 'Who are these that seem so crushed beneath their plight?' And Sam Beckett (still in the grave voice of Virgil) answered:

> These miserable ways
> The forlorn spirits endure of those who spent
> Life without infamy and without praise.

Norman Mailer once wrote in uncharacteristic humility that Beckett's work 'brings our despair to the surface, nourishes it with air, and therefore alters it. . . . The last ten years have been part of the great cramp of our history . . . that cramp which will finally destroy Will and Consciousness and Courage, and leave us in the fog of failing memory, expiring desire, and the vocation for death.' Both in his work and in his life, Sam Beckett has quietly defied that threatened destruction of the Will. In *Godot*, he began the construction of a bridge across the abyss, offering through unremitting work, sometimes despairingly, sometimes with wry humour, a way back for man's stricken, paralysed Will. Madness is never an uninvited stranger who moves into the house of the lost and the lamenting, Sam Beckett said to me on that first night. It is simply the strapping, and binding, and handcuffing by man himself on his own Will; and Will is nothing more than courage by another name. Both Beckett and Dante repeated to me that, in Hell's anteroom, the torture of the detained is to be committed to the company of those who, like themselves, were too cowardly (these are Dante's exact words) to choose one side or the other, or to speak out (again Dante's words) of their beliefs.

The line of action which Sam Beckett's life has followed, a progression of decisive choices, traces another way out of the anteroom of detention which Dante has described. Like Joyce, Sam mistrusted the various pressures in his own country, and although he was appointed assistant to the professor of French at Trinity College, he knew (as he has put it) that he could never settle down to the work of teaching, and after the fourth term he resigned. 'I didn't like living in Ireland', he said 'You know the kind of thing – theocracy, censorship of books. . . . I preferred to live abroad.' So he left Ireland, but was back on a visit to his family when war broke out in Europe in 1939. Of the decision he took then he says quite simply: 'I immediately returned to France. I preferred France in war to Ireland in peace. I made it just in time. I was here [Paris] up to 1942, and then I had to leave . . . because of the Germans.' The German army units entered Paris in the spring of 1940, and thus Beckett's casual remark indicating that he spent two years there under the Occupation reveals nothing at all of the peril and pain and actual hunger that he chose to endure. Of his work in the French Resistance, Beckett says: 'I couldn't stand there with my arms folded.' It was for others to say that he was decorated for his services to England and France.

It might be supposed that I would have, through the years, continued to learn from Beckett's patient and forbearing wisdom, but I did not. For instance, when I first saw *Waiting for Godot* in New York City in 1956, I insisted on interpreting it as an evaluation of France during World War II. Vladimir and Estragon in their eternal waiting for liberation were discarded man, man relegated to the gutter, which, during an occupation, is his designated place. When Lucky comes out upon the stage carrying a heavy bag, a folding stool, a picnic basket and a great coat, it is clear that these objects are the property of the man, Pozzo, who holds him tethered by the rope around his neck. These are not the belongings of the slave but of the conqueror. Pozzo's directions to Lucky (the sign and symbol of a defeated people) are as clipped as military orders. He cracks his whip and barks: 'On! Back! Up, pig! Up, hog! Back! Stop! Turn! Coat! Stool! Stop!' Lucky, the subjected, the shackled, has no choice but to comply. Pozzo admits that he might just as well have been in Lucky's shoes, and Lucky in his, 'if chance had not willed otherwise'; that is, if the history of the war had been re-enacted and rewritten.

The symbolic meaning of the figure of Pozzo is further confirmed at the moment of his meeting with Gogo and Didi, at which time he shouts out his name to them. 'P-O-Z-Z-O!' he tells them, but Didi is not certain whether he has said 'Bozzo' or 'Pozzo'. There is no explanation as to why the average Prussian invariably pronounces 'p' as 'b', but so it is. As if this were not clue enough, Beckett sits Pozzo down on the stool that Lucky has carried and has him eat a sumptuous meal from the basket that has been a part of Lucky's burden, a picnic lunch that includes chicken. In contrast, Gogo eats a carrot fished out of the miserable débris of Didi's clothes, preferring it to a turnip. (Carrots and turnips, turnips and carrots: these were staples of the actual diet of the occupied under the occupier.) Pozzo dines like a king, like a general, it might be said, before the famished tramps and the tethered Lucky, the ironically named shackled victim, the abject figure of the paralysed will.

When the meal is done, Estragon asks tentatively of Pozzo: 'Er . . . you've finished with the . . . er . . . you don't need the . . . er . . . bones, Sir?' Pozzo turns the bones with the handle of his whip, and when he speaks the blood runs cold through the heart, for it is as if one heard the commander of an extermination camp saying: 'Do I need the bones? No, personally, I do not need them any more.'

In the second act, Pozzo, the tyrant, is blind (no longer able to see the vision of conquered, subjected humanity), for the liberation (in my version) which Didi and Gogo have waited for is now on its way. When Lucky collapses in exhaustion, Pozzo too falls to his knees, crying out for help. It is that moment that Vladimir exhorts Estragon to act.

During the German Occupation of France, there was one hazardous way out of France and that was the clandestine crossing of the Pyrenees into Spain. In the last act of *Godot* (the second act, when a few leaves appear on the previously barren tree), Estragon says: 'We'll go to the Pyrenees. . . . I've always wanted to wander in the Pyrenees.' Vladimir says: 'You'll wander in them', but although they know that 'down in the hole, lingeringly, the grave-digger puts on the forceps', still they do not, cannot go. 'Hope deferred maketh the something sick', quotes Vladimir from *Proverbs*, but he cannot remember the conclusion, 'but when the desire cometh, it is a tree of life'.

When I submitted this *explication de texte* to Beckett in 1957, he said there wasn't a word of truth in it, but he has never held that or anything else against me.

Source: essay-chapter ('All Mankind Is Us'), in Ruby Cohn (ed.), *Samuel Beckett* (New York, 1975), pp. 15–19.

Sean O'Casey *Not Waiting for Godot* (1956)

. . . Beckett? I have nothing to do with Beckett. He isn't in me; nor am I in him. I am not waiting for Godot to bring me life; I am out after life myself, even at the age I've reached. What have any of you to do with Godot? There is more life than Godot can give in the life of the least of us. That Beckett is a clever writer, and that he has written a rotting and remarkable play, there is no doubt; but his philosophy isn't my philosophy, for within him there is no hazard of hope; no desire for it; nothing in it but a lust for despair, and a crying of woe, not in a wilderness, but in a garden.

The earth isn't either a grave-yard or a roaring camp – save in a war, when it is both; but today war is a *non est*, for with the new nuclear explosive power, all are within range of death; the rich and the poor, the ones who go out to fight, the ones who remain at home; the Catholic pope and the Catholic peasant share its shivers, and so aren't ready to nod the head in favour of strife. And there is life and energy even in decay (not Beckett's, but nature's), for dead leaves turn to loam, and dry bones to phosphates.

What witnesses does this Beckett call? A dowdy and a doleful few: Camus, Kafka, Orwell, Graham Greene, Huxley, with T. S. Eliot a wan follower, cross on breast and hands clenched in an obscure prayer. And what witness have we? A cloud of them: Copernicus, Newton, Beethoven, Angelo, Shelley, Whitman, Balzac, Faraday, Titian and, yes, by God, and Shakespeare, too, with ten thousand others close up to the greatest! . . .

SOURCE: extract from article in *Encore* (Easter 1956); reproduced in O'Casey's *Blasts and Benedictions* (London and Basingstoke, 1967), pp. 51–2.

Sidney Homan 'Playing Prisons' (1984)

. . . If waiting is the sole choice, then the audience's own waiting is the one activity shared by those off- and on-stage. Our style of waiting is thus no less an issue, and audiences for *Godot* have ranged from the impatient Coconut Grove tourists who walked out of the American premier to the New Yorkers who, finding the play an anti-play, also despaired of Beckett, to the inmates at San Quentin and at the ten prisons visited by my troupe who literally took the play to heart, to the countless literary 'audiences' of more recent times who, according to my own well-worn edition, have sent the play to its fifty-fourth printing.

It is little wonder, then, that *Godot* is so conscious of its audience. We are the 'inspiring prospects' surrounding one side of its world; the tree frames the rear, and the exits, which prove to be no exits, frame the other two sides. Estragon advances to front-stage, '*halts facing auditorium*', and, looking at us, sees those 'inspiring prospects', that phrase itself followed by the cynical and deflating 'Let's go'. Our prison production allowed the actors at times to play literally to the audience as we alternated between actor-to-actor contact and – whenever demanded by the inmates who wanted to be let into the production – actor-to-audience contact. Because actor is linked to audience and audience to actor, we are 'tied' together. If the tree denies a way out, figuratively and literally, the same is true for us, that bog on the opposite side. All that we have is the present, the 'charming spot' stripped of hierarchy and meaningful dichotomy, and of any time or space beyond that framed by the audience. Beckett is even conscious of the critics in his audience, professional or self-styled. At the end of the list of curses that Vladimir and Estragon hurl at each other – Moron, Vermin, Abortion, Morphion, Sewer-rat, Curate, Cretin – is 'Crritic!'.

Vladimir's greeting to Estragon, 'Together again at last!', thus bursts the confines of the stage and embraces the audience as well. We are all in it together; another curtain has risen. In the words of *How It Is* we are 'glued together'. Now, for audience and actors, no less than for Vladimir and Estragon, what shall we do? How shall we pass the time as we singly and mutually wait for our personal Godot? Together at last. 'We'll have to celebrate this?' How easy it is to forget that the theatre is a place for and of entertainment sustained by both actors and audience. The issue here is: what will be the level of that entertainment? The hat trick, or vaudeville, or Beckett's finer, more profound 'hat' trick? Vaudeville or Chaplin or Beckett – this is the order of ascent. To celebrate is half the answer; the other half, which Vladimir quickly supplies, is a second question: 'But how?'.

The image of the audience doubles back on the play. Audiences surrounding the stage are balanced with audiences on-stage. Vladimir performs for Estragon, Estragon for Vladimir; audience-like, the clowns watch Pozzo. The real Pozzo, Beckett's parody of a self-conscious actor ('Is everybody looking at me?', performs his discourse on the night for Vladimir and Estragon, complete with a request for audience feedback; appropriately, his 'How did you find me?' is met with 'Tray bong, tray bong'. In our prison production the actor playing Pozzo, more than any other character, played to our audience, giving them his best half with only cursory attention to his 'likes' on stage.

At one point, the audience almost degenerates to a collection of voyeurs, including Lucky, Pozzo, Estragon and – if we so choose – ourselves: we watch characters watch Vladimir off-stage going to the bathroom. I have seen members of the audience strain their necks to see if the reference to nature taking its course is faked or real, as Vladimir off-stage, but accompanied by an on-stage chorus from Estragon, empties his bladder. In a larger sense, many of the play's rhetorical questions – like the intrusive question from the public address system that shatters the illusory world of the movies: 'Is there a doctor in the house?' – are addressed as much to the audience as to anyone on-stage: 'He wants to know if it hurts'. By extension, the line might even be shouted so as to reach the ears of the absent Godot. Indeed, the number of audiences multiplies: Godot, we assume though at our peril, observes his subjects (above or below or all around, to echo Hamlet's incantation of his father's ghost); we face the boards from our side, while the Boy, who has been there unseen for some time, overhears from the wings, even as characters onstage watch other characters on-stage and, in the case of Vladimir's emptying his bladder, off-stage. As we watch Hamlet and Horatio observe Claudius in attendance at *The Murder of Gonzago*, or as we observe Oberon and Puck observe Thesesus and his court mock Bottom and his rustic actors, we experience the microcosmic-macrocosmic metaphor inherent in the Renaissance theatre. In his meta-theatre Beckett also reminds us by his mirror-audiences and by his allusions to the real audience that we are part of the stage action. Our sense of participation (we validate the play by our witness; the play is itself validated by being a mirror of ourselves as audience) is a vital contribution to that classic goal of any art: *utile et dulce*. What distinguishes *Godot*, I believe, is that rather than being imposed from above or from outside the play proper, that usefulness and pleasure are determined at performance, by those on- and those off-stage. . . .

SOURCE: extract from chapter ('*Waiting for Godot*: The Art of Playing') in *Beckett's Theaters* (Lewisburg, Penn., 1984), pp. 41–3.

Eric Gans Beckett and the Problem of Modern Culture (1982)

The most obvious problem of modern culture is that there doesn't seem to be very much more of it. The dearth of 'great' writers today is unjustly dismissed as a problem of perspective. For there are scarcely even any *major* writers, those known outside the côteries of specialised amateurs of 'nouvelle poésie', 'nouveau (nouveau) roman', 'nouveau théâtre'. There remains, to be sure, at least one . . . writer who constitutes an exception to this generality. But Beckett's greatness lies in his lucidly paradoxical refusal of greatness. To understand Beckett, and above all to understand the problem of modern culture, we must take seriously his description of Bram Van Velde as an exemplary modern artist: 'Van Velde . . . is the first to admit that to be an artist is to fail, as no other dare fail, that failure is his world and the shrink from it desertion, art and craft, good housekeeping.'[1] That this statement is paradoxical, Beckett freely admits. The failure, as a new criterion of authenticity, becomes a new form of success, that failure to express succeeds in becoming 'an expressive act, even if only of itself, of its impossibility, of its obligation'. Beckett the Nobel-Prize winner is perhaps even more acutely aware today than when, as a little-known post-war novelist, he expressed these paradoxes in his 'Three Dialogues' with Georges Duthuit. But paradox is not nonsense, and Beckett's analysis of modern culture may well be the best point of departure we have.

Taken at face value, this analysis very nearly implies the impossibility of art. The 'successful' artist is relegated to 'arts and crafts', to what we might otherwise call 'mass' or 'popular' culture. His success is the sign of artistic inauthenticity, of his having set himself a problem that is *a priori* of no esthetic interest precisely because it can be solved. Solving problems was possible, Beckett says or implies elsewhere, for Proust or Joyce; it is no longer possible for artists today. There are no more significant solvable problems left unsolved: success in art is paid for by insignificance, not to say outright plagiarism of earlier solutions. The artist-as-failure, if he is to exist at all, is thus condemned to tread a narrow line between inauthentic success and the truly irremediable failure to produce anything at all. He has nothing to express except his failure to express, which poses a particularly difficult problem, or perhaps I should say 'meta-problem' of expression. Yet all this would be of little interest did there not exist artists, and in particular literary artists, whose works constitute worthy solutions of this problem. There are perhaps a few other candidates for this honor; but the most obvious and significant case is no doubt that of Beckett himself, particularly in his theatrical masterpiece *Waiting for Godot*.

If we take Beckett's statements seriously, we should avoid approaching this play in the first place as a success in doing what it does. We must avoid falling into the critical trap of discussing what happens on stage. What happens is precisely what the play succeeds in presenting; but what should interest us is rather what does not happen, what fails to happen, not because the author chooses to make something else happen, but because he fails to make it happen. We should seek in this play, in other words, a two-level structure corresponding to the distinction in Beckett's esthetic between the 'problem' that the artist cannot solve, that is, the level on which he 'fails to express', and the 'meta-problem' that he solves as a result of failing on the first level – the meta-problem, that is, of expressing his failure to express.

That these two levels indeed exist in this play, are in fact structurally evident, is already apparent from its title, particularly in its original French version. *En attendant Godot* is not so much 'waiting for Godot' as '*while* waiting for Godot'. The 'action', such as it is, takes place in an interval of waiting for something else. The primary dramatic action is thus the waiting itself. This primary action may be said to 'fail' in a peculiarly Beckettian way. This is not because Godot never shows up; indeed, his absence is the *sine qua non* of *successful* waiting, since as soon as he arrived the waiting would be over. Vladimir and Estragon are in fact very good at waiting. But this waiting, as the title demonstrates, fails to express itself in the concrete action of the play. To be sure, there is much talk of waiting. But what the characters actually do, even when they talk about waiting, is not waiting but something else. The playwright fails and indeed must fail to portray waiting in this play, because waiting is not action at all, but simple abstract presence on stage. As soon as the characters do anything at all, even if it be standing around in silence – of which they do rather little – it is not waiting itself but what they do *while* waiting, which is to say, the entire action of the play, that successfully expresses Beckett's failure to express waiting. To sum up, then, the very choice of 'waiting' as dramatic action condemns the writer to failure, but this is a failure that can be perfectly well expressed in its own right, since everything that happens, or can possibly happen, expresses it.

Both Beckett's 'failure' and his 'success' in *Waiting for Godot* are of exemplary interest for the understanding not only of 'the problem of modern culture', but of culture in general. For not only does his play 'succeed' in exemplifying modern culture, it 'fails' as an attempt at classical dramaturgy and thus exemplifies, albeit in a negative sense, traditional culture as well. And to the extent that we can imagine the possibility of another play 'succeeding' precisely where this one fails, we may derive from Beckett's play a model of successful insignificant, or 'popular' culture. In these works, of course, Godot always arrives.

The 'failure' of *Godot* as traditional high culture is its only possible means of succeeding. But the precise nature of this failure enlightens us concerning the essence of this culture as well as the present impossibility of pursuing it. For the waiting Beckett proposes as his dramatic subject-matter must be understood not as a fortuitously success-proof theme but as a critical comment on the illusions of the cultural enterprise from which he has disassociated himself. Beckett has qualified this enterprise, with especial reference to James Joyce, as that of 'mastery'. Joyce was a master, he has said; I no longer claim to be one. Now of all activities, dramatic or not, waiting is certainly the least masterful. It is not, to be sure, the characters but the author whose mastery is in question here; neither in tragedy nor in comedy are the protagonists masters of their situation. The difference is that they are its presumed or potential masters. Whether kings or commoners, they seek to dominate their universe, and their failure is the sign of a higher mastery of their world from without, a mastery with which the hidden author is identified. Dramatic characters are the playthings of a fate that only the author can grasp as a whole. The spectators are said to identify with the hero in his tragic or comic fall; but their primary identification is with the author, who, like them, witnesses and judges the hero's actions from off-stage. The identification with the hero is what is, in Aristotle's term, 'purged'; but this is only possible because the spectators identify not only with the hero but with the author as agent of purgation. It is in Sophocles's, not Oedipus's, hands that we place ourselves in our search for esthetic *catharsis*.

Now what characters like Oedipus or Antigone do could scarcely be qualified as 'waiting' – they do what they can to resolve their problems, problems which are not merely their own but, in tragedy at least, explicitly those of their society as a whole. Yet because their projects either fail or succeed as the dramatist knew they would, the end result of all their activity is not really very different from that produced by Vladimir and Estragon. No doubt Oedipus contributes to his own demise, but only as an unknowing instrument of fate. The end, for Oedipus as for Beckett's heroes, is really only a matter of time. This the spectator well knows, whose evening in the theatre is sandwiched between other worldly activities like eating dinner and undressing for bed. Whatever the nature of the action on stage, its ultimate effect is to take up the time required to bring about a conclusion determined in advance by the dramatist. This end may be staved off or hastened by the actions of the characters, but it is in no way subordinate to them. What Beckett shows by explicitly reducing his character's primary activity to waiting is that this extra-dramatic conclusion is in effect always of a higher level of necessity than any dramatic activity. The dramatist's apparently superior understanding of the world his heroes attempt to dominate really only reflects an *a priori* structural necessity. For however well or badly motivated his plot, it is he and not the heroes who will have the last word.

But even if the dramatic hero may be said to 'await' his fate, surely there is a difference between his awaiting something that will of necessity take place within the world of the play and Beckett's heroes' awaiting a character who never arrives. Precisely. The 'fate' of the hero *within* the play is in reality decided *outside* the play by the dramatist. The characters function within a framework the workings of which are outside them – that of the 'catharsis' in which spectators and author collaborate. What is being awaited is a process external to the world of the characters. Godot personifies this process. It is worth spending a few minutes on the tiresome question of 'whether or not Godot is God' because, like many tiresome questions, it is not so much insignificant as badly posed. Whether Beckett had the English word 'God' in mind when he decided to use the French name 'Godot' is not a legitimate subject for inquiry. But 'God' or not, Godot plays a transcendent role with respect to the scene that is not without clear parallels with sacred phenomena. Godot belongs to the world of the play, but not to that of the stage, and in Beckett's dramaturgy presence on stage possesses a considerably more rigorous significance than in the classical theatre. It is Godot's absence that maintains the world of the stage on which the awaiting takes place. Without Godot, our heroes would have nothing to wait for and no place to wait. Their time and place in the stage-world are justified by their orientation to this 'other-worldly' personage, who can never arrive without violating the condition set in the title of the play – that the action takes place 'en attendant'. Now this is precisely the role of the sacred in Judaeo-Christian society: God never makes himself present, but belief in his presence off-stage allows for worldly activity to go on while waiting for his return. And more generally, the role of the sacred in all societies is to guarantee their internal values from without, to constitute the *real* expression of these values that men can only strive to realise imperfectly under the watchful eyes of the gods. In rituals, to be sure, the gods make themselves present; but in secular culture, notably in the theatre, the gods generally wait in the wings, appearing at best *ex machina* to conclude the action on stage. This presence is a shadowy one that the characters sometimes attempt to provoke but usually try to put off as long as possible. Beckett's heroes, more humble and more realistic, are content to wait. And by making waiting their central activity, they insure in effect that Godot will never come.

The foregoing remarks suggest some preliminary conclusions concerning the modern culture of artistic 'failure' exemplified by this play. The refusal of mastery displays itself in the reduction of the action to a secondary level, in the renouncement of any *dramatic* conflict which would make the world of the stage itself appear – illusorily, as we have seen – as a place of decision. We identify with only one desire of the characters – that for Godot's arrival, about which they can do nothing, and which, because its object coincides with the end of the play's action, is effectively paradoxical within the context of the play. If traditional drama was, as Aristotle put it, the 'imitation of an action', modern drama is the imitation of an inaction that reveals the ultimate insignificance of all dramatic action. Yet our remarks concerning the sacred suggest that, precisely, in the demystification of our identification with such action, this play reveals an essential structure of all culture. The 'society' formed by Vladimir and Estragon, because its members have no individually dramatic purposes and accomplish no individually dramatic acts, is a qualitatively more universal model of human society than can be provided by the *dramatis personae* of a traditional play. Or to put it more schematically, traditional culture is historical, whereas modern culture is anthropological. Instead of a significant event, *Godot* portrays a period of pure insignificance; but it is precisely for that reason that Beckett's characters form a model of society, that is, an on-going, essentially stable set of insignificant interactions. Such a model no doubt 'fails to express' any significant experience, but it can all the better express the anthropological reality that lies beneath significant experiences. For we may go beyond Beckett's self-irony to point out the positive mastery involved in the failure to express. This 'failure' is in fact a transcendence of the subjective desire that imprisons the individual within temporal experience. What must be mastered is not the world but the self; the artist, no longer able to create on the basis of his desire, must eliminate all desire from his creation. And in doing so, he arrives at insight into the fundamental problem of social organisation, which is the limitation of the conflicts engendered by desire – the very conflicts that form the subject-matter of the traditional theatre. Vladimir and Estragon do not become caught up in the illusion that they are participating in significant experiences because they are only acting *en attendant* – but Beckett can only discover this mechanism for avoiding the conflict that arises from 'self-expression' because it already exists at the basis of society. . . .

From the standpoint of a creator of 'high' culture, such as Beckett undoubtedly is, modern culture is problematic and at the limit paradoxical. If to be an artist is to fail, then the choice of art as a career can only be explained as the result of a quasi-pathological inner necessity, an ironic modern version of the divine curse with which the Romantic artist – particularly the unsuccessful one – was customarily afflicted. To quote for one last time from 'Three Dialogues', modern art takes as its content 'the expression that there is nothing to express, nothing with which to express, nothing from which to express, no power to express, no desire to express, *together with the obligation to express*'. But we may ask whether this 'obligation to express' is not the heritage of an all-but-defunct high culture rather than a living cultural imperative. If Beckett's non-expressive expression can already be credited with considerable anthropological insight, this is because to the abandonment of the expressive there corresponds an organisation of the fictional world according to reversible anthropological structures rather than irreversible historical ones. But the fruitful prolongation of these insights cannot be obtained by continuing to express the impossibility of expression, but by abandoning expression altogether for the construction of scientific hypotheses. The future of the high culture, in this perspective, lies with the social sciences, however inadequate they are in their present state to assume this role. The enormous interest of American literature departments in the works of French social and humanistic thinkers from Barthes and Foucault to Derrida and René Girard – an interest which contrasts with nearly total uninterest in recent French literary productions – is a notable sign of this trend. What is suggested by this development, and what I should like to suggest in conclusion, is that we should learn to expect little from either the 'high' or the 'popular' culture, and busy ourselves in creating the only culture we can create: the culture of rational reflection – of human science.

SOURCE: extract from article, 'Beckett and the Problem of Modern Culture', *Sub-Stance*, no. 35 (1982), pp. 3–7, 14–15.

NOTE

1. 'Three Dialogues', in Martin Esslin (ed.), *Samuel Beckett: A Collection of Critical Essays* (Englewood Cliffs, N.J., 1965), p. 21.

Alec Reid 'An Act of Love' (1968)

. . . Before we examine *Waiting for Godot* as an example of how Beckett has changed and enlarged the theatre, we must remind ourselves that *Godot* is an outstandingly successful play. Since its première in Paris on 5 January 1953, it has been performed by all sorts of actors in all sorts of places, by negroes in Harlem, by convicts in a German prison, by pupils of Beckett's old school in the North of Ireland. It has been played in more than twenty different countries from Finland to the Argentine, and has been translated into at least fifteen different languages, as different as Serbo-Croat and Japanese. Clearly we are not dealing with a play of limited appeal, or, as many insist, with an elaborate intellectual hoax. *Godot* has turned out to be world theatre.

No one could have been more surprised at this than the author. At their first meeting Beckett told his director, Roger Blin, that he confidently expected *Godot* to play to almost empty houses, probably, as he added, the ideal conditions for it, and ninety-nine people out of a hundred would agree. It is hard to imagine anything less likely to prove an international success, a play in which as the critic Vivian Mercier says, 'Nothing happens, *twice*'. There is no story, no 'message', no spectacle, no star part, no sex, not even a woman in the cast. Why, then, has it succeeded? Why does it still succeed, and why has it become widely recognised as possibly the most important play of the last fifty years? These questions are hard to answer, but a remark of Tyrone Guthrie's provides a good starting point for our investigations. 'Take a situation of general human application', he once said, 'charge it with the overtones of myth, and no wise man will refuse to listen to you.'

At first sight *Godot* would seem to bear scant reference to the human predicament. We feel little inclination to identify ourselves with these garrulous unkempt vagabonds indifferent to all the concerns of civilised life as we know it. Even if we were so tempted, Beckett has deliberately withheld every detail that would make this possible. Godot sounds as if he might have some significance; but a glance at the programme tells us that he will not appear. If, however, we forget about the civilised world for a moment, close our programmes, and simply watch what is happening on the stage, we will realise that Vladimir and Estragon, or Didi and Gogo as they call each other, are waiting, and that the waiting is of a particular kind.

They are not like men at the proper stop, expecting a bus which they know will come at a fixed time or within a given period. They may say they are waiting for Godot, but they cannot say who or what he is, nor can they be sure that they are at the right place, or if it is the right day, or what will happen when Godot comes, or what would happen if they gave up waiting. Their position more closely resembles that of travellers miles from home waiting late at night at what could be the right or the wrong stop for the last bus which may already have gone anyway. They cannot be sure because they have no watches, no timetables, and there is no one from whom they can get information. Possibly they are at the wrong stop but could still catch the bus if they knew where to go; on the other hand, perhaps they are at the right stop and still in time, but if they move, the bus may come and go without them. Maybe the bus has already gone, and by remaining they are jeopardising their chances of finding a taxi, and all to no purpose. If only they were sure they could decide what was the best course open to them; but they cannot get the essential knowledge – they are ignorant – and without it they cannot act – they are impotent.

We are all familiar with the sense of baffled helplessness which comes welling up in us when we are forced to remain in an obscure situation over which we have no control. We know it, for instance, as we sit in an airport lounge hoping the fog will soon clear, as we watch the post for a love letter or for news of a job, as we wonder when the hospital will have something to tell us. The greater our fears or frustrations, the more eagerly we look for some means of taking our minds off things, some way to make the time pass more quickly. Almost anything will serve, however trivial, provided it helps to fill the vacuum, if only for a few minutes.

This is exactly what Estragon and Vladimir are doing from the beginning of the play. They tell stories, sing songs, play verbal games, pretend to be Pozzo and Lucky, do their physical exercises, but all these are mere stop-gaps, valuable only to occupy the twenty-four hours that must separate one possible meeting with Godot from the next. They understand this perfectly. 'Come on Gogo', pleads Didi, breaking off a reflection on the two thieves crucified with Christ, 'return the ball, can't you, once in a way?' and Estragon does; as he says later, 'We don't manage too badly, eh Didi, between the two of us', ... 'We always find something, eh Didi, to give us the impression we exist'. Here we have the very essence of boredom –

actions repeated long after the reason for them has been forgotten, and talk, purposeless of itself, but invaluable as a way to kill time.

We are fast approaching the heart of the matter, the crux of *Godot*. . . . *Waiting for Godot* is not about Godot or even about waiting. It *is* waiting, and ignorance, and impotence and boredom, all made visible and audible on the stage before us, direct expression to which we respond directly, if at all because in it we recognise our own experience. We may never have waited by a tree on a deserted country road for night to fall or for a distant acquaintance to keep his appointment, but we have sat in an airport lounge on a foggy day, we have watched the post, we have wondered when we would hear from the hospital – we have lived through these situations or innumerable others like them. So, after all, we find ourselves on common ground with Vladimir and Estragon; we feel with them and, as it seems, with millions of others, Finns and Argentines, Japanese and Serbs, with everyone who has known ignorance, impotence and boredom. Here is that situation of general human application postulated by Tyrone Guthrie. 'I think', said Beckett in 1956, 'anyone nowadays, who pays the slightest attention to his own experience finds it the experience of a non-knower, a non-can-er' (i.e. of someone ignorant, therefore impotent). The history of *Godot* seems to bear him out.

Yet before Beckett, no one in the theatre had come to grips with this experience; indeed as long as the dramatist and the public thought along the traditional lines of a well-made play with a strong story involving conflict, character development and a final solution, nothing could be done with it. Impotence cannot produce action, and without action there can be neither conflict nor solution. The only possible character development for a non-knower is to turn him into a knower, thereby destroying him altogether. Movement, therefore, is clearly impossible, but, as was generally accepted in the theatre, *le mouvement, c'est la vie* – a static drama was a contradiction in terms. By substituting situation for story, and sensuous, direct impact for logical, indirect description, Beckett has cut through this difficulty and has bridged the gulf between a widely felt emotion and the expression of it on the stage. But he has done more than solve one specific artistic problem; he has in effect created a whole new concept of drama much as the Impressionists created a whole new concept of painting. Just as the artist who has grasped the Impressionist technique is not confined to painting only bridges or sunflowers, so the dramatist who has grasped this concept of direct expression through total theatre is not confined to working with ignorance and impotence. Beckett himself has applied it to time in at least three different ways, and to awareness, and James Saunders has made notable use of it in *Next Time I'll Sing To You*, where he brings it to bear on identity.

Beckett belongs to no school of dramatists, so current labels like The Theatre of Cruelty or The Theatre of the Absurd bear no relation to his work. Nor does he seem likely to found any school unless it be The Theatre of The Non . . . . His achievement can, perhaps, be gauged through a parallel with flying; with *Godot* we move from the age of the propeller aircraft into that of the jet. Range and power have been increased enormously and things cannot ever be quite the same again.

Beckett's own use of his discovery has been intensely personal. He does not relate it to any overall system of belief as a Marxist, an Existentialist, a Nihilist or any other 'ist' might do. The new kind of play which he has evolved directly serves his individual needs as a creative artist, and these needs are, he insists, strictly his own. He sees no evidence of any system anywhere, he has no message to give, yet he cannot escape an imperative urge to try to say the unsayable, if only to satisfy himself that he exists. In a very real sense, Beckett's is an art of involvement.

He does not, cannot, describe ignorance, impotence, with clinical detachment standing back as a doctor might noting symptoms, incidence, probable causes, effects and possible cures. As he struggles to capture ignorance and impotence, he is tortured by these emotions himself. He is no Henry the Navigator sitting in his tower at Belem reading the reports of his captains; he is one of the captains actually on the deck, Vasco da Gama, say, or Columbus, as he rounds the last charted headland and goes on into the unknown, never sure of what lies ahead, or of whether he may not sail off the face of the earth altogether. Beckett has justly described himself as a man whose world has no outside; 'It is impossible for me to talk about my writing because I am constantly working in the dark', he once explained, 'it would be like an insect leaving his cocoon. I can only estimate my work from within.' Hence, as Dan Davin puts it, in an article significantly entitled *Mr Beckett's Everymen*, 'It is his own feelings, his own life, he is directly expressing and not the lives of characters with whom we can be expected to identify ourselves.'

The thing *itself* not something *about* the thing, creation not description, first hand not second, this is what makes *Godot* far more than a brilliantly original solution to a problem in play-writing. If it had only been a technical *tour de force* we could have treated it as such, arguing about it, analysing it, but never feeling it through our own experience. *Godot* springs directly from Beckett's own anguish – he has called it a howl – and we respond directly or not at all, because we, too, are human beings so made that we must feel as well as reason. . . .

. . . In his monograph on Proust, written over twenty years before *Godot*, Beckett has described 'the perilous zones in the life of the individual, dangerous, precarious, painful, mysterious and fertile, when for a moment the boredom of living is replaced by the suffering of being'. Now, before our eyes, Vladimir enters one such zone changing from clown into poet. He no longer feels any misery or anger on his own account. A few minutes earlier he had weakened Estragon for no better reason than that he was bored and frightened, but now as his awareness increases, Vladimir's concern goes beyond himself, beyond his friend, to embrace all sorts and conditions of men. Here is a piercing consciousness of the human condition, of the sadness implicit in being a living mortal. But there is nothing deadening or paralysing about the suffering, quite the opposite, for, as Beckett says, 'it is the free play of every faculty'. With this free play comes an end to self-deception. Vladimir had earlier admitted quite cheerfully that 'The hours are long, under these conditions, and constrain us to beguile them with proceedings which – how shall I say – which may at first sight seem reasonable until they become a habit'; and as he says later, 'habit is a great deadener'. Now habit can no longer insulate him from the truth as with every faculty he feels the happenings of the day for what they are, a series of pathetic attempts to pass the time: 'But in all that, what truth will there be?' Estragon, too, has suffered, and in the end what has he learned? 'He'll know nothing. He'll tell me about the blows he received and I'll give him a carrot.' Ignorance, impotence, remain unassailable; only time has passed imperceptibly. Vladimir now knows and accepts that life can be no more than the distance between birth and death, 'Down in the hole, lingeringly, the grave-digger puts on the forceps. We have time to grow old.' The lament is for all mankind, springing from a union of compassion and anguish as fundamental to Beckett's work as the sense of impotence and ignorance which directly inspires it. The anguish is not a thing of the intellect or of the body in isolation; it permeates the whole being. . . . Suffering transcends the immediate, and thus makes of Beckett's work, for all its savagery and irony, what one critic has called an art of goodwill, and another, an art of love.

At first sight this seems a strange claim. Physically, Beckett's people are nearly all repellent grotesques; Vladimir has bad breath and a weak bladder, Estragon's feet smell, Krapp is constipated, Willie can only crawl on all fours and eats his mucus, the man in *Play* suffers from flatulence, Nagg and Nell are toothless cripples, Hamm, a blind haemophiliac, cannot stand up, while Clov cannot sit down. . . . Bereft of all physical dignity, Beckett's people have few pleasant character traits either, being, for the most part, cruel, violent, obscene, selfish, blasphemous, finding a corrosive pleasure in their own squalor and the abject helplessness of others. . . .

What cannot be cured must be endured, and in this process Beckett's people reveal unexpected virtues, charity, compassion, love, and an unbreakable determination to endure. Estragon, the smaller of the two though eager enough to die, will not hang himself first. Vladimir's greater weight might break the branch, leaving him to face the world alone. For his part, Vladimir is deeply protective, watching over Estragon as a fond parent watches over a sleeping child. For Winnie, the mere knowledge of Willie's proximity is adequate reason for going on, while a sound or even a sign from him is more than enough to make her day. Nagg and Nell, as eternally apart in their dustbins as the figures on the Grecian urn, speak a love duet heart-piercing in its tenderness. Even the nameless heads in *Play*, 'emptied, ruined, impotent creatures', as *The Times* critic called them, can each feel pity and hope for the others, thus saving themselves from despair, and saving us with them. If pity and hope are possible in such a place, and in such a world, for such people, then they are possible anywhere for anyone, for us here. Nobody need be excluded. Beckett has reached rock-bottom, and, not very surprisingly, has revealed rock. . . .

Each of us comes to Beckett by a different road because each of us has led a different life. Our discussion of *Godot* has included bus stops, airport lounges, love letters and hospitals – not one of which is mentioned in the play. These objects have not been used as symbols or metaphors; they stand for nothing beyond themselves. They have been introduced because, for the present writer, they occur in that area of his experience recognisable to him as the area of experience presented in *Godot*. Other people describe it differently. There is, for example, the cricketing enthusiast who likens *Godot* to waiting outside the Tavern at Lords for it to open – which it won't because the licence has been revoked – watching two deadly-dull batsmen but hoping that Sobers or Dexter will come in next – which they won't because they have gone home. One of the convicts in California said simply, '*Godot* is the outside'. The Public Orator of Dublin University called it a modern equivalent of the Psalmist's *Expectans, Expectavi.* The cricketing enthusiast, as it happens, was an atheist, the convict had never seen a cricket match, and the professor had never been in prison, yet all three recognised the one experience – there is no divergence here like that separating the Roman Catholic critic and the Existentialist over the alleged meaning of *Godot*. Beckett's play is valid for cricketer, convict and professor alike because each is assimilating the general anguish into his particular experience and then translating it into his own terms. . . .

SOURCE: extracts from *All I Can Manage, More Than I Could* (Dublin, 1968), pp. 50–1, 52, 52–4, 54–5, 56, 57.

Christopher Mosey (1986) 'The Ultimate Test'

Stockholm – It was perhaps the ultimate test of Sweden's famously liberal prison system: a national tour by five inmates of the country's top maximum security jail to perform in Samuel Beckett's play *Waiting for Godot* (Christopher Mosey writes).

Their would-be audience is still waiting.

Four out of the five, all drug offenders, absconded through an open dressing room window just before the first night at the City Theatre in Göteborg.

The play's director, Mr Jan Jonsson, said yesterday he had discerned in the 'body language' of at least one of the cast 'a longing for freedom'.

Referring to the content of Beckett's enigmatic play, he said: 'Each rehearsal has been like a primal scream for freedom.'

SOURCE: news-report, 'Audience Wait and Wait for Prison Godots', *The Times* (31 April 1986).

CHRONOLOGY OF BECKETT'S WORKS

Compiled with the generous assistance of James Knowlson. Dates are those of *completion*, sometimes approximate. Titles are given in the language in which a work was originally written; and Beckett's translations from French are noted in parentheses. Collections are set in **bold** typography. An asterisk (*) signifies an unpublished work.

Year	*Poetry*	*Fiction*	*Drama*	*Criticism*
1929		Assumption Che Sciagura		Dante . . . Bruno. Vico . . Joyce
1930	Whoroscope From the only Poet . . . For Future Reference			Proust
1931	Return to the Vestry Yoke of Liberty Hell Crane to Starling Casket of Pralinen . . .		*Le Kid [lost]	The Possessed
1932	Home Olga	*Dream of Fair to Middling Women Dante and the Lobster		
1934	Gnome	More Pricks than Kicks		Recent Irish Poetry Feuillerat rev. Mörike rev. Leishman rev. MacGreevy rev. Pound rev. Papini's *Dante* rev. O'Casey rev.
1935	**Echo's Bones** Cascando	*Echo's Bones		
1936		Murphy		Jack Yeats rev.
1937			Human Wishes	
1938	Ooftish			Denis Devlin rev. Les Deux Besoins
1939	**Poèmes 1937–39**			
1944		Watt		

Year	*Poetry*	*Fiction*	*Drama*	*Criticism*
1945	Saint-Lô			rev. of MacGreev book on Jack Y
1946	Mort d'A.D.	La Fin (The End 1954) Le Voyage de Mercier et Camier autour du pot dans les bosquets de Bondy (Mercier and Camier 1974) Premier Amour (First Love 1972) Le Calmant (The Calmative 1967) L'Expulsé (The Expelled 1962)		
1947		Molloy (Eng. vers. 1951)	Eleuthéria	
1948	**Six Poèmes** (trans. 1961)	Malone meurt (Malone Dies 1956)	En attendant Godot (Waiting for Godot 1954)	Peintres de l'empêchemen
1949		L'Innommable (The Unnamable 1958)		Three Dialogues
1950		Textes pour rien (Texts for Nothing 1967)		
1954				Hommage à Jack Yeats
1955				Henri Hayden
1956		From an Abandoned Work	Fin de partie (Endgame 1958) Acte sans paroles I (Act Without Words I 1958) All That Fall	
1958			Krapp's Last Tape	
1959			Embers Acte sans paroles II (Act Without Words II 1959) Fragment de théâtre I (Rough for Theatre I 1976)	
1960		Comment c'est (How It Is 1964)	Fragment de théâtre II (Rough for Theatre II 1976)	
1961			Happy Days	

Year	*Poetry*	*Fiction*	*Drama*	*Criticism*
			Words and Music Pochade radiophonique (Rough for Radio I 1976)	
1962	Song		Play Cascando (Eng. vers. 1963) Esquisse radiophonique (Rough for Radio II 1976)	
1963		All Strange Away	Film	
1965		Imagination morte imaginez (Imagination Dead Imagine 1966) Assez (Enough 1967)	Come and Go Eh Joe	
1966		Le Dépeupleur (The Lost Ones 1972) Bing (Ping 1967)	Breath	
1969		Sans (Lessness 1970)		
1972		**Foirades** (**Fizzles** 1976)	Not I	
1973		Sounds As The Story Was Told		
1974	hors crâne Dread Nay Something there	For To End Yet Again Still	That Time	
1975		La Falaise	Footfalls	
1976	Roundelay thither neither		Ghost Trio . . . but the clouds . . .	
1977			A Piece of Monologue	
1978	**Mirlitonnades**			
1979		Company		
1980		Mal vu mal dit (Ill Seen Ill Said 1981) One Evening	Rockaby	
1981			Ohio Impromptu	
1982			Quad Catastrophe (Eng. vers. 1983)	
1983		Worstward Ho	Nacht und Träume Quoi où (What	

Year	*Poetry*	*Fiction*	*Drama*
			Where 1983: rev. 1986)
1986		two fragments	

SELECT BIBLIOGRAPHY

TEXTS

En attendant Godot, published by Les Éditions de Minuit (Paris, 1952) preceded the first production in January 1953; it was reprinted with corrections in 1953, and subsequent French editions are based on this revision.

Waiting for Godot was first published in the United States, by Grove Press (New York, 1954), two years before the first American production of the play. This version differs from the 'censored' edition published by Faber (London, 1956) in the year after the first British production. The first British unexpurgated edition was not published until 1965 (in hardcover and paperback, with subsequent reprints). This edition was authorised by Beckett as 'definitive'. In 1986, a version of the play corresponding to that of 1956, not of 1965, was published by Faber as part of the *Complete Dramatic Works*. There are unsatisfactory aspects to this 1986 revival of the 1956 British edition (see Hersh Zeifman's article in Part Two of this Casebook, especially note 14).

The 'acting edition', published by Samuel French Ltd (London, 1957) incorporates unauthorised changes. A new 'performance text' edition of the play, in its English version, is in preparation by Dougald McMillan. This is part of a joint venture between Faber (London) and Grove Press (New York) under the general editorship of James Knowlson which will also provide his volume on *Krapp's Last Tape* and S. E. Gontarski's on *Endgame*.

BIBLIOGRAPHIES

Raymond Federman and John Fletcher, *Samuel Beckett: His Works and His Critics* (Berkeley, California, 1970) is the fullest bibliography, but needs updating. Robin J. Davies, *Samuel Beckett: Checklist and Index of His Published Works, 1967–1976* (Stirling, 1979) is useful but also needs updating.

BIOGRAPHY

Deirdre Bair, *Samuel Beckett* (London and New York, 1978) should be read with caution and scepticism, except where documented.

CRITICISM

Since Beckett criticism is a minor industry in vigorous production, selection here is stringent, omitting works from which excerpts are included in the Casebook's selection.

H. Porter Abbott, *The Fiction of Samuel Beckett: Form and Effect* (Berkeley, California, 1973).

Richard Admussen, *The Samuel Beckett Manuscripts* (Boston, Mass., 1970).

Linda Ben-Zvi, *Samuel Beckett* (Boston, Mass., 1986).
Richard N. Coe, *Samuel Beckett* (London and New York, 1964).
Ruby Cohn, *Back to Beckett* (Princeton, N.J., 1973).
Martin Esslin, *Mediations* (Baton Rouge, 1980).
Beryl S. and John Fletcher, *A Student's Guide to the Plays of Samuel Beckett* (London, 1985).
Lawrence Harvey, *Samuel Beckett: Poet and Critic* (Princeton, N.J., 1970).
Hugh Kenner, *A Reader's Guide to Samuel Beckett* (New York, 1973; London, 1973).
James Knowlson and John Pilling, *Frescoes of the Skull: The Later Prose and Drama of Samuel Beckett* (New York, 1979).
Charles R. Lyons, *Samuel Beckett* (London and Basingstoke, 1983).
Michael Robinson, *The Long Sonata of the Dead* (London, 1969).
Clas Zilliacus, *Beckett and Broadcasting* (Abo, Finland, 1976).

NOTES ON CONTRIBUTORS

JACK ANDERSON was a staff reporter for the *Miami Herald*.

ANSELM ATKINS studied literature and theology.

LINDA BEN-ZVI is Professor of English in Colorado State University, at Boulder. She has published widely on Beckett and is completing a study of Susan Glaspell.

MARY BENSON is a free-lance writer who has edited the notebooks of Athol Fugard.

ERIC BENTLEY, born in England, is the doyen of American theatre critics as well as a dramatist. Among his many publications are *The Life of the Drama* (1964), *The Theatre of Commitment* (1967) and *Theatre of War* (1972).

KAY BOYLE, a widely published American poet, essayist and fiction-writer, is one of Beckett's oldest friends.

DAVID BRADBY, who lectures in French culture in the University of Kent at Canterbury, publishes on both French and popular theatre.

MARIA MINICH BREWER is Professor of French in the University of Minnesota.

HARRY COCKERHAM lectures in French literature at Royal Holloway College, University of London.

JACQUES DUBOIS is a Belgian scholar with interests in the modern theatre and contemporary literature.

COLIN DUCKWORTH – actor, critic and drama director – is Professor of French in the University of Melbourne.

MARTIN ESSLIN, one of the most influential theatre critics of our time, is a former Head of Radio Drama at the BBC. For the last decade he has been Professor of Dramatic Art in Stanford University, California. His publications are legion, including *Brecht: A Choice of Evils* (1959), *The Theatre of the Absurd* (1961; rev. edn 1968) and the edited volume, *Samuel Beckett: A Collection of Critical Essays* (1965).

JOHN FLETCHER is Professor of Comparative Literature in the University of East Anglia; he has published widely on French literature in general, and on Beckett his works include *The Novels of Samuel Beckett* (1964; rev. edn 1970), *Samuel Beckett's Art* (1967) and – with John Spurling – *Beckett: A Study of His Plays* (1972; rev. edn 1978).

MARCEL FRÈRE was a reporter for *Combat*, a post-war French newspaper no longer published.

ERIC GANS is Professor of French in the University of California, at Los Angeles. His publications include studies on Flaubert, Mérimée, de Musset, Racine, and *Essais d'esthétique paradoxale* (1977) and *The Origin of Language: A Formal Theory of Representation* (1981).

PETER GIDAL is an avant-garde film-maker.

PEYTON GLASS III has taught at Oklahoma State University.

STANLEY E. GONTARSKI, erstwhile academic, is a free-lance critic and director, and also editor of the *Journal of Beckett Studies*.

MEL GUSSOW is a theatre critic for the *New York Times*.

SIR PETER HALL, outstanding in university drama at Cambridge in the early 1950s, was a bold pioneer, almost unknown in London, when he directed there the first British production of *Godot* in 1955. Director since then of many plays and operas, he concluded in 1987 a long term of service as Artistic Director of the National Theatre of Great Britain.

DAVID H. HESLA is Professor of English at Emory University, Georgia.

SIDNEY HOMAN, scholar and drama director, is Professor of English in the University of Florida at Gainsville.

PHILIP HOPE-WALLACE (1911–79) was drama critic (1946–71) then opera critic (1971–79) of *The Manchester Guardian* (subsequently retitled *The Guardian*). His publications include *A Key to Opera* (1939 – with Frank Howes) and *A Picture History of Opera* (1958).

JAMES KNOWLSON, Professor of French and founder of the Beckett Archives in the University of Reading, has published widely on Beckett, drama and French literature; he is editing Beckett's 'production notebooks' for publication.

FRIEDRICH LUFT is a well-known German theatre critic.

HANS MAYER (b. 1907 in Cologne): doyen of German literary critics, he has published many books on all aspects of German literature from Lessing to Brecht.

JAMES MAYS is Lecturer in English at University College, Dublin. He has published widely on English literature, and is currently editing the works of Samuel Taylor Coleridge.

DOUGALD MCMILLAN is a publisher and scholar; author of many pieces on Beckett, he has also written books on Hugh Macdiarmid and on *transition* (the inter-war *avant-garde* journal in Paris), and he is currently preparing a 'performance text' edition of *Waiting for Godot*.

CHRISTOPHER MOSEY is an English journalist covering Scandinavia.

ANNE C. MURCH teaches French culture at Monash University, near Melbourne.

SEAN O'CASEY (1880–1964), fiery Irish dramatist, should need no introduction to readers of this Casebook.

KENNETH REA is a reporter for *The Guardian*.

ALEC REID (died 1986) was a widely published Irish critic.

ANTONIA RODRÍGUEZ-GAGO is a Spanish critic, drama director and translator who has applied all these talents to Beckett.

ALAN SCHNEIDER (1919–85) was Beckett's loyal American director, as well as the energetic producer of many other plays.

DINA SHERZER is Professor of French in the University of Texas, at Austin; she has published widely on French literature.

RICHARD KELLER SIMON has taught at the University of Texas, at Austin.

ALAN SIMPSON (died 1980) was director of the Pike Theatre in Dublin.

BERT O. STATES, Professor of Dramatic Art in the University of California, at Santa Barbara, has published widely on theatre.

DAN SULLIVAN is the theatre critic of the *Los Angeles Times*.

YASUNARI TAKAHASHI is Professor of English in the University of Tokyo, and the author of many publications on English literature.

ELMAR TOPHOVEN, Beckett's German translator, has translated several authors from the French, and is founder of an institute for translation.

RAYMOND WILLIAMS is one of the most distinguished contemporary critics of culture. Professor of Drama in the University of Cambridge until retirement in 1984, his many publications include *Modern Tragedy* (1966), *Drama from Ibsen to Brecht* (1968) and *Writing in Society* (1984).

KATHARINE WORTH, Professor of Drama and Theatre Studies at Royal Holloway College, University of London, has published widely on drama and her books include *The Irish Drama of Europe from Yeats to Beckett* (1978) and *Beckett the Shape Changer* (1975).

HERSH ZEIFMAN is Professor of Drama in York University, Toronto; he has published many articles on drama.

ACKNOWLEDGEMENTS

The author and publishers wish to thank the following for permission to use copyright material: Jack Anderson, review, 'Mink Clad Audience Disappointed in *Waiting for Godot*', *Miami Herald* (4 Jan. 1956), by permission of United Feature Syndicate, Inc; Anselm Atkins, 'A Note on the Structure of Lucky's Speech', *Modern Drama* (Dec. 1966), by permission of the University of Toronto; Mary Benson, extract from 'Blin on Beckett', *Theater* (Fall, 1978), by permission of Theater Magazine; Eric Bentley, extract from *The Life of the Drama*, Atheneum (1964), by permission of Laurence Pollinger on behalf of the author; Linda Ben-Zvi, 'All Mankind is Us: "Godot" in Israel, 1985', by permission of the author; Kay Boyle, extract from 'All Mankind is Us' in *Samuel Beckett*, ed. Ruby Cohn (1975), by permission of the author; David Bradbury, extract from *Modern French Drama* (1984), by permission of Cambridge University Press; Marie Minich Brewer, extract from 'A Semiosis of Waiting' in *Theatre Journal* (March 1985), by permission of Johns Hopkins University Press; Harry Cockerham, extracts from 'Bilingual Playright', in *Beckett the Shape Changer*, ed. Katherine Worth, by permission of Routledge & Kegan Paul; Jacques Dubois, extract from 'Beckett and Ionesco' *Modern Drama* (Dec. 1966), by permission of the University of Chicago; Colin Duckworth, extracts from Introduction to *En Attendant Godot* (1966), by permission of Nelson-Harrap; Martin Esslin, extract from *The Theatre of the Absurd*, Eyre and Spottiswoode (1961; 1968), by permission of the author; Martha Fehsenfeld and Dougald McMillan, extract from *Beckett in the Theatre* (1987), by permission of John Calder (Publishers) Ltd; John Fletcher, extract from *Beckett: A Study of his Plays*, Methuen (1972) by permission of Associated Book Publishers; Eric Gans, extracts from 'Beckett and the Problem of Modern Culture' *Sub-Stance* (1982), by permission of The University of Wisconsin Press; Peter Gidal, extract from *Understanding Beckett* (1986), by permission of Macmillan Publishers Ltd; Peyton Glass III, extract from 'Beckett: Axial Man', *Educational Theatre Journal* (Oct. 1977), by permission of Johns Hopkins University Press; Stanley Gontarski, extract from *The Intent of Undoing* (1985), by permission of Indiana University Press; Mel Gussow, 'Theatre: South Africans in *Godot* at Long Wharf', *New York Times* (12 May 1980), by permission of The New York Times; Peter Hall, extract from 'Waiting for What?', BBC Radio interview broadcast (14 April 1961), by permission of the interviewee; David H. Hesla, extract from review article, *Journal of Beckett Studies* No. 7, by permission of John Calder (Publishers) Ltd; Sidney Homan, extract from *Beckett's Theaters*, Bucknell University Press (1984), by permission of Associated University Presses; Philip Hope-Wallace, review, 'Two Evenings with Two Tramps', *Manchester Guardian* (5 Aug. 1954), by permission of Miss J. Hope-Wallace; James Knowlson, extract from 'The Production Notebooks of Samuel Beckett' in part published in *Revue d'Esthetique* and *Modern Drama*, by permission of the author; Friedrich Luft, 'Beckett produces Beckett in West Berlin', *Die Welt* (10 March 1975), by permission of the author. English translation published in *The German Tribune*, by permission of Friedrich Reinecke Verlag GmbH; Hans Meyer/Jack Zipes, article 'Brecht's Drums, A Dog, and Beckett's Godot' from *Essays on Brecht* (1974) by Hans Mayer, trans. by Jack Zipes, by permission of the University of North Carolina Press. First published *Theater Heute* (6 June 1972); James C. C. Mays, article 'Allusion and Echo in *Waiting for Godot*', by permission of the author; Christopher Mosey, 'Audience wait and wait for prison Godots' in *The Times* (31 April 1986), by permission of Times Newspapers Ltd; Anne C. Murch, extracts from 'Quoting from *Godot*', *Journal of Beckett Studies*, No. 9, by permission of John Calder (Publishers) Ltd; Sean O'Casey, extract from *Blasts and Benedictions* (1967), by permission of Macmillan Publishers Ltd; Kenneth Rea, review article, 'En Attendant Godot', *Guardian* (8 Aug. 1978), by permission of the author; Alec Reid, extract from *All I Can Manage, More Than I Could* (1968), by permission of Dolman Press Ltd; Antonia Rodríguez-Gago, extract from 'Staging Beckett in Spanish', by permission of the author; Alan Schneider, extract from *Entrances*. Copyright © 1985, 1986 by Eugenia R. Schneider, Executrix of the Estate of Alan Schneider, by permission of Viking Penguin Inc; Dina Sherzer, extracts from 'De-Construction in *Waiting for Godot*', in *The Reversible World: Symbolic Inversion in Art and Society*, ed. Barbara A. Babcock, by permission of Cornell University Press. Copyright © 1978 by Cornell University; Richard Keller Simon, extract from 'Beckett, the Critics and the Problem of Comedy: A Study of Two Contexts', by permission of the author; Alan Simpson, extract from *Beckett and Behan and a Theatre in Dublin* (1962), by permission of Eileen Colgan (Mrs Alan Simpson); Bert States, extracts from *The Shape of Paradox* (1978), by permission of University of California Press; Dan Sullivan, article, 'Waking up *Godot*', *Los Angeles Times* (30 Jan. 1977), by permission of *Los Angeles Times*. Copyright © 1977 by Los Angeles Times; Yasunari Takahashi, extract from 'Qu'est-ce qui arrive? Some Structural Comparisons of Beckett's plays and Noh', in *Samuel Beckett: Humanistic Perspectives*, eds. M. Beja, S. E. Gontarski and P.

Astier, by permission of Ohio State University Press; Elmar Tophoven, 'Ein Franzosischer Dramatiker aus Irland', *Die Neue Zeitung* (6 Sept. 1953) no. 208, by permission of the author; Raymond Williams, extract from *Modern Tragedy* (1979), by permission of Verso and New Left Books; Katharine Worth, extract from *The Irish Drama of Europe from Yeats to Beckett* (1978), by permission of the Athlone Press; Hersh Zeifman, article 'The Alterable Whey of Words', in *Educational Theatre Journal* (March 1977), by permission of Johns Hopkins University Press.

Every effort has been made to trace all the copyright holders but if any have been inadvertently overlooked the publishers will be pleased to make the necessary arrangement at the first opportunity.

INDEX

French and English titles of Beckett's works are given separately in the alphabetical listing. Names of characters in his plays and novels are denoted by SMALL CAPS. Page numbers in **bold type** signalise items in this Casebook's selection.